The Critical Reception of Alfred Döblin's Major Novels

Alfred Döblin (1878–1957) was one of the major German writers of the twentieth century. His experimental, ever-changing, avant-garde style kept both readers and critics off guard, and although he won the acclaim of critics and had a clear impact on German writers after the Second World War (Günter Grass called him "my teacher"), he is still largely unknown to the reading public, and under-researched by literary scholars. He was a prolific writer, with thirteen novels alongside a great many other shorter fiction works and non-fiction writings to his credit, and yet, paradoxically, he is known to a larger public as the author of only one book, the 1929 novel *Berlin Alexanderplatz,* which sold more copies in the first weeks of publication than all his previous novels combined. *Alexanderplatz* is known for its depiction of the criminal underground of Berlin and a montage and stream-of-consciousness technique comparable to James Joyce's *Ulysses;* it became one of the best-known big-city novels of the century and has remained Döblin's one enduring popular success. Döblin was forced into exile in 1933, and the works he wrote in exile were neglected by critics for decades. Now epic works like *Amazonas, November 1918,* and *Hamlet oder Die lange Nacht nimmt ein Ende* are finding a fairer critical evaluation. Wulf Koepke tackles the paradox of Döblin the leading but neglected avant-gardist by analysis of contemporary and later criticism, both journalistic and academic, always taking into account the historical context in which it appeared.

Wulf Koepke is Distinguished Professor Emeritus at Texas A&M University.

Studies in German Literature, Linguistics, and Culture:
Literary Criticism in Perspective

Edited by James Walker

About *Literary Criticism in Perspective*

Books in the series *Literary Criticism in Perspective* trace literary scholarship and criticism on major and neglected writers alike, or on a single major work, a group of writers, a literary school or movement. In so doing the authors — authorities on the topic in question who are also well-versed in the principles and history of literary criticism — address a readership consisting of scholars, students of literature at the graduate and undergraduate level, and the general reader. One of the primary purposes of the series is to illuminate the nature of literary criticism itself, to gauge the influence of social and historic currents on aesthetic judgments once thought objective and normative.

The Critical Reception of
Alfred Döblin's Major Novels

Wulf Koepke

CAMDEN HOUSE

First published 2003
by Camden House

Camden House is an imprint of Boydell & Brewer Inc.
668 Mt. Hope Avenue, Rochester, NY 14620 USA
and of Boydell & Brewer Limited
PO Box 9, Woodbridge, Suffolk IP12 3DF, UK

ISBN: 1–57113–209–0

Library of Congress Cataloging-in-Publication Data

Koepke, Wulf, 1928–
    The critical reception of Alfred Döblin's major novels / Wulf Koepke
        p. cm. — (Studies in German literature, linguistics, and culture. Lit-
    erary Criticism in perspective)
    Includes bibliographical references and index.
    ISBN 1–57113–209–0 (alk. paper)
        1. Döblin, Alfred, 1878–1957—Criticism and interpretation. I. Title.
    II. Studies in German literature, linguistics, and culture (Unnumbered).
    Literary criticism in perspective

    PT2607.O35Z71776 2003
    833'.912—dc21
                                                                        2003048934

Contents

Preface

ALFRED DÖBLIN belonged to the generation of Thomas and Heinrich Mann, Franz Kafka, Carl Sternheim, Lion Feuchtwanger, and Hermann Hesse. He was a prolific writer in many genres, but he is primarily remembered as a novelist. The experimental nature and the complexities of his texts have earned him the praise of many writers and critics, but only one of his major novels has enjoyed enduring popular success internationally: *Berlin Alexanderplatz* (1929), which was hailed as the outstanding German big-city novel and as a German equivalent to the narrative strategies of James Joyce's *Ulysses* and John Dos Passos's *Manhattan Transfer*. Döblin is recognized as one of the leading German prose writers of the twentieth century, and his impact has been acknowledged by no less a writer than Günter Grass, who has praised Döblin as "my teacher."

But the reception of Döblin's works was severely hampered by his exile in 1933, and by the reluctance of German publishers after 1945 to reacquaint readers with his texts. The considerable but belated scholarly attention given to Döblin's works has not translated into popular success, and among them only *Berlin Alexanderplatz* is widely known to the public, not least because of Rainer Werner Fassbinder's monumental television series of 1979. So Alfred Döblin, despite being recognized as one of the great German writers of the twentieth century, remains virtually unknown to the reading public.

This book traces the reception of Alfred Döblin's major novels, which, despite lack of popular success relative to *Alexanderplatz*, are still debated by scholarly critics. Most important among them (in addition to *Alexanderplatz*, of course) are *Die drei Sprünge des Wang-lun* (The Three Leaps of Wang-lun, 1915), *Wallenstein* (1920), *Amazonas* (1937–38), *November 1918* (1948–50), and *Hamlet oder Die lange Nacht nimmt ein Ende* (1956). As will become clear from the discussion of the texts, the word "novel" is in many of these cases a misnomer. Furthermore, the line I draw between novels and other, usually shorter, narrative works is arbitrary at best. Döblin wrote autobiographical texts, short stories, and novellas, plays — including radio plays —, many essayistic works of varying lengths, and a host of shorter texts of all kinds, not to mention political commentaries, texts of popular science, and scientific papers in the field of medicine (he was a medical doctor). There is a good deal of literature by now on Döblin's aesthetics and poetics, on his philosophy of nature, on his political views, on his attitude toward Judaism and Zionism, and on his conversion to Catholicism and his writings on Christianity. Although there is not yet a satisfactory comprehensive biography of Alfred Döblin, much has been written on his life, his family, and his professional and literary activities. None of this is within the scope of this book. Still, the study of the critical literature on Döblin's novels gives a good idea of the complexities surrounding his life and work.

With the issue of scope in mind, I have found it necessary to limit myself to the discussion of the novels, and to draw the line where such discussion turns to general issues concerning Döblin and his place in the cultural history of the first half of the twentieth century. I am aware of the drawbacks of my approach: most of Döblin's texts on aesthetics and poetics are directly connected with specific narrative works, and he had a habit of commenting on his works and their genesis. However, to go deeper into literary theory and provide more information on the cultural, social, political, and religious background, beyond providing a listing of secondary literature, would have made this project unmanageable. As it is, I hope that the limitation to the critical reception imposed by the focus of the Literary Criticism in Perspective series will meet with understanding, and that this work will serve to stimulate future scholarship beyond those bounds: to encourage exploration of other avenues of investigation into Döblin and his works.

There are a sufficient number of useful bibliographies, beginning with Louis Huguet. Matthias Prangel and Klaus Müller-Salget offer "user-friendly" overviews, and the periodical volumes of the colloquia of the International Alfred Döblin Society include up-to-date bibliographies of recent publications. The compilation of contemporary reviews by Ingrid Schuster and Ingrid Bode, *Alfred Döblin im Spiegel der zeitgenössischen Kritik* (1973), offers an excellent selection of the divergent views on Döblin's works at the time of their publication. I spent a good deal of time and effort locating and reading the original sources, and came to the conclusion that, by and large, Schuster and Bode's selections are indeed representative and reliable in their texts, so that I can with good conscience refer the reader to their anthology, which is widely available. I am certain that what I do offer in this book is a representative choice of the divergent and sometimes contradictory views on this difficult writer and his texts, which are notorious for their complexities and their style, which can be characterized as aggressive, overwhelming, hard-to-grasp, opaque, emotionally charged, irrational; in any event: not easily accessible.

It is typical for such a writer that much of the secondary literature has come in the form of dissertations on very specific problems. Since 1980, the International Alfred Döblin Society has organized periodic symposia, usually every two years. These symposia have a particular, although not exclusive, focus on specific periods and themes. The published papers of these symposia offer the best insight into current thinking and research on Döblin's work. Another source for an introduction into Döblin's work are the "Nachworte" of the later volumes of the complete edition of his works, still modestly named *Ausgewählte Werke in Einzelbänden*.

It is inevitable that at the point of completion, the author sees most clearly the faults of and gaps in his work. For those who disagree with my presentation, who find it distorted, partial, or incomplete, please go ahead and improve upon it. This is what scholarship is all about. Döblin's works are so little known in the English-speaking world that we must welcome every attempt to spread the word about them. I hope I have done my part with this book.

Major Novels by Alfred Döblin

(With date of first publication and first translation, if any.
All novels before 1933 were published by S. Fischer Verlag, Berlin.)

Die drei Sprünge des Wang-lun, 1915. Translated by C. D. Godwin as *The Three Leaps of Wang-lun*, Hong Kong: Chinese University Press, 1991.

Wadzeks Kampf mit der Dampfturbine (Wadzek's Struggle with the Steam Turbine), 1918.

Wallenstein, 2 volumes, 1920.

Berge Meere und Giganten (Mountains Oceans and Giants), 1924; a simplified version was published as *Giganten. Ein Abenteuerbuch* (Giants. A Book of Adventures), 1932.

Manas. Epische Dichtung (Manas. Epic Work), 1927.

Berlin Alexanderplatz. Die Geschichte vom Franz Biberkopf, 1929. Translated by Eugene Jolas as *Alexanderplatz, Berlin*. New York: Viking, 1931.

Babylonische Wandrung (Babylonian Migration). Amsterdam: Querido, 1934.

Pardon wird nicht gegeben. Amsterdam: Querido, 1935. Translated by Trevor Blewitt and Phyllis Blewitt as *Men without Mercy*. London: Gollancz, 1937; New York: Fertig, 1976.

Amazonas. First Part: *Die Fahrt ins Land ohne Tod* (The Voyage to the Land without Death). Amsterdam: Querido, 1937.

Amazonas. Second Part: *Der blaue Tiger* (The Blue Tiger). Amsterdam: Querido, 1938.

November 1918, Eine deutsche Revolution. Erzählwerk. (November 1918. A German Revolution. Narrative Work)

> First Part: *Bürger und Soldaten 1918* (Citizens and Soldiers, 1918). Amsterdam: Querido, 1939.

> Second Part: *Verratenes Volk*, Munich: Alber, 1948, translated by John E. Woods as *A People Betrayed*. New York: Fromm International, 1983.

> Third Part: *Heimkehr der Fronttruppen* (Return of the Army from the Front). Munich: Alber, 1949, partially incorporated into the translation of *A People Betrayed*.

Fourth Part: *Karl und Rosa*, Munich: Alber, 1950. Translated by John E. Woods as *Karl and Rosa*, New York: Fromm International, 1983.

Hamlet oder Die lange Nacht nimmt ein Ende. Berlin (East): Rütten & Loening, 1956. Translated by Robert and Rita Kimber as *Tales of a Long Night*. New York: Fromm International, 1984.

Introduction

ALFRED DÖBLIN WAS one of the great novelists of the twentieth century. Over a period of fifty years he wrote a dozen novels, in addition to a very large number of other fictional, critical, political, and philosophical texts, and was recognized early on as a major avant-garde writer. He has been compared to James Joyce. And yet, only once in his life did he manage to attract the attention of a large audience and of the majority of literary critics: with his 1929 novel *Berlin Alexanderplatz*. While the (still incomplete) collection of his works now numbers well above thirty volumes, only this one volume seems to matter. Not much energy has been spent on explaining this paradox, since most critics and scholars remain unaware of the dimensions of Döblin's oeuvre. Analyzing the reception of Döblin's major novels may offer answers to the riddle of why this is so.

There is no doubt that the nature of Döblin's texts forbids easy consumption as entertainment. But what exactly is it that makes *Wallenstein* such a forbiddingly monumental avant-garde epic and *Berlin Alexanderplatz* a bestseller for the ages? There is by now a sizable body of scholarship, yet this and related questions remain unanswered. Still, the immediate reception of Döblin's novels offers a fascinating insight into German cultural and political history. But the flipside of Döblin's high degree of relevance to German culture is another aspect of his reception that has limited scholarly attention to his works: while *Berlin Alexanderplatz* has been accepted as one of the great epic works of Western civilization in the twentieth century, along with works by writers such as Joyce, Proust, Thomas Mann, André Gide, and John Dos Passos, it, like most everything else that Döblin wrote, has proven to travel poorly in translation. His reception has been a German affair, in spite of his international reputation. Therefore, the rupture of 1933 was much more devastating for him as a writer and for the reception of his works than for writers who enjoyed a greater readership outside of Germany, for instance, Thomas Mann, Lion Feuchtwanger, Erich Maria Remarque, or Stefan Zweig. Döblin, however, shares this fate with other great writers, for instance Heinrich Mann. Döblin's reception in postwar Germany followed a similar pattern: while *Berlin Alexanderplatz* was reprinted many times, his other works, especially those written in exile, did not find their audiences until long after his death. His monumental epic work *November 1918* did not attract a sizable number of serious readers until it was reissued in paperback in 1978!

Since the story of the reception of Döblin's novels is intertwined in a unique and complex way with the political history of the time, with Döblin's own biography, with ruptures in literary taste and critical judgment, it will be necessary to analyze the comments of critics not only with reference to what they say about Döblin, but what they say about themselves and their prejudices. From the beginning, Döblin's texts have polarized his audiences and critics. It seemed to be impossible to be neutral or "objective." While the public at large may have been unaware of his texts before *Berlin Alexanderplatz*, his readers were always fascinated or repelled. Döblin's reception moves along the fault lines of German criticism.

Döblin began writing novels as a student in the Gymnasium; but his first published novel, *Die drei Sprünge des Wang-lun*, did not appear until he was thirty-seven years old. He wrote incessantly, and in a vast array of genres: short stories; book and theater reviews; essays on aesthetics and poetics; political articles and essays; accounts of his travels, historical events, and personal experiences; articles on popular science; medical papers; essays on the philosophy of nature, on religion, and on the Jewish question; autobiographical sketches; documentary literature; stage and radio plays; screenplays. Döblin's novels do not contain only strictly narrative texts: rather a montage of heterogeneous materials is typical for this writer. He always wrote several works simultaneously, and therefore, the novels are influenced by the concurrent preoccupations. Most of all, until 1933, Döblin was a practicing physician, and valued that occupation more than that of a writer. All of his texts are informed by the diagnostic gaze of the physician and psychiatrist.

Döblin has frequently been called a "Proteus," since each new novel presented the reader with a surprise, being different in subject matter and style. On the other hand, the continuity of Döblin's thought, style, and approach is unmistakable. To understand this paradox, a chronological approach is in order. There were several turning points in Döblin's life and career: one coinciding with the First World War; the next, less pronounced, in the mid-twenties, before *Berlin Alexanderplatz*; the third some time into his exile; a fourth was his conversion to Catholicism of November 1941; and a fifth coincided with his return from exile in 1945. The aesthetic and literary consequences of these turning points were not always clear and direct, but they need to be considered. The reader cannot expect this to be a book on Alfred Döblin. However, the reception of his works, the reflection of the texts in the minds of critics and readers, should shed light on the texts themselves as well.

Part One:
Contemporary Reviews

1: Contemporary Reviews before 1933

Döblin's Concept of the Novel in Crisis, and the Move to the "Epic"

"A N ROMANAUTOREN UND IHRE KRITIKER," Döblin's commentary on the genre of the novel, written in 1913 after the completion of *Wang-lun*, was a polemic against what Döblin considered the then-dominant type of the novel, the psychological novel. With the negation of psychology as the central concern, Döblin turned against the predominance of subjectivity and the focus on the fate of individuals. This implied, for him, a break with the form of the novel as it was then understood. Döblin was never comfortable with the word *Roman* and the idea of fiction, as he valued scientific observation and reality. *Schöne Literatur*, fiction in particular, was morally suspect. This view had been reinforced by Döblin's materialistic family environment, above all his mother, so that as a youth Döblin had felt ashamed to admit that he was writing fiction, and had hid the fact from his family.

Döblin's new concept was the "epic," with the narrator as a self-eliminating medium. Döblin had already experienced what would later be termed the crisis of the novel, and the impossibility of writing novels in the traditional vein had been exemplified by the major anti-novels of the twenties, such as Joyce's *Ulysses,* Gide's *Faux Monnayeurs,* and Thomas Mann's *Zauberberg,* to which we should add Döblin's *Wallenstein* and *Berlin Alexanderplatz.* Whereas the new epic would be exemplified by *Wallenstein,* its concept was clearly present in Döblin's first published novel, *Die drei Sprünge des Wang-lun.*

Imagining China: *Die drei Sprünge des Wang-lun*

Döblin's novel is not exoticist, but the image of the exotic Far East was prevalent at the time. It had three dominant aspects. First, the political actualities were the emergence of Japan as a modern power after the Russian-Japanese war of 1904–05 and the revolution in China, which led to the declaration of the Republic of China in 1911. Second, culturally, the impact of Japanese painting and graphic arts on the turn-of-the-century art in Europe had been considerable. And third, Europeans, going beyond the pilgrimage to India, had discovered Chinese mysticism, as the texts of Lao-tse and his followers were translated into German for the first time.

Döblin, however, was equally attracted by another aspect that has since equally dominated the image of China and Japan: mass psychology. China is routinely seen as the most populous country, the country of the (dangerous) masses, and a megalopolis like Tokyo also invokes the image of masses of human beings. Mass psychology was very much in vogue, not only because of Nietzsche's dichotomy of elites and masses, but also as a new area of research beginning with Gustave Le Bon. It is clear that, in spite of the title of Döblin's book, the masses are the real hero of the text.

For most of the critics, Döblin was a new author, as many of them had overlooked his collection of short stories of 1913, *Die Ermordung einer Butterblume*. While the war year 1915 did not seem favorable for a novel on eighteenth-century China, major critics took notice of a new voice on the German literary scene. Beyond the expected diversity of views, they agreed on these points: Döblin's representation of China was "echt," authentic, even if it was purely imaginary. Döblin convinced through the power of his language. Döblin's text, although uneven and of unnecessary length, was great literature. Ludwig Rubiner began his 1917 review in *Zeit-Echo* with the sentence: "Das Buch des bisher unbekannten Döblin gehört zur Weltliteratur" (Sch 38).[1] Some critics had noticed that Döblin was a doctor in a military hospital at the time of the publication and recognized the significance of his profession for the book. In 1916, Döblin received the Fontane Prize for this novel, and critics mentioned this fact, sometimes dispairingly (*Tägliche Rundschau*, 23 August 1916, Sch 18–19).

Remarkably, all critics, even those who doubted the accuracy of Döblin's facts, agreed on the authenticity of Döblin's eighteenth-century China. Wolf von Dewall considers it a collection of Chinese peculiarities (*Frankfurter Zeitung*, 1 August 1916; Sch 21), and Lion Feuchtwanger sees Eastern feeling and thought, forced into a rounded Western form (*Schaubühne*, 12 November 1916; Sch 23). He adds that "eine neue ungeahnte Welt ist da, Menschen und Dinge stehen da, ungeheuer fremd und seltsam, aber sie sind da." E. Pernerstorfer, writing in the *Berliner Tageblatt*, even poses the question whether the novel is a translation from the Chinese or an imitation of a Chinese original? (27 November 1916, Sch 25). Kasimir Edschmid, however, relativizes the point: "China ist nur Materie, Stoff, Andeutung. Das Buch erfüllt sich nicht darin" (*Masken* 12, 1916/17; Sch 28). Günter Mürr underlines that the Chinese element in the novel is not make-up or perfume, but its natural form (*Hamburger Correspondent*, 24 June 1917; Sch 35). Writing later, in 1922, Otto Jensen defines it as Döblin's "großer chinesischer Kulturroman" (*Freiheit*, 19 March 1922; Sch 46).

Döblin describes the masses, but the text of his epic is also massive. Kurt Glaser, writing in *Das literarische Echo,* thinks that the novel rises to the level of a truly great epic in its portrayal of monstrously flooding masses of humanity (18, 1915/16; Sch 18). Otto Jensen observes a mutual effect between the masses and the individual (Sch 47).

Critics noticed analogies with new forms in the visual arts. For instance, Kasimir Edschmid finds that the fundamental artistic problem for Döblin is that of cubism, and that he pares his sentences accordingly (28). For Karl Korn futuristic-cubist technique and expressionistic psychology dominate the novel (*Die Glocke*, 1917; Sch 30). Alfred Lemm sees the impact of Expressionism, writing that "Der vielverleumdete Expressionismus hat als unschätzbar Gutes die Voranstellung des gestaltenden Willens zum Nachteil des gestalteten Stoffes gebracht" (*Die Weißen Blätter* 4,1, 1917; Sch 32). Camill Hoffmann sees the book as inspired through art, which he sees as its source, adding that "Die Metaphysik der Farben birgt sich hinter den Bezauberungen durch Exotik" (*Das Kunstblatt* 2, 1918; Sch 42, 44).

With this high praise, the critics also pointed out some weaknesses that would become a standard in the criticism of Döblin's texts. Adolf Behne dislikes the "elegiac speeches" at the end (*Die Aktion* 6, 1916; Sch 19), Wolf von Dewall the "metaphysical meditations" (23). He also suggests that the book should have been shorter. Alfred Lemm takes this one step further: he considers the abundance of detail arbitrary, and thus says that *Wang-lun* is an important, but unfortunately not a compelling book (32). As a first messenger of strictly ideological critique, the *Posener Neueste Nachrichten* of 12 September 1917 believes that the religious currents represented here stem from lack of faith and may therefore not be welcomed by every reader (Sch 38). A satirical poem by Karl Otten about *Wang-lun* appeared in *Die Aktion,* culminating in the verses "wie ist dir der vierte gelungen / Der Sprung in die Lächerlichkeit" (8, 1918; Sch 44): the opinion being that Döblin had made the fourth leap — from the sublime into the ridiculous.

However, a remarkable chorus of critics praised the book as a major event in German letters. Adolf Behne expected a masterpiece from Döblin following on this great novel. Edschmid pronounces *Wang-lun* "ein dichterisches Buch" (28). Julius Levin, writing in the *Vossische Zeitung,* says that the novel, viewed as a test of talent, is one of the most convincing of the decade (33). For Ludwig Rubiner the novel belongs to world literature, and he adds: "Döblins Buch ist die vollkommenste Romanschöpfung, wirkliche Schöpfung, die in deutscher Sprache seit dem Tod der großen Dichter geschrieben wurde. Döblins Buch ist eines der vollendsten Sprachkunstwerke, die die deutsche Literatur besitzt" (38). For Otto Jensen the book is not just a novel, but like every great work of art it is also a picture of a time ("ein Zeitbild") (47).

The critic Karl Korn describes vividly his battle with *Wang-lun*. First he finds it impossible to read, but then he succumbs to its fascination, which he compares to the effects of modern paintings: "Von ähnlichen Wirkungen einer künstlerischen Attacke berichten ja die Gläubigen der kubistischen und expressionistischen Malerei" (29). "Attacke" is a telling word: Döblin attacks the reader with his prose and forces him or her into the narrator's dynamic. And from this point on readers would either engage with and follow his "attacks" or choose not to do so.

Wadzeks Kampf mit der Dampfturbine

Döblin followed *Wang-lun* with his first Berlin novel, *Wadzeks Kampf mit der Dampfturbine*, 1918, a book characterized by grotesque humor and a wild imagination paired with apparent realism. The expectations of readers and critics at the time were disappointed and subsequent generations have never warmed up to this tale. The appearance of the grotesque as the prevailing mood would repeatedly recur in Döblin's texts, especially in the first novel of his exile period, *Babylonische Wandrung*, and it did not necessarily endear them to critics and readers.

The strongest blast against *Wadzek* came from one M. B., who wrote in the *Zeitschrift für Bücherfreunde* of 1918/19 that "Unsere Großstädte überkommt es von Zeit zu Zeit, daß sie sich vor der staunenden Provinz der Gase in ihrem Innern hörbar zu entledigen wünschen; sie erzeugen einen Schriftsteller, der diesem Unterleiblichen zur entsprechenden Kunstform verhilft" (Sch 58). In short: Döblin has turned a fart into a novel; *Wadzek* is bad-smelling hot air. But the book also had its strong defenders, all of whom agreed on the term grotesque as a descriptor. According to Hans-Georg Richter, Döblin had written a "humoristic-satirical" novel that was at the same time a "grotesque-cubistic" work (*Leipziger Tageblatt*, 8 December 1918; Sch 55). But Oskar Maria Graf finds "eine bis zur grotesken Verzerrung ausgerenkte Ironie" (*München-Augsburger Abendzeitung*, 25 August 1918, Sch 53). Kl., in *Geschichtsblätter für Technik, Industrie und Gewerbe* (6, 1919) observes that Döblin attempts unsuccessfully to copy the style of modern Expressionists like Edschmid and Sternheim (Sch 60).

It had to be expected that the new novel would be compared to *Wang-lun*. The anonymous reviewer in Berlin's *Die Post* starts by referring to *Wang-lun*, which he ranks among the strongest literary accomplishments of recent times (9 August 1918; Sch 52). In *Wadzek* he praises a masterful imagination that risks bold images and scenes (52). However, he detects "dangers" for Döblin, writing that the shortcomings of the work give an impression of overheatedness, deliberate exaggeratedness (52). Another anonymous critic, in *Die Neue Zeit*, admits that "the modern art of expression celebrates a triumph here" (20 September 1918; Sch 53). But the same critic then turns his praise on end, saying that when the reader comes to the book's end he thanks God and wishes never to read such a book again. Karl von Perfall, writing in the *Kölnische Zeitung*, remarks that *Wang-lun* had caused a sensation, and justifiably so ("berechtigtes Aufsehen," 25 August 1918; Sch 54). He has doubts about *Wadzek*, though it has a different, clearer power behind it than do the overexcited mindgames ("überreizte Gehirnspiele") of writers of the most modern school (54). Returning to Hans-Georg Richter's review in the *Leipziger Tageblatt*, he talks about a deficiency in the novel's character ("Mangel seines Wesens," 55), whereas Franz Herwig, writing in *Hochland*, says that if Döblin had told the same story in a simple manner it might have become a good novel (16, 1918/19; Sch 58). The review in the *Geschichtsblätter* speaks of platitudes and notes that the plot goes nowhere ("verläuft im Sande," 61). One critic, Hanns Johst, writing in *Die neue Rundschau*, turns this seeming weakness of plot into a strength, stating that the fragment is the essence of true German art ("das Wesen der wahrhaften deutschen Kunst ist das Fragment," 30, 1919; Sch 59) and Döblin's work is shockingly fragmentary ("erschütternd fragmentarisch," 59). However, he sees it as an inherent danger that the achievement of Döblin's personal argument with the world will stiffen into mania (60). In a more general sense, the critics saw the danger of Döblin's style becoming manneristic and repetitive, the author becoming the prisoner of his own language. It is an ironic twist to note that Johst, who called Döblin a true German writer, was prominent among those who burned his books in 1933.

The Crisis of German History:
Coping with the First World War

In 1914, Döblin was swept along in the general outbreak of fervent patriotism and the optimism about the short duration of the war. Later, his perspective changed dramatically, not least because of his experiences as a doctor in military hospitals in Alsace-Lorraine. After the war had been lost, having ended with a bad armistice and a peace treaty that was even worse, Döblin was ready for a radical new beginning. He joined the USPD (Unabhängige Sozialdemokratische Partei Deutschlands), the "independent" left wing of the Social Democrats, and he wrote political commentaries under the pseudonym of "Linke Poot," or "left hand" in Berliner slang. He was disappointed by the Weimar Republic and its compromises that allowed right-wing groups to flourish and eventually opened the door for National Socialism. Preceding this intense involvement in politics, Döblin had written a historical novel during the later parts of the war. It dealt with the deepest crisis of German history before the twentieth century, the Thirty Years' War (1618–48), and Döblin gave it the title *Wallenstein*, after the most notorious and successful of the war's generals, assassinated in 1634. The modern image of Wallenstein in Germany had been largely determined by Friedrich Schiller's dramatic trilogy *Wallenstein,* but shortly before Döblin, the author and historian Ricarda Huch had published her three-volume work on the subject, *Der große Krieg in Deutschland* (1912–14). Döblin's *Wallenstein* appeared in 1920 in two volumes. While Wallenstein is one of the central figures in the text, Döblin's primary focus is on the devastating effect of the war on all people; on violence, destruction, and the efforts to find a way out of the vicious circle of violence begetting violence.

Critics were faced with the massiveness of the tale, the overabundance of facts and details, and, generally, a totally new variety of a hitherto despised genre, the historical novel. They also had to acknowledge that *Wallenstein* was indeed, for better or worse, a major work by an author who had established his reputation on the literary scene and among the avant-garde, if not with the public at large.

The Historical Novel in Germany

The development of the historical novel in Germany during the nineteenth century had been intertwined with the rise of German nationalism and struggle for the restoration of a true German Reich. The historical novel had established itself as a popular genre for a national audience, dealing primarily with German or Germanic history. With the overwhelming influence of the Scottish novelist Walter Scott (1771–1832) on form and style, German authors dealt with the overriding issue of German unification. While earlier historical novels chose regional themes, such as the very popular eight "Vaterländische Romane" by Willibald Alexis, which appeared during the period 1830–50 and treated the history of Brandenburg-Prussia from the Middle Ages to the present, the novels and *romans fleuves* after 1871 stressed the commonality of all

Germans. This was especially true of *Die Ahnen* by Gustav Freytag (1816–95), which appeared in six volumes between 1872 and 1881 and was the outstanding work of the genre, but also, albeit indirectly, of the immensely popular four-volume *Ein Kampf um Rom* (1876–78) by Felix Dahn (1834–1912), which tells the story of the tragic end of the Ostrogoths in Italy. Both Freytag and Dahn were professors and popular writers. Freytag had preceded his novel with his historical work, *Bilder aus deutscher Vergangenheit* (1859–67, 5 volumes), and also wrote the novel *Soll und Haben* (1855, 3 volumes), which is still read, but is most controversial because of its negative portrayal of Jews.

The genre of the historical novel in Germany was therefore determined by particular political and nationalistic ideologies, especially German nationalism. It tended to cater to popular tastes in a manner similar to that of historical movies. Other historical novels and novellas, although popular, had impressed themselves much less on the collective mind of the nation: the works of the Swiss writer Conrad Ferdinand Meyer come to mind, specifically his novel *Jörg Jenatsch* (1878), Theodor Fontane's *Vor dem Sturm* (1878), Luise von François's *Die letzte Reckenburgerin* (1871), and Victor von Scheffel's *Ekkehard* (1855). There were also other foreign models of different kinds: Tolstoi's grand epic *War and Peace*, Flaubert's exotic tale *Salammbô*, de Coster's *Thyl Ulenspiegel*, novels by Victor Hugo, Scandinavian tales, to name a few. But any German writer portraying the past had to contend with the long shadows of Gustav Freytag and Felix Dahn.

Wallenstein and the Overwhelmed Critics

The two volumes of *Wallenstein* were a hard test for the patience of the critics in those turbulent and fast-paced years. It was not easy to get a handle on this monstrous volume of eruptive language. The critics groped for comparisons. Ricarda Huch's *Der große Krieg* came to mind, as did Flaubert's *Salammbô*, and then, inevitably, Schiller's *Wallenstein* and Leopold von Ranke's *Geschichte Wallensteins;* even Heinrich Mann's *Die Herzogin von Assy* and Hermann Löns's *Der Wehrwolf* were mentioned. Lion Feuchtwanger spoke of Döblin as the "Homer of the Thirty Years' War" (*Die Weltbühne*, 1921, Sch 95).

Many critics complained about the efforts they had to make to read the book. Victor Klages, writing in Bremen's *Weser-Zeitung* on 27 November 1920, moans: "O, es gibt Bücher, von deren Wert man überzeugt ist, die aber dennoch keiner bezwingen kann ohne Stöhnen und kalten Schweißerguß. Philosophische Bücher? Auch Romane!" (Sch 81) Friedrich Burschell, writing in *Der Neue Merkur*, puts it more bluntly, stating that "Döblin ist ein irritierender Mann." Lion Feuchtwanger, an admirer, admits: "Sie sind ein schwerer großer Brocken, zäh und saftig, an dem man lange zu kauen hat, und den man doch nicht aus den Zähnen lassen mag" (93). And he asks, with good reason, who at this time would have the nerves for this work, which he considers to be as demanding as it is profitable for the reader ("so voll von Anspruch wie von Verdienst," 95–96). Gregor Knipperdolling, writing in *Die Glocke* in 1921, sums it up: "Er macht es dem Leser nicht leicht" (105): this is not a reader-friendly book.

The critics often used two attributes to classify Döblin. The first is "baroque": "Seine Schreibweise ist nun allerdings sehr barock" (Kasimir Edschmid, Sch 92); "Döblin ist Barockkünstler"(Otto Ernst Hesse, *Der Tag*, September 1921, Sch 102); it is no accident that he wants to express the spirit of the Baroque age. But "baroque" was a dubious compliment, as is shown by Hesse's explanation of what he sees as baroque in Döblin's text: "Seine Menschen gehen nicht richtig, sie springen, schleichen, torkeln, stolpern; sie reden nicht, sie krächzen, lispeln, schnarren, brüllen; sie atmen nicht, sie keuchen, husten, röcheln speien; sie essen nicht, sie fressen, schlingen, gurgeln, rülpsen" (102). Döblin's characters don't just walk, speak, breathe, and eat; rather, their actions are most often described in more exaggerated terms: they jump, creep, stagger, and stumble; they croak, whisper, rasp, and bellow; they pant, cough, rattle, and spit; they devour, gulp, gurgle, and belch.

The second attribute critics applied to Döblin, one related to that of "baroque," is "grotesque." *Wallenstein* reinforced the views the critics had gained from *Wang-lun* and *Wadzek*. Karl von Perfall describes what Döblin does this way: "Döblin macht nämlich aus Wallenstein und anderen Gestalten seiner Zeit ein Riesengemälde ganz grotesken Charakters, so daß wir einen bunten Maskenzug spukhaft verzerrter Erscheinungen an uns vorüberziehen sehen, untermischt von Bildern des Grauens" (*Kölnische Zeitung*, 5 December 1920, Sch 83). For Friedrich Burschell this uncanny, carnevaleske "Maskenzug" is the predominant impression of Döblin's grand narrative: "In diesem Wallenstein geht es auch wirklich toll zu" (Sch 85). Döblin's images are confusing due to their colorfulness and harshness ("Buntheit und Grellheit") according to Hans Friedeberger (Sch 87). For Franz Blei, Döblin has transformed the monstrous panorama of the war into a chaos of boiling steel (*Das Tagebuch*, 1920, Sch 90). Kasimir Edschmid, however, sees only fragmentation and not a whole picture: it is so hacked-up that instead of sirloin steaks one gets a huge portion of hamburger (Sch 92). And he reproaches Döblin for "Unkonzentriertheit" (93). Moritz Goldstein, an old acquaintance from Döblin's Gymnasium days, expresses a fundamental criticism when he writes "Grotesken schreiben immer Leute, die nicht gestalten können": grotesques are always written by those who cannot create (*Vossische Zeitung*, 13 November 1921, Sch 100). But he admits that the grotesque is carried out masterfully: "Wie ist das gekonnt!" But Otto Ernst Hesse sees the other side of this artistic mastery, saying that Döblin's artisticness is oppressive, and the artist himself gloomy, dismal (102). The reviewer in the *Kölner Tageblatt* of 10 February 1921 considers the grotesque limiting, and misses the liberating voice of humor in this horrible phantasmagoria (107).

With all these reservations, most critics were overwhelmed by the achievement and considered that *Wallenstein* fulfilled the promise of *Wang-lun*. For instance, Otto Ernst Hesse wrote that *Wallenstein* represented a giant leap forward after what he saw as the small jumps of *Wang-lun* and *Der schwarze Vorhang* (102). Friedrich Burschell describes the progression from *Wang-lun* to *Wallenstein*:

> Als man "die drei Sprünge des Wang-lun" gelesen hatte, wußte man, daß hier der bedeutendste Romanschreiber der heutigen Deutschland sich ankündigt. Er besaß etwas, das abhanden gekommen zu sein schien, Phantasie, Spieltrieb, und dies in reichster, aufschließender Kraft zentralen mystischen Problemen zugewendet. Sein zweites großes Buch enttäuschte darum um so mehr. Es war in einem unmöglichen gehetzten Tempo geschrieben, die Menschen und Ereignisse waren äußerst belanglos, es war quälend, sich durch tausend Zerfaserungen hindurchzukauen. Der Wallenstein hat diese Scharte wieder ausgewetzt. Es ist unleugbar, daß Döblin Distanz braucht. (84)

Not all critics were of such a positive opinion, however: Victor Klages exclaims: "Wohin ist dieser Mann geraten, der so prachtvoll mit dem "Wang-lun" begann?" (Sch 81). But for Hesse, Burschell, and others, Döblin had rehabilitated himself. This became something like a pattern of Döblin criticism: the critics who were won over by one work were disappointed with the next, but appreciated later ones. *Wadzek* in particular had not been well received, and it is evident that *Wallenstein* confirmed Döblin's status and convinced critics that *Wang-lun* had not been a one-time affair.

All critics agreed that *Wallenstein* was one of the most unusual works of the time. Karl von Perfall calls it one of the most notable ("denkwürdigsten") books, one that provided new illumination of Döblin's intellectual character (Sch 84). Friedrich Burschell defines it as an exceptional achievement, which however must not be taken without criticism ("Widerspruch") (Sch 84). Lion Feuchtwanger writes that "Wallenstein ist etwas durchaus Neues, Andres, Abwegiges,"meaning this in a positive sense (Sch 93). Hans Friedeberger calls it "ein Werk von so starker und bezwingender Wahrheit, daß es im deutschen Schrifttum einen hohen Rang behaupten wird" (Sch 96). Otto Ernst Hesse considers it a unique work that even attained the level of world literature (Sch 103). Otto Zarek, who considered it the decisive task of the novelist to bring into words the experience of time, argues that this is precisely what *Wallenstein* does: "diese Leistung ... bedeutet ... *Wallenstein*" (108).

Wallenstein was an "epic" and not a "novel"; Döblin's rejection of the psychological novel and his idea of a new "epic" is reflected by the critics who agree or disagree with the direction the genre of the novel is taking. At the same time, the problematic label of "historical novel" is mentioned only to say that it does not fit. Karl von Perfall indicates that Döblin's work does not fit the labels when he admits that it is problematic in literary terms, but full of imagination and originality, and a proof of extraordinary craftsmanship (Sch 83–84). Friedrich Burschell sees a fatal indecisiveness between novel and "Legende": one cannot serve two masters at once; one has to decide between the narration of history and the elucidation of its meaning (Sch 86). This statement indicates the ideological standpoint of a reviewer who judges a literary work by its religious message. Franz Blei focuses on the genre problem, saying that perhaps the word "novel" does not fit: "Vielleicht paßt das Wort Roman, wie man es braucht, auf dieses Werk nicht. Vielleicht besser das Wort Epopöe, wenn ich mir für dieses Wort ein Werk denke, das weitesten Horizont oben und unten umspannend eine Diktion hat, voll von heißem Atem eines erregt Sprechenden" (Sch 90). Willy Cohn, however, feels lost in the superabundance of details; the text has many good qualities and shows what the author tried to accomplish, yet the end result is that one can't forget the author, who hovers above the material, and the manneristic nature of the language is at times unbearable (Sch 91). Lion Feuchtwanger praises the epic flow but stresses that the two volumes are not a novel, and certainly not a historical novel (Sch 93). He likens *Wallenstein* to an old Indian epic, saying that the book is the first German epic in a very long time. Döblin is the "Homer of the Thirty Years' War" (Sch 94–95). This is countered by Moritz Goldstein's personalizing statement: "Ein schwer Kurzsichtiger, der die Objekte ganz dicht an die Augen bringen muß, hat ein Kolossalgemälde für Kurzsichtige zustande gebracht" (100). Döblin is near-sighted, myopic (as he was in real life), and his painting is made for people like him. Lulu von Strauss und

Torney expands the genre question when she asks how it is possible that in spite of the mastery of its creation, this big novel does not convey "jenes innere Bild . . . eines edlen kristallisch-strengen Formgebildes, wie es uns sonst ein ganzes und starkes Kunstwerk läßt — jene tiefe unbewußte Freude, mit der wir die Erfüllung geistiger Gesetze in sichtbarer Gestalt erleben?" (Sch 112). Hanns Johst had spoken about the fragment; here is the expression of a neo-classical concept of art that feels confused by the overpowering dynamics of Döblin's language and the endless series of facts and details, in short by Döblin's self-proclaimed "Naturalism." Von Strauss und Torney, herself a poet of historical ballads, did not miss the chance to point out the limits of a naturalistic view of history; the naturalistic work of art can only convey as its deepest and last message "was das Leben selbst uns gibt," and that is determinism, fatalism, and senselessness in everything that occurs (Sch 113).

In connection with the genre problem, the critics did not fail to point out that the title of the work was a misnomer, and many of them identified the Emperor Ferdinand as the real hero, whereas others expressed the doubt, evidently generated by Döblin himself, whether great men really have any formative impact on history. If so, this Wallenstein seemed anything but a great man. Hans Friedeberger acknowledges Döblin's very personal view of history and historical characters (Sch 97). They are all dependent on deeper-lying forces: "Tiefste mystische Verflochtenheiten, wie sie sich schon im Wang-lun fanden, kehren hier wieder" (Sch 98). Moritz Goldstein wants to name the novel "Kaiser Ferdinand" (101). Otto Ernst Hesse sees Döblin as debunking the myth of "Wallenstein" as a great figure, an idea that he sees as tantamount to fraud (103).

Döblin had provoked and irritated a whole set of traditional values: the well-rounded, noble work of art as the model for a novel; the heroic myth of war; the tragic image of Wallenstein created by Schiller and perpetuated by the historians; the idea of the Thirty Years' War as a war about religion, specifically between Catholics and Protestants; the image of Emperor Ferdinand II as a relentless fighter for "Re-Catholization"; the idea of an epic narrative with a prescribed narrative curve; the notion of "heroes" and great men in history. The critics responded to some of these provocations, expressing annoyance about being irritated in this fashion. Their criticisms of language, style, structure, narrative flow, and lack of unity were often grounded in identifiable ideological positions. *Wallenstein* was the first of Döblin's novels to provoke such ideologically-based responses, but this would become typical for the reception of all of his subsequent works. At the time of the publication of *Wallen-*

stein, Döblin the political essayist, writing under the pseudonym of "Linke Poot," was just emerging, but in the extremely polarized cultural scene of 1920/21, each text was regarded as a political statement. Karl von Perfall recognized "pacifistic intentions" (Sch 83) in Döblin's novel. Friedrich Burschell looked in vain for a religious orientation; the word "mystisch" recurs frequently (e.g. Hans Friedeberger, Sch 98). Kasimir Edschmid and Lion Feuchtwanger looked for the great epic that would lift the reader above the confusing analytical (and decadent) novel of the bourgeois middle class. Herbert Ihering brings in the materialistic perspective, pointing out that the first mention of Wallenstein comes in connection with a financial operation. He writes that "Wallenstein is an exploiter and extortioner, a speculating capitalist and statesman, leader of gangs and of armies, uninhibited robber and fanatic of discipline." He destroys the German states and builds the Reich. He is so mean that those who use him are ashamed of his company. He is so great that the most powerful are humiliated before him. He is the demon of material power and therefore challenges the demons of spiritual power: the Jesuits. Ihering admires the work and detects its relevance for the present: Döblin needed the experience of the present to become "hellseherisch" (clairvoyant) for all the undercurrents of the past age (104).

Whereas Ihering counts on the socialist leanings of the author, Lulu von Strauss und Torney has reason to doubt his "Germanness," specifically, Döblin's commitment to the Reich of yesterday, as well as his commitment to a conservative or restorative view of art's function in society. Thus she shares a deep suspicion about the power and fascination of Döblin's view of history and the human race with those who see modern art as dangerous, as it reflects the disintegration of the old structures and values and the uncanny dynamics of modernism.

Linke Poot

It is noteworthy that Döblin's collected political glosses, published in 1921 with the title *Der deutsche Maskenball*, found a positive response. Kurt Tucholsky in *Die Weltbühne* (writing as Ignaz Wrobel) greets Linke Poot as a like-minded comrade in the same struggle; Helmut Falkenfeld in *Freiheit* welcomes him as independent of political parties, championing the right causes and chastising the enduring mentality of Imperial Germany. Hanns Brodnitz, in *Berliner Tageblatt*, draws the connection between *Wallenstein* and these glosses and sees Döblin as a major satirist of the age. Moritz Goldstein, who was so critical of *Wallenstein*, finds, writing in *Vossische Zeitung*, an epic talent and breath in the narrations of these glosses. It is obvious that the reviewers valued the narrative talent, the sharp wit, and the political independence of Linke Poot, and this is what shaped the image of Döblin in the twenties: his readers expected wit, fresh insights, unprejudiced opinions, and a lively way of telling real-life events. Döblin became the exemplary Berliner.

The Dubious Future of the Human Race: Science Fiction and *Berge Meere und Giganten*

It is significant that there is no German word for science fiction. The German genre that emerged in the later nineteenth century, predating the genre of science fiction proper, was called the "Zukunftsroman": fiction of the future, or imaginings of how life will be in the near or distant future. The novels of Jules Verne and — to a lesser extent — of H. G. Wells were popular reading in Germany. Bernhard Kellermann produced a bestseller of the genre with *Der Tunnel* in 1913. While the genre usually stressed technological advances and their sociological consequences, Döblin included biology in his novel *Berge Meere und Giganten*.

Space travel, including voyages to the moon, were the first type of such futuristic visions, followed by descriptions of the power of robots, of artificially created humans, as well as the vision of future cities, utopias. With the age of Romanticism and its fascination with the power of the subconscious, the double and the uncanny, the optimistic Enlightenment hopes for the future had been countered by nightmare visions, especially of the evil and destructive power of humanoids, exemplified by the figure of Frankenstein. The First World War brought the first taste of the power of the human race to destroy itself through the technology it had created, and the theme of the "Decline of the West" became a household word, especially in Germany where the title of the book by Oswald Spengler (1880–1936) sounds much more radical in the original language: *Der Untergang des Abendlandes*. The book appeared in two volumes in 1918 and 1922 and generated a long-lasting and worldwide debate. Spengler saw the causes for the decline and eventual downfall in the dominance of technology, or "Zivilisation," equated with Americanism, over the spiritual/humanistic values of "Kultur," or the European tradition.

Döblin, the expert in physiology, internal medicine, psychiatry, and creator of a philosophy of nature, looked far ahead into the third millenium, but detected the root causes for the imagined future in the present. Typically, his vision can be termed neither optimistic nor pessimistic, although it does not predict a rosy future, and indeed contemplates the mutation of humans into a superhuman race of giants, not Nietzsche's supermen, but something much more frightening and grandiose. Döblin did not adhere to the popular genre of the *Zukunftsroman*, but created a more serious tale of the human potential to outdo itself and thus lose its humanity.

In 1924 Döblin published his novel about the future of humankind, *Berge Meere und Giganten*. If the critics had a hard time coping with the two volumes of *Wallenstein*, they were even more helpless before this monstrous creation, and the words "chaos" and "chaotic" recur routinely in their reviews, indicating both the predominant impression gained from reading the text and the worldview emanating from it. Döblin's vision was taken very seriously, but the text was certainly not regarded as a "novel." It was the content, Döblin's dystopia, that preoccupied the critics; language, style, and structure were mentioned as an afterthought, and usually with some reservations. It is important to note the intense impact the book had on the critics, as it did not attract a large number of readers, and its non-reception caused Döblin to fashion a simplified and popularizing version, entitled *Giganten*, in 1932, which found, however, neither a positive popular nor critical response, as the few reviews lamented that Döblin had amputated the limbs from his own work.

In 1924, the original *Berge Meere und Giganten* was welcomed as an important event. Erik Ernst Schwabach writes in that year's *Zeitschrift für Bücherfreunde* that three centuries before, such a visionary as Döblin would have been burned at the stake, and asks that his readers not mistake Döblin's greatness (Sch 141).

Although the text names a considerable number of individuals in the course of the narration, the critics saw them only as part of the masses. It is a sign of the fascination of this text that the critics tended to use an expressionist style to describe it. Max Krell, writing in *Die Literatur* (aka *Das literarische Echo*) in 1923/24, writes: "Den Roman beherrscht das Menschenmassiv, das Chaos mit allen Möglichkeiten" (131). Krell praises the book as a unique achievement: "I don't know any work of literature that melts together the human and the divine in such a bold manner, bundles up with one gesture everything, throws together all abilities, thoughts, desires, loves that make up the material to build new forms and contents. This text perhaps reveals the true face of expressionism for the first time, beyond all the groping experiments of the past ten years; here its true form has come to life. And a Homeric power wrote it" (Sch 131). Ernst Blass, writing in *Die Neue Rundschau* (1924), calls it "ein tobendes, rasendes unheimliches Gebilde, mit einer erdrückenden Kraft wirft es sich auf den Leser, wirbelt ihn herum, umschlingt ihn, verschluckt ihn" (Sch 131). Again and again the critics note the aggressiveness of Döblin's attack on the reader. Moritz Goldstein in the *Vossische Zeitung* of 30 March 1924 cannot blame a reader who revolts against such excesses of imagination and throws the book into a corner (136). Fred Hillenbrandt believes that many well-educated readers had to put the book down after thirty or forty pages, feeling they had to escape from it (138). Franz Herwig, writing in *Hochland* (1924/25), laments that it is like loud, dissonant music that destroys all quiet and tenderness that can reside in the human heart (143). And yet in Ernst Blass's estimation it is a powerful book that will be read, studied, interpreted for decades (133). How wrong Blass was, in spite of the fact that it is a huge and powerful book.

Döblin's offensive against the unsuspecting reader takes place on two fronts: his radical departure from the expected language and style, and in the content of the "action." Fred Hillenbrandt sees Döblin as the destroyer of a taboo: he delves into things one should not talk about, because "dann das Paradies verloren geht. Das ist die Weltangst und der Weltfluch, das ist der Raum ohne Gott und ohne Satan, die fahle Wüste und das entleerte Meer, das erstickte Wort, der zertrümmerte Sinn, das verdampfte Idol, ein furchtbarer Salto mortale in die Ewigkeit, die starrt von Leere" (138). Döblin's world is chaos rather than cosmos; without God and Satan, without a religious dimension, it is "Weltangst" and "Weltfluch." Heinrich Zillich, writing in *Klingsor* (Kronstadt) in 1924, considers Döblin the "prophet of a new pagan worldview" (141) und defines its vision as "Leben, sinnloses Befruchten, Gebären, Sterben, gesehen in Bildern, die die Welt umspannen" (142).

For Carl August Bolander, writing from a "neutral distance" in Stockholm's *Dagens Nyheter* on 5 April 1924, Döblin's novel was one of the consequences of the phenomenon of Spengler's *Untergang des Abendlandes:* "Wie ein großer schwerer Stein fiel Spenglers Arbeit über den Untergang des Abendlands in den stillen See der deutschen Literatur. Es gab es Brodeln und Wellen, das noch heute nicht beendet ist" (133). Not all of the literary reactions to Spengler's work are very original, but one of the more original is *Berge Meere und Giganten* (135). Bolander sees it as a direct outcome of the war, and assumes that the man who wrote this mythical excess must have been in the trenches (134). Even though this assumption was wrong, Döblin had treated enough wounded and traumatized soldiers from the trenches that he had been deeply affected by the war experience. Bolander considers *Berge Meere und Giganten* another outgrowth of German Romanticism: "Es ist ein Schriftsteller von der deutschen Gespensterschule. Er versagt sich auch nichts" (134). Indeed, from Bolander's vantage point outside Germany this monstrous product is typically German and "so inhuman, such a feast of the most brutal sensations and the coarsest effects" (135).

Such a text could not have appeared in any other country except Germany. "German" is here anything but a compliment, it is equated with inhumanity, brutality, sensationalism and cheap effects, a reflection of the Allied image of the "Huns" during the war.

Heinrich Zillich, an aspiring young writer and poet from Kronstadt in the German-speaking area of Romania (born 1898), considered *Berge Meere und Giganten* disquieting for different reasons. He, like many in his generation, was looking for new models to follow. "Döblin's novels 'Die drei Sprünge des Wang-lun' and 'Wallenstein' seemed when they appeared to be works that were more significant than the novel production of the last ten years in Germany" (141). They impressed so much through their elementary vitality that people saw in their author not just a great writer, but also the prophet of a new pagan worldview (141). This is what Zillich was looking for: the expression of a new "pagan" Weltanschauung, but already in *Wallenstein* Döblin had transcended the region of epic clarity (141). Döblin had always tended to the extreme, the titanic (141), and this is now the dominant impression: "the chaotic is the impression that lasts" (142). The Weltanschauung Döblin puts forward here is successful in its vision, yet remains artistically open, and Zillich understands that his and Döblin's ways will part. Döblin's is a visionary imagination, but one that does not achieve an individual Gestalt. Döblin may be a guide ("Wegweiser") for a young generation of writers in a way that Thomas or Heinrich Mann are not, but he is unable to fulfill the promise of the great German epic (142–43).

It is somewhat surprising that reviewers of *Berge Meere und Giganten* were so fascinated by the novel's gigantic dimensions, the technological imagination expressed in it, such as the project of the de-icing of Greenland, and overlooked the struggle for the human soul. Moritz Goldstein is one of the few who paid attention to this dimension, inquiring about the situation of human beings in this book of forces and counterforces, and finding that they mostly appear as parts of the masses who are carried up and down on the waves, stream forth, and go under (137). But there is a change two-thirds of the way through the book, when humans begin to conquer nature, recognizing and fulfilling its conditions (138). Goldstein grants Döblin true insight into the way that man can live with nature, with power, knowledge, and humility, which is the opposite of the technological arrogance flaunted by Western civilization. Goldstein greets the author Döblin as the most improbable genius of the age: "Ein kleiner schwer kurzsichtiger jüdischer Berliner Nervenarzt: seltsames Gefäß Gottes" (138).

Each reviewer arrives at the same conclusion, although for vastly different reasons: this is a monstrous and chaotic product, and yet one cannot deny its greatness and its impact. Klaus Herrmann, writing in *Die Neue Bücherschau* in 1925, views this from another, though familiar, angle: there is no reliable tradition of the German novel, as opposed to the situation in France and England, so all German novelists had to find their own way, their own model (145). Now came Döblin, whose *Wang-lun* first demonstrated his powerful way of swirling the masses into a chaos, of representing hundreds of human beings, who then pass by and vanish into the collective (146). The depiction of the crowds was the great achievement. *Wallenstein* followed, boldly shattering the existing form of the novel and unmasking history "schon hier wucherte Legende"; life degenerated into myth (146).[2]

For Herrmann, *Berge Meere und Giganten* came as a real shock after *Wallenstein*: he writes that it is the most problematic German book, surpassing even Nietzsche. He sees it as combining a long, dull list of disgusting psychoanalytic complexes and desires with sections akin to a technological encyclopedia, but also with the most interesting adventure stories since Karl May. Not that Hermann is in any way attracted by these supermen, -animals, and -things ("Übermenschen, Übertiere, Überdinge)" in this "Überwelt" (146). He doubts whether it is possible to write a true epic in the twentieth century because it would require a new mythology, independent from the past and from tradition. Döblin is not content to be Germany's foremost novelist, he wants to be a creator of new myths, and does not see the pitfalls of his hubris. This is simply too much, and for his effort Döblin achieves only the strangest hodge-podge ("Gemengsel") of novel and epic, of "Überkultur und Unkultur," creating a mongrel creature of a lifeless world ("Zwitterwesen einer leblosen Welt") rather than giving Europe a new mythology. (147). One has to say here that the reviewer's expectations were very high; Döblin, in his view, tried the utmost and failed. Should he have been more modest? Döblin's preoccupation with myth did not end here, but the experiment of the mythical novel *Berge Meere und Giganten* remained unique.

The Transition to a New Form of the Novel

When *Berlin Alexanderplatz* appeared in 1929, critics noted significant changes in form compared to Döblin's previous works, and a consensus of Döblin scholars today agrees. Between 1924 and 1929 Döblin published numerous texts, but no novels. However, these texts indicate in various ways a reorientation toward a concern for and involvement in social problems, so that it may be helpful to point some of them out. In particular, one narrative work stands out, the verse epic *Manas*. While not a novel per se, it is another of Döblin's many experiments within the epic genre.

Döblin continued his explorations of the innermost workings of nature, but in an essayistic fashion, culminating in his two books *Das Ich über der Natur* (1927) and *Unser Dasein* (1933). At the same time, he was always intensely involved in the political and cultural struggles of the Weimar Republic, and was himself searching for a metaphysical or religious orientation. This became evident when he published his experiences in the Jewish communities in Poland, entitled *Reise in Polen*, in 1926. The majority of his reviewers, however, were less interested in Döblin's discovery of the East European Jews and their way of life than in his views on the new state of Poland and its treatment of the German minorities. After all, Germany never recognized the new German-Polish border, and German animosity against Poland remained strong.

It was indicative of Döblin's preoccupation with his immediate social environment that he wrote the first volume of a new fourteen-volume series edited by Rudolf Leonhard and titled "Außenseiter der Gesellschaft: Die Verbrechen der Gegenwart," in which writers presented noteworthy criminal cases in a factual style. Some of the other authors were Egon Erwin Kisch, Ernst Weiß, Iwan Goll, Theodor Lessing, Karl Otten, and Arthur Holitscher. Döblin's contribution, *Die beiden Freundinnen und ihr Giftmord* (1924), emphasized, as the reviewers duly noted, the unfathomable psyche of people who find pleasure in murdering others. In its documentary style and stylistic restraint, the text offered an impressive case study for a crime-ridden city and an age where crime seemed to destroy the foundations of society, an image of Berlin impressively visualized in Fritz Lang's film *M*. *Die beiden Freundinnen und ihr Giftmord* was an indication of Döblin's increasing preoccupation with the city of Berlin and the environment where many of his patients lived. The reviewers did not detect a new genre, the documentary novel, but they welcomed the combination of factual reporting and psychological analysis, especially since Döblin's analysis acknowledged its own limits.

The Excursion to India: *Manas*

One of the greatest surprises of Döblin's writing career was that in 1927, in the midst of professional, political, and cultural involvement in current affairs in Berlin, with a clear trend towards a confrontation with the present, Döblin published an epic poem, *Manas*, which was based on ancient

Indian mythology. From today's perspective, it is also surprising that this verse epic was considered a major literary event and was widely reviewed.

One needs reminding that the genre of the verse epic was well and alive, and even at times popular with readers, although usually in a trivialized form such as in the case of Victor von Scheffel's *Trompeter von Säckingen* (1854). But Walt Whitman's poems, which began to be translated and make an impact after the First World War, were received as epics of the new American nation and its Civil War, and Gerhart Hauptmann published his epic in hexameters, *Eulenspiegel,* one year after Döblin's *Manas.* Many poets wrestled with the epic form as the fulfillment of their careers, among them Detlev von Liliencron with his *Poggfred* (1891). Döblin's concept of the new epic narrative vs. the psychological novel had brought his attention back to Homer and to the mythological epics of ancient India. Döblin was a prose writer, and the free verses of *Manas* are not quite distinguishable from prose, yet it seems that this was another experiment that was necessary for him.

Why far-away India and its mythology? This obvious question was asked by Guido K. Brand in *Die Literatur* (1926/27). He criticized *Manas* as fundamentally remote, conceptual and foreign in it symbolism, "a dead epic," and asked when Döblin would write the great, humanly accessible epic of the day ("das große menschennahe Epos unserer Zeit")(Sch 178). Wolfgang von Einsiedel, in *Die schöne Literatur* (1928), was even more critical, reproaching Döblin for his lack of true creative power (194–95). If one analyzes Döblin's style, one sees how artificial the literary means are that he uses to create atmosphere; he created the poem's whole mythological apparatus in order to fake life where there is only emptiness; nothing grips you, and all remains superficial. This leads to Einsiedel's final devastating judgment: "*Manas* ist keine epische Dichtung in neuer Form, sondern ein Ausstattungs- und Zauberfilm für Intellektuelle, mit der Fata Morgana einer tieferen Bedeutung" (195). Instead of considering the influence of film on Döblin's epic technique, this reviewer considers the content, the substance of *Manas* nothing more than that of an intellectualized, trivial costume movie. Döblin's writing was often characterized as directed by the brain and not the heart, an innocent-sounding characterization until one remembers the anti-Semitic image of the Jews as heartless creatures of the intellect.

In the case of *Manas,* however, the positive judgments were much weightier, and characterized it as a great work. Axel Eggebrecht, in *Die literarische Welt* (1927), writes that it is, next to *Berge Meere und Giganten,* the greatest triumph of the human spirit over its physical and cultural limits, the extreme victory of an epic poet and one that could only be a product of the present age. Eggebrecht acknowledges that *Manas* is hard to read: the flowing river of Döblin's hymnic language tires out the indifferent, casual pleasure reader ("gleichgültigen Zufallsgenießer") — though it is hard to imagine who would have taken up this book for casual entertainment — and even the penetrating reader gets lost in the unreal, limitless world of ghosts and demons that the poet has created. Yet finally one is swept along by this endless world of deserts, mountains, and oceans. It all ends with a wild triumph over our narrow, empirically-determined world, so that even the sober reader is carried along by power of the imagination to a world beyond, far from causal and material restraints (179). *Manas* offers liberation from material and utilitarian everyday life; it is an escape from the prison of our society.

Fritz Landsberger, writing in *Die Neue Rundschau* in 1927, was one of the reviewers baffled by both the idea and the achievement of the poem. How can anyone in the Eastern (proletarian) part of Berlin be serious about writing an Indian epic? Landsberger believes that myth fascinated Döblin due to the boundless freedom it allows the imagination. But equally astonishing is that the text is totally suspenseful, unique, and serious, a great, thrilling gushing-forth ("*ganz* spannend, *ganz* eigen, *ganz* ernst, ein großes, hinreißendes Entströmen" (180). In view of Döblin's subsequent turn to the present in *Berlin Alexanderplatz*, it is noteworthy that the reviewers praise and bemoan Döblin's boundless imagination, his need to travel into the realm of the fantastic. However, in the case of *Manas*, Landsberger notices the tight structure (181). The structure of the action, with a clear beginning, crisis, and ending, derives from a newly decisive element, the individual: "for the first time with Döblin, a very few actively intervening individuals are at the center, not as before the chaotic powers which overwhelm even the strongest individuals" (182). Although paradoxically set in a framework of ancient myth, *Manas* is a story of the fate of individuals, their sacrifices and their redemption.

"*Manas* heißt das jüngste unter den wenigen Werken der Gegenwart, die den Ruhm der deutschen Literatur in die Zukunft tragen werden": with this emphatic statement, Oskar Loerke begins his long review in the *Vossische Zeitung* of 24 May 1927 (184). Loerke continues by saying that, Döblin is younger than the young generation, younger than he had been ten years before. Loerke turns the conventional view that the epic poem had been superseded by the prose novel on its head, asking whether the end of the age of the novel may be near. In any case, he says, "Döblin schleudert ein Epos hin, und zahllose Romane bekommen in seiner frischfunkelnden Nähe einen altmodischen Schimmer"

(184). Döblin brings back the pathos of tragedy, and Loerke asks whether the spiritual weightiness of the events, the Faustian nature of the passions involved have been noticed (186). Inevitably the striving Manas becomes a Faustian figure. But the individuals are not there by themselves: they are surrounded by the masses, as always in Döblin's texts. Finally, contrary to the consensus of most reviewers, Loerke the poet feels immediately and intensely the lure of Döblin's world: "Wir fühlen uns von Anfang an aufgenommen in die Welt des Manas, so sehr wirkt eine einheitliche Schwerkraft durch ihre Dinge" (187).

The most significant among the reviews of *Manas* is the long review by Robert Musil in the *Berliner Tageblatt* issue of 10 June 1927. Musil lived in Berlin at the time; he had published his novellas *Drei Frauen* in 1924 and was working on *Der Mann ohne Eigenschaften,* the first volume of which appeared in 1930. Musil's review (in a daily paper!) discusses the fundamental generic problems of epic and novel, and comes to a radical conclusion: "Mit einem Wort, unser Roman hat das Epos so gründlich überwunden, daß sich an der Spitze der Entwicklung bereits wieder das Bedürfnis nach einer Gegenschwingung merken läßt, was durchaus nicht das gleiche ist wie eine Umkehr" (190). Whereas a countermovement would mean dialectical progress, a simple return to old forms would be retrograde. Contrary to Musil's expectations, however, who stated that the novel had shed all mythical elements, the "epic" novels of the thirties and forties, beginning with Thomas Mann's *Joseph und seine Brüder,* incorporated old and new myths in a new way. Did Döblin's *Manas* indicate a way to the future, as Oskar Loerke thought? Indeed, according to Musil, Döblin tries to gear the old turtle, the epic, to a new fast pace, with an admirable recklessness ("Rücksichtslosigkeit") that shows the signs of greatness (190). Musil analyzes Döblin's language and verse with an grudging respect and grave reservations as to its barbaric depth: "was Döblin schreibt, ist eine Art Urvers, roh und leidenschaftlich, dabei eine ganz unstabile, fortwährende Mischung und Entmischung" (191), magically prepared out of the prosaic structure of the language. This achievement is as great as it is surprising, and here lies the problematic nature of the text for those who don't want to be convinced by it. Everything else would be acceptable in Musil's view, even the wild excesses of the myth. Musil sees a natural resistance to this text, and thus wonders what impact it might have. But although Musil tries to remain cautious, he still predicts that the work will be of the greatest influence (192). This did not turn out to be the case. But Musil was by no means the only prophet; Wolf Zucker, writing in *Die Weltbühne* (1927), concludes his review by saying that despite the difficulty of predicting the future in the fast-changing present day, Döblin's epic seems to be a book that will survive the years, due not only to its ethical but also to its poetic message (194). It is the work's message as much as its style that speaks to this reader; the new epic needs a new message, it cannot be a purely formal experiment, but must be an appeal to readers to change their lives.

Around the Alexanderplatz: Novels of Berlin

Berlin, the exemplary big city in Germany, the city of royal and then imperial power and of new industry, a city of newcomers, especially from the East, began to produce its literature and its myths during the nineteenth century. Willibald Alexis's *Ruhe ist die erste Bürgerpflicht* was followed by the Berlin novels of Theodor Fontane. Berlin was the preferred locale of Naturalism, its bourgeoisie and its proletariat lived side by side and offered obvious contrasts. The overhasty growth of the city in the later nineteenth century produced terrible living conditions in tenements called *Mietskasernen,* and after the First World War Berlin offered the material for socialist and communist criticism as well as for the conservative image of the decadent and diseased metropolis. In the later twenties, a new generation of proletarian as well as bohemian writers discovered the metropolis, as did the visual arts, film, and the stage..

The image of Berlin stretched from Georg Hermann's *Jettchen Gebert* (1906) and Otto Julius Bierbaum's *Stilpe* to Gerhart Hauptmann's *Die Ratten* (1911) and on to Erich Kästner's *Fabian* (1931), Hans Fallada's *Kleiner Mann, was nun?* (1932), Hermann Kesten's *Glückliche Menschen* (1931), Irmgard Keun's *Das kunstseidene Mädchen,* Ernst Erich Noth's *Die Mietskaserne,* and Walter Schönstedt's *Kämpfende Jugend.* The movie images included *Berlin — Symphonie einer Großstadt* by Walter Ruttmann, Fritz Lang's *Metropolis* and *M,* and eventually, *Berlin Alexanderplatz,* which was filmed in 1931 by Phil Jutzi.

It is significant that the literary image centered on the social life in the city, not the city as an urban organism; Berlin was never represented as beautiful, but it was fascinating in its modernity, its bustling life, its speed, and its entertainment possibilities. From the beginning, Berlin had its dark secrets, as described by Willibald Alexis; it shared this dark image with London and Paris as big cities that were sites of crime, anxiety, misery, brutality, and above all, existential uncertainty. The city is in constant flux; there is no safe haven, no trust, no mercy.

The area close to the Alexanderplatz that was most familiar to Döblin had two distinct features of direct concern for him. While one of the symbols of the Alexanderplatz was the Polizeipräsidium, which had played a fatal role in the uprisings of 1918/19, the adjacent areas were proletarian in nature. One of these areas was called the Scheunenviertel, and was predominantly Jewish, that is, it was the mostly transitory station of the immigrating East European Jews, many of them orthodox and wearing their traditional clothes, and therefore standing out as a foreign element in the center of the city. The densely inhabited houses of the Scheunenviertel were also a refuge for criminals, so that it was considered both exotic and disreputable.

Whereas the factory workers of Siemens, Borsig etc. lived in the districts close to the factories, the proletariat around the Alexanderplatz consisted typically of street vendors, workers in service jobs, temporary workers who went from job to job and had to live by their wits, and members of an underground economy on the margin of society and always in conflict with the law. There were plenty of beer joints, cheap amusement places, and brothels. All of this contributes to the environment represented in *Berlin Alexanderplatz*, and in a different way in Brecht's *Dreigroschenoper*.

Döblin on the Literary Scene in Berlin

Döblin began his political activities soon after the end of the First World War with his "Linke Poot" articles. He was active in the "Schutzverband Deutscher Schriftsteller," or SDS, and became its president in 1924. He wrote for newspapers: *Vossische Zeitung, Berliner Tageblatt, Prager Tageblatt, Frankfurter Zeitung;* he gave readings from his works, mostly in bookstores, and offered lectures; he participated in the meetings of the "Gruppe 1925," an informal gathering of left-liberal to communist writers; he signed manifestoes; he became active in the then-developing medium of radio by reading from his texts, giving lectures, and taking part in debates; he acted as judge for literary prizes, such as the Kleist Prize, and in 1930, he was instrumental in the granting of the Frankfurt Goethe Prize to Sigmund Freud. In 1928, he was elected member of the Literary Section of the Prussian Academy of the Arts, and tried to institute cooperation between the university and the Academy. When severe conflicts developed in the Literary Section between the political right, represented by Erwin Guido Kolbenheyer, Josef Ponten, Wilhelm Schäfer, and Emil Strauß, and members on the left, Döblin was most vocal in the defense of the left-wing position.[3]

For his fiftieth birthday in 1928, Döblin wrote his first autobiographical memoir or *Rückblick*, and he was honored by the Berlin radio station and in the *Neue Rundschau* and the *Literarische Welt*. In 1929, after the publication of *Berlin Alexanderplatz*, the prominent critic Herbert Ihering proclaimed Döblin as the only worthy German candidate for the Nobel Prize — which was awarded in that year to Thomas Mann. Given Döblin's stature at the time it made sense for the young student Gustav René Hocke to ask him for help in finding a political orientation in this time of crisis; Döblin's "open letters" grew into his 1930 book *Wissen und Verändern!*

When the communists founded the Bund proletarisch-revolutionärer Schriftsteller Deutschlands, or BPRS, in 1928, breaking off the previous cooperation with the liberal and socialist left, their journal *Die Linkskurve* chose *Berlin Alexanderplatz* as a prominent target for its polemics, not simply because of the immense success of the book and its working-class milieu, but also because of Döblin's prominence as a writer and political activist. Döblin was undoubtedly one of the most visible progressive writers in the Berlin of the Weimar Republic and could be identified with its independent leftist intellectuals and artists. His career and public involvements were typical for the literary and political life in Berlin in the twenties. While he and writers of his persuasion were usually in opposition to the ever-changing governments, they were active within the existing cultural institutions, especially in Prussia with its mostly progressive cultural policies, and in spite of the many warning signs and the evident crises both in the economy and in politics, the end of the era on January 30, 1933, came as an unforeseen shock.

Berlin Alexanderplatz appeared in October 1929. The worldwide economic depression was about to begin. In German letters, the preoccupation with the trauma of the First World War reached its peak with the anti-war novels *Der Streit um den Sergeanten Grischa* by Arnold Zweig (1927), *Krieg* by Ludwig Renn (1928), and *Im Westen nichts Neues* by Erich Maria Remarque (1929). An "inside" perspective was that of Ernst Glaeser's *Jahrgang 02* (1928). And in a very different way, Hermann Hesse reached a traumatized audience with *Steppenwolf* (1927), as he had reached the immediate postwar audience with *Demian*. But, of course, there was also Hans Grimm's *Volk ohne Raum* (1925) and Edwin Erich Dwinger's *Die Armee hinter Stacheldraht* (1929). In 1930, Lion Feuchtwanger described the background of Hitler's Munich putsch of 1923 in *Erfolg,* a novel that Munich, which was also Feuchtwanger's hometown, never forgot or forgave.

On the Berlin stage, the unbelievable success of Brecht and Weil's *Die Dreigroschenoper,* written and first performed in 1928 and published in 1929, was followed in 1931 by Carl Zuckmayer's satiric comedy *Der Hauptmann von Köpenick,* also a great success. There were also Friedrich Wolf's *Tai Yang erwacht* and *Zyankali — § 218* (both 1929), and Leonhard Frank's *Karl und Anna* (1927). Ferdinand Bruckner's 1928 play *Die Verbrecher* attacked the entire system of justice, while Ernst Toller's *Hoppla, wir leben!* attacked the whole society. Döblin's own play against the ban on abortions, *Die Ehe*, came out in 1930, and its performances aroused stormy protests.

Thus the literary scene, stage, and film were no strangers to controversial and provocative products when *Berlin Alexanderplatz* appeared on the market. Its immediate success with the reading public is therefore all the more remarkable. The numerous reviews were prompted not only by Döblin's reputation and by the text itself, but also in equal measure by the book's unexpected popular success.

Berlin Alexanderplatz

The S. Fischer Verlag had insisted that the title *Berlin Alexanderplatz* should be accompanied by a subtitle indicating the action of the novel: *Die Geschichte vom Franz Biberkopf.* The critics generally paid attention to the two aspects, the view of Berlin around the Alexanderplatz, and the story of Biberkopf from his release from prison to an uncertain end. The description of the city included a montage of heterogeneous materials, whereas the story was told in a language that seemed to be taken directly from the conversations of real-life people in that district. The critics had to cope with both of these unusual elements.[4]

A review by R. Rang in the *Hefte für Büchereiwesen* (1928/29) began by saying that Döblin had created against the background of Berlin a picture of the time, one that was pitiless, bold, visionary ("erbarmungslos, kühn, visionär") (Sch 207). It was the task of reviews in this publication to decide whether books were suitable for public libraries, and Rang's answer, though he conceded the book the status of a "modernes Volksbuch," was a qualified "yes" (207). Berlin however, according to Rang, is more than a background for the novel: instead, Berlin, as a city and a metropolis, is shown in a dynamic fashion never before seen in literature: dynamic, vivid from outside and in, true to an extreme degree (208). Julius Bab, writing in *Der Morgen* in 1929, was equally impressed: "Berlin speaks to us, grips us, carries us along, as it intrudes in a hundred different ways into the nerves of the passer-by, the head of the observer, the soul of the participating person" (210). From all of these pieces of sense impressions results a rhythm that carries the reader along. Efraim Frisch, in the *Frankfurter Zeitung* Literaturblatt of 29 December 1929, points out that there has not been a Berlin novel since Fontane, that is, until this long-awaited Berlin epic by Döblin. Such a work had long been expected from this author; it was his task but he had avoided it, escaping instead to China, the Thirty Years' War, Utopia, India, and only now has he finally come home (217). But has Döblin really written the epic story of Berlin or of the Alexanderplatz? Hardly, answers Frisch; rather, he has written the epic of the outsiders, of the poor and the free, of the underworld (219). Willy Haas, writing in *Die Neue Rundschau* in 1929, sees the author Döblin struggling with a new form of epic narration — which he has not yet achieved, but to which he has created an invaluable transition stage. But Berlin vs. Biberkopf is a contradiction that doesn't add up. It is either/or, and Biberkopf wins. Herbert Ihering, in the *Berliner Börsen-Courier* of 19 December 1929, sees Biberkopf only as one of the "Menschentausend" that Döblin brings together and sets into motion (227). For Ihering, this mass of people is the city in motion. While critics asked the obvious question whether the "extraneous" documentary materials were really integrated into the action in an aesthetically satisfactory way, Hans Sochaczewer, in the *Berliner Tageblatt* of 18 October 1929, found that Döblin's image of Berlin was merely that of a particular historical moment, 1927–28 (234). Others saw a more general significance. Wilhelm Westecker in the *Berliner Börsen-Zeitung* of 15 November 1929 points out that although the Alexanderplatz is a area of questionable repute for Berliners from the western suburbs, to whom its atmosphere seems quite miserable, the human desires there are the same as on the Kurfürstendamm — only the clothes people wear are different. For Westecker the novel is relevant to all, because it offers not only atmosphere — an unbelieveably colorful one masterfully created from the perspective of the people of the Alexanderplatz — but also human destinies, which are easily separated from that atmosphere (236). Later, however, Emanuel Bin Gorion in *Die Neue Revue,* 1931, considered everything in the book phony: a textbook example of what one calls "Pseudo-Dichtung." Even the dialect is wrong: it is not even a true dialect but instead a phony Berlin or Jewish slang ("gemachtes Berlinern oder Jüdeln") that runs counter to anything one would hear spoken around the Alexanderplatz or in the Grenadierstraße (258). S. Stang, on the other hand, writing in 1931 in *Stimmen der Zeit,* considers the language authentic, and sees the two aspects of the novel well integrated: the double title corresponds to a double content, whose two parts are tied to one another in unison and in contrast ("im Zusammenspiel und Gegensatz") (264)

Biberkopf's Way

The prominence of individual fates in the novel should have alerted the reviewers that Döblin had entered a new path. R. Rang, in his review for librarians, considered the Biberkopf story "the exterior aspect of the course of the action" (208), yet he also spoke of "the despairingly courageous vision of Job," but criticized the book's "Steckenbleiben im Materiellen" (209), the ambivalent ending and uncertain message, and warned against lending this book out to unprepared readers.

Julius Bab defines the downward spiral of Biberkopf's life until his final breakdown as a temporary triumph of the city, that is, of Berlin-Alexanderplatz, over the individual. The more Biberkopf is weakened, the more the city enters into his nerves, his brain, and his soul, and its terrible force replaces his individual life. But the city does not win in the end. Bab sees Biberkopf's gradually mounting resistance as a re-enactment of the story of Job: in the manner of these verses of Job the poet's voice rises in the soul of Franz Biberkopf, who is ready to die (211). Bab sees the highest significance of Döblin's work in the fact that he finds a power within the individual human being that is equal to and able to resist the power of the world outside. And this process of dying and becoming ("Stirb und Werde") of the individual, who, in his weakness, proves to be stronger than the power of the city, is a process of renewal (212).

For Bernhard von Brentano, however, writing in *Der Scheinwerfer* in 1929, *Berlin Alexanderplatz* is nothing but the bad old bourgeois novel, only in the disguise of an avant-garde style. With his bourgeois story, Döblin is unable to create authentic characters, except for some episodic figures. Von Brentano claims that the character of Biberkopf is the least interesting of all, since the old psychological manner of presenting him in his daily life ("Franz Biberkopf wie er leibt und lebt") overpowered even Döblin's style and devoured this, the only character he created. In von Brentano's view, the reason for the impossibility of Döblin's text is the fact that bourgeois society does not exist anymore (214). What Döblin describes is nothing but petty bourgeoisie, albeit in its economic depths, and not the proletariat.

E. Kurt Fischer, in his review in the *Leipziger Neueste Nachrichten* of 11 November 1929, has a much simpler and more obvious description: If you read the book in its entirety, you find more than the story of one poor devil ("armer Teufel"). You find the story of all poor devils, the story of an entire class of poor Berliners who think like Biberkopf, try to overcome all obstacles, and come into conflict with society ("die Gesellschaftsordnung"). This is "ein Stück dunkles Europa" (216) presented with a passionate empathy.

"Wer ist dieser Held Franz Biberkopf?" asks Willy Haas in *Die neue Rundschau* in 1929, and answers: "Ich möchte ihn den *herausfordernden* oder *provozierenden* Typus nennen. Er lebt drauf los. Er provoziert das Leben" (223). And since he is this provoking type, he provokes others, but he provokes himself even more. "Und da es nicht anders geht, als daß er stirbt, so reißt er sich selbst in Stücke und stirbt, und spricht mit dem Tod, wie kein anderer es kann, der nicht auserwählt ist vom Schicksal, zu sich selbst zu kommen, bis er wirklich zu sich selbst kommt — und weiterlebt" (22). Again, there is the prototype of Job, but in a different version: Biberkopf provokes his fate, he asks for his own destruction, he tears himself into pieces — only to be renewed and to live on. This final renewal appears somewhat miraculous, also in this description. The provocation takes place not only on the level of the action, the narrator and by extension the author Döblin also provoke through their probing. Döblin would later call Biberkopf "eine Sonde," a probe into new depths of human existence.

For Hans Henny Jahnn, writing in *Der Kreis* in 1929, the title of the book should be "Franz Biberkopf." Franz Biberkopf, who is driven by an engine within himself, a principle that says "yes" to life in spite of everything (228). This is what Jahnn finds repeated throughout the text, fanatically: this dirty and mean life is nevertheless life — all that we have. Death will come soon enough anyway (228). Is such a vitalism really Döblin's last word?

Hans Sochaczewer, writing in the *Berliner Tageblatt* of 18 October 1929, sees the Franz Biberkopf of the main body of the story and the one at the very end, when Biberkopf takes a job as a *Hilfsportier,* or porter, at a factory, as two very separate characters with no transformation of one into the other, but then he detects, to his regret, a third Biberkopf. There is the Biberkopf of the story, a real authentic person, who is well enough understood by the reader, there is the Biberkopf who survives at the end — the *Hilfsportier* — but then there is another Biberkopf, invented by Döblin out of the blue. This is the Biberkopf who has visions of death, who experiences "während er mit dem Tode ringt, nicht die Änderung seines Seins, sondern er hat den Intellekt seines Gestalters zu schlucken, der Prophetenwort und Übersinnliches auf ihn niederrieseln läßt, der ihn, obwohl ihm an Körperkraft unterlegen, zwingt, zwischen dem ersten und zwischen dem dritten Biberkopf in sich zu erdulden. Ein Wunder, daß Franz Biberkopf mit dem Leben davonkommt . . ." (234). And with some sarcasm, Sochaczewer characterizes the ending: "Wahrlich ein Wunder, daß er als Hilfsportier endet. Da ist ihm der grandiose Gestalter und Dichter Döblin rasch noch zu Hilfe gekommen, indem er den Grübler Döblin gründlich narkotisierte" (234). Döblin the creator and poet is in serious conflict with Döblin the thinker who wants to bestow a metaphysical meaning on this medical case.

Döblin has achieved the integration of Biberkopf's story with the story of Berlin perfectly, according to Wilhelm Westecker in the *Berliner Börsen-Zeitung* of 15 November 1929, because Biberkopf is embedded in his milieu, but still remains in the forefront (238). Not every reviewer was of this opinion, as we have seen already. But H. A. Wyß, in the *Neue Zürcher Zeitung* of 8 November 1929, agrees that everything revolves around Biberkopf: this average person who boasts and pretends to be stronger than fate until the awareness of himself begins to grow is the novel's center. There are the masses, but the merry-go-round of the world turns around Biberkopf (240–41). It is the individual alone that counts. Wyß finds a religious dimension, and he finally uses the word that one would have expected more often as a descriptor of the work: "Ein Erziehungsroman," an educational novel. But he adds to this the phrase "ohne moralische Absicht": without moral intention (241).

Although Axel Eggebrecht seems to say the same thing in a review in *Die Weltbühne* in 1929/30, it is by no means the same; the city, the streets, people, animals, and all kinds of exterior phenomena circle around "den lustigen, armen, umgetriebenen, immer wieder von vorn beginnenden Franz" (243). It is not a novel of education, but of resistance, resilience, of vitality: "Der Mann Biberkopf stellt sich dem Moloch Stadt. Er durchbricht das Dickicht der Städte. Er überwältigt die Hure Babylon. Nach hundert Niederlagen erweist er sich — um eine frühere Prägung Döblins zu benutzen — als der größere Mensch über der großen Natur" (245). Biberkopf survives, he conquers the "Moloch Stadt." Eggebrecht alludes not only to Brecht ("Dickicht der Städte"), but also to the Expressionist view of the big city, and to movies like *Metropolis.* Döblin's "Ich über der Natur," at first sight, seems to belong in a different context, but if the big city Berlin is considered to equal nature, the analogy may work.

Walter Muschg, in *Schweizer Monatshefte* 1929/30, characterizes the novel as a "Bänkelsang von einem deutschen Proleten" (popular ballad of a German proletarian), which for him is probably the most interesting and important German novel since the war (246). Biberkopf himself is great, unforgettable despite the disharmony and pollution in the very air he breathes and the people, objects, and events that circle around him, appearing from the unknown and then disappearing again into the jungle (247). Again, he is the center of his world.

For Bertha Badt-Strauss, writing in the *Jüdische Rundschau* in 1930, Biberkopf is only one figure of the "Masse Mensch," and his fate is in no way special. She focuses her attention on the Jewish episodes, and she finds them appropriate as part of the action: "A large community, no individual is prominent. But it is the community of the miserable, and here the Jews too have their traditional place" (249).

The most quoted review is that by Walter Benjamin, published in *Die Gesellschaft* in 1930. Benjamin writes about the epic and the novel, and he defines *Berlin Alexanderplatz* as an epic that baffles readers, since they cannot understand the meaning of the montage technique. Benjamin writes about the transformation of the Alexanderplatz, the momentous construction going on there, and how Berlin expresses itself in the text. Biberkopf's problem, he says, is that "Hunger nach Schicksal verzehrt ihn" (253). Biberkopf asks for trouble, he is hungry for it, he wants more than his daily bread. How this hunger is satisfied for good, how it is replaced with satisfaction with one's daily bread, how the petty criminal becomes a wise man: that is the crux of the story (253). But then the ending returns to novelistic conventions — Biberkopf the porter transposes us into a different world — it represents the last, most extreme and advanced, fraudulent stage of the old bourgeois Bildungsroman (253–54). But Biberkopf's last transformation is, for Benjamin, not a positive step into a new life, but simply into "Gescheitertsein": being a failure (253).

Félix Bertaux, in *La Nouvelle Revue Française* in 1930, compares Biberkopf to Faust, as his conscience awakens rather late in the game, but one might also see the Faust analogy in terms of "Stirb und Werde," of transformation. This is what Wilhelm Michel makes more explicit in *Die schöne Literatur* in 1930: "Aber was sich an dieser vollzieht, ist das eine große Menschenleben zwischen Himmel und Erde, und darin vor allem die eine große *Wandlung*, der Durchgang durch die vollkommene Zerschmetterung, die den Menschen für das wirkliche Leben erst reif macht. Döblins Dichtung ist eine Art 'Faust' des kleinen Mannes, ein 'Don Quichotte' am Berliner Boden" (255).

If several reviewers wanted to see in the novels the victory of Biberkopf, the Everyman of 1928, over the hostile metropolis, Friedrich Muckermann, writing in *Der Gral* of 1930/31, reads it in exactly the opposite way: the protagonists are not free personalities, but instead "Vergewaltigte des zwingenden Ablaufs der Ereignisse": victims of the violence of the coercive force of events. The book is a tragedy of the good will, that is, the will to resist outside forces is destroyed. It is a book without hope, says Muckermann, adding that it would be impossible to write one more hopeless (257).

Comparisons

Döblin's *Berlin Alexanderplatz* was seen as outside the accepted norms of the novel, and that is perhaps why critics were groping for analogies and models, both for the depiction of Berlin and for the life of Biberkopf. The closest model that the critics found was that of James Joyce's *Ulysses* (1925), a novel that was considered scandalous at the time not only in the English-speaking world and was thus published in German in a "private" edition by the Rhein Verlag in Basel in 1927. Döblin reviewed it in 1928 and told his colleagues: Read it! Read it! Another book that came to mind was John Dos Passos's *Manhattan Transfer* (1922), also translated into German in 1927, though it is not documented that Döblin read this book. But the Joyce connection was there, and ill-meaning critics called Döblin a plagiarizer, while the vast majority of reviewers lauded his originality. Döblin had praised Joyce, but the insinuation of plagiarism caused him to mount a vigorous defense and rightfully point out fundamental differences between the two texts. Still, critics looked everywhere to locate the roots of Döblin's phenomenal new work.

Julius Bab expressed the consensus of many critics about the influence exerted by the Irishman "Yoice" and contemporary American writers with their "Sekundenstil" (210). Döblin's eventual affirmation of life in the conclusion of the text reminded Bab of Gerhart Hauptmann, whose work showed the same principle of "Stirb und Werde" (212). Bernhard von Brentano, who denies Döblin status as a proletarian writer, considering him bourgeois, brings up other names, such as Thomas Mann and Gustav Freytag, to put Döblin's novel down: sarcastically, he says that Döblin has far more talent than they (214). For E. Kurt Fischer, Biberkopf is "ein guter Mensch" like Woyzeck, and such a poor devil (216). Efraim Frisch looked for the new Berlin novel that had not been written since Fontane — but the only point of comparison of Fontane with Döblin seems to be the colloquial style, the oral qualities of the dialogue; however, Döblin's dialogues are not real dialogues, certainly not of the quality of Fontane's.

Willy Haas mentions Balzac, Stendhal, and Flaubert, only to realize that Döblin belongs to a very different tradition exemplified by Rabelais, Grimmelshausen, and the *Arabian Nights* (221). Herbert Ihering, who thought that Döblin was the only German writer worthy of the Nobel Prize, noted with irony that the Nobel Prize winner Thomas Mann, when asked about Döblin, commented that he was hard to read — which, in Ihering's view, disqualified the author of *Der Zauberberg* from speaking about truly innovative works of German literature, such as *Berlin Alexanderplatz*.

Döblin had affirmed his affinity with Naturalism and had praised Arno Holz. This was reason enough for Max Rychner, writing in the *Neue Schweizer Rundschau* in 1929, to compare *Berlin Alexanderplatz* to Holz's *Die Familie Selicke*, only to disqualify Döblin's novel as a work of literature; this kind of "art" would not last very long, unless it had the luck to have been written by Zola (229).

Fritz Schulte ten Hoevel, writing in *Der Scheinwerfer*, 1929, comes back to Thomas Mann in an even more perfidious way. There is nothing new about either Döblin's technique or the substance: the method comes from Thomas Mann, the conceit ("der Trick") from the portfolio of the social novel (230). For ten Hoevel, Thomas Mann is the better writer (231). It is obvious that such comparisons, positive or negative, were galling for both writers, and the anti-Thomas-Mann campaign in Döblin's journal *Das Goldene Tor* after 1945 has its roots in part in these comparisons of 1929.

Hans Sochaczewer is on more solid ground when he writes that readers who were familiar with the latest American literature could not be surprised by *Berlin Alexanderplatz* (233). Even if Döblin was not familiar with it, the similarities were there. Axel Eggebrecht considers the obvious similarities with *Ulysses* and *Manhattan Transfer* to be secondary, even negligible, and emphasizes the originality of the text, refuting Max Rychner's degradation of *Berlin Alexanderplatz* as an example of outmoded naturalism. For Walter Muschg it is obvious that the work had come into being under the influence of Joyce's *Ulysses* (246).

Walter Benjamin uses no comparisons, but instead a timely contrast: André Gide's *Faux-Monnayeurs*, and especially the following *Journal des Faux-Monnayeurs*, both of 1926. *Berlin Alexanderplatz* and the *Journal* are extreme examples of two strains of a new novelistic or epic art, extremes that may be hard to surpass.

The Ending

One of the most enduring controversies about *Berlin Alexanderplatz* concerns the ending, Biberkopf's "return" from insanity and the abrupt departure of his taking a new position as *Hilfsportier* in a factory, evidently far away from the Alexanderplatz and his previous milieu. Was this transformation, this outer and inner change, believable (indeed, was it meant to be believable?), and where did it all lead? Döblin's later explanation that he had contemplated a continuation of the story, a second book, was not known to reviewers of 1929 and 1930, and they took the ending as final and accepted or rejected it. Their evaluations show that the religious implications of the change were well understood, but that the political message seemed to be very much in doubt. Also, a distinction should be made between the narrator's and/or author's direct message and the reviewer's evaluations of Biberkopf's new existence, the latter of which we will now turn our attention to.

For Julius Bab, Biberkopf is "wiedergeboren," born again, at the end of the book (212). For Bernhard von Brentano this is an impossibility: Döblin allows his hero Biberkopf to singlehandedly prevail and live on, but this is something of which no proletarian is capable (215). The author intervenes in the "death" scenes and lifts Biberkopf up into a new life, which the social conditions of capitalism would deny him, because he knows that "there are no [alternative] destinies for those who are not in possession of the means of production, but only one fate" (215). Herbert Ihering, whose evaluation of the book is otherwise as positive as Brentano's is negative, agrees that the ending is not convincing: it has no "geistige Überzeugungskraft." Döblin draws an intellectual conclusion as if from a medical cure, says Ihering. Biberkopf is no longer alone. But how this is so is not specified, only hinted at (227). E. Kurt Fischer ignores the solution; he praises the diagnosis of a professionally trained observer, a physician of body and soul who does not lose himself in accusations, who does not adorn the background of his story with a utopia, but simply tells the story (216). Willy Haas accepts the logic of Biberkopf's way to the end, until "er wirklich zu sich selbst kommt — und weiterlebt" (224). Ihering invokes a comparison with Brecht's *Dreigroschenoper,* writing that the theme of *Alexanderplatz* is that of "'Mann ist Mann' in der Sphäre eines Berlinischen 'Dreigroschenepos'" (227). While Hans Sochaczewer considers Biberkopf's transformation and his final station as brought about intellectually by an author ex machina, Wilhelm Westecker is convinced by the healing process: Biberkopf has lost his mind and has to be brought to the psychiatric clinic in Buch. He is healed and returns to Berlin and to life. He becomes gatekeeper in a factory. He is a changed man and has the strength to remain respectable ("anständig") (237–38). Even Friedrich Wolf, who said in relation to *Alexanderplatz,* "Dieser Roman ist ein großer Beginn" (248), did not criticize the ending, which might have looked less than authentic to him, he being after all not only a medical expert but a communist as well.

The Story and the Message

The critics looked for the author's message both in Biberkopf's story and especially in its ending, in the style and the montage technique, in the depiction of the city, and in the narrator's voice and commentary. They drew different, in some cases even opposite, conclusions.

E. Rang warned the naive reader that the lack of overall resolution of the whole, the entrapment in the material sphere, and the problematic and daring experimentation of Döblin's work would limit whatever deeper impact the author had perhaps desired (209). For Julius Bab, it is the final victory of the individual over the violent and murderous city environment that is the real message. Efraim Frisch bemoans that Döblin writes (or has to write) in a way that will never reach his intended audience:

> Wollte Döblin ein Volksbuch mit praktischer erziehlicher Tendenz schreiben, das untere Volk aufrütteln, zueinander finden? Wem singt er sonst diese köstlichen Moritaten, die Rhapsodien der Kühnheit, wem sonst gälte diese naiv gereimte Prosa, dazu geschaffen, sich ins Ohr zu schleichen, mit dem Rhythmus des Schlagers das Gedächtnis zu unterwerfen, für die Vielen ein Leit- und Marschlied zu werden? — Tragische Ironie des Dichters von heute: durch die Kompliziertheit seiner Form wird die einfache Zwiesprache mit denen, die er meint, zu einem kunstvollen Monolog, der ihm Bewunderung und Anerkennung derer einträgt, die er nicht meint. (219)

But did Döblin really want to reconnect with the "Volk," that mystical foundation of a nation and of a society that may not really exist except in the imagination? Is not *Berlin Alexanderplatz* rather a demystification of that elusive "Volk"? In any case, it is certainly true that many passages of the book carry the reader along with a melody, a rhyme, and a rhythm that are hard to resist.

Willy Haas, writing in *Die neue Rundschau,* sees *Berlin Alexanderplatz* as a prologue to an epic saga of life vs. death in the metropolis, and expects great things from Döblin: he was to do for Berlin and for his age what Balzac's "Comédie humaine" had done for the Paris of his time — of course with a different approach (225). This would be the human comedy a century after Balzac, in the face of the explosive advances in technology, mass media, and the aggressiveness and conflicts associated with what was then generally considered declining capitalism. It is doubtful that Döblin would have fulfilled that promise, but Willy Haas's aperçu still gives a glimpse of the potential that was destroyed by the catastrophe of 1933. Wilhelm Westecker, in a review in the *Berliner Börsen-Zeitung,* on the other hand, has the intuition that *Alexanderplatz* is probably a unique, one-time accomplishment (239).

H. A. Wyß, as noted above, had coined the intriguing description of *Alexanderplatz* as an educational novel without a moral intention ("Ein

Erziehungsroman ohne moralische Absicht") (241). Wyß also found the novel to be a religious book, finding in it the coming-to-himself of Biberkopf in slow inner enlightenment that involves many obstacles, leading to his dialogue with death, at which point he looks inside himself and is transformed (241). Döblin has told a paradigmatic tale that is not only valid for the poor, the proletariat, but for everyone: What happens to Biberkopf can happen to anyone: whether rich, middle class, or poor, and it is valid for all time (241). There is no "moral" intention, yet the text describes the education of Biberkopf and appeals to the readers to transform themselves through suffering and self-enlightenment.

For Franz Herwig, it is the lack of a message that condemns this book. The text is an uninhibited stream of notations of sense impressions; Döblin inserts everything that crosses his path, so that the only message is that of the chaos of the big city. Herwig maintains that Döblin's style is revolutionary nearly to the point of nihilism, and says that it could be a suitable tool in the hands of a great, clear-minded master. Perhaps Döblin would be the one, but in another future book (246).

For Walter Muschg, who sees in *Berlin Alexanderplatz* a translation of Döblin's 1927 *Das Ich über der Natur* (which he calls "die schönste naturphilosophische Konfession") into epic narration, the popularity of the book seems a misunderstanding: it has been written for other writers, just like its model, by which he means *Ulysses*. Walter Benjamin, who typifies the novel as depicting "the sentimental education of a petty criminal" (253), tells us that this "Bildungsroman" leaves the reader out in the cold to fend for himself. For Benjamin, Biberkopf is "gescheitert," and he can sit in his "Portiersloge" to think about his "Gescheitertsein." But this does not concern the reader any longer: "Wir aber sehen ihm in seine Loge nicht nach. Denn es ist ja das Gesetz der Romanform: kaum hat der Held sich selber geholfen, so hilft uns sein Dasein nicht länger" (253). *Berlin Alexanderplatz* ends like a conventional novel in a sphere outside of real life.

For Wilhelm Michel, Biberkopf's transformation does take place and it is exemplary:

> ... bis zum Schluß die neue Nüchternheit dasteht, ein neuer bestimmter Biberkopf in blankgescheuerter Szenerie, der gelernt hat, sein Leben wie ein Unbeteiligter zu leben, in einer Mischung von Unterwerfung und Tätigkeit, Gehorsam und Kühnheit, die das wichtigste und schwierigste Produkt aus der Alchemie des Lebens ist. (255)

Would Döblin have approved of this description of the "new" Biberkopf? In any event, it is evident that the ending allows for many readings, all centered around the magical words "Verwandlung" and "Veränderung." For Friedrich Muckermann, contrary to others, it is obvious that Döblin lacks the faith. Biberkopf's is a terrible, unlivable world, and the author should show a way out, but does not: "Fast scheint es mir, als fehle hier einem Dichter, der das Letzte ahnt, einfach der Mut, nun die Hände zu heben und um Gnade zu flehen. Ist es so schwer, aus dem Kerker herauszukommen, den der Freisinn dem modernen Schriftsteller zum Aufenthaltsort angewiesen hat?" (258) The Döblin of 1942 might have agreed with this appeal of a militant Catholic writer.

The long, damning review of Emanuel Bin Gorion, who finds everything false and phony, from the details and slang to the action, wonders what the sense and purpose of the novel is, saying that a poet is either a bird that sings because he has the voice to, or one that cries because he is so shaken by the misery he sees (263). But Döblin does neither, and instead only strews refuse as if emptying a garbage can through the streets, which requires no talent to do (263).

S. Stang finally points to the nature of Döblin's religion. Whereas Herwig, who was a novelist as well, had seen a search for God, Stang sees Döblin on another track. There is no trace in the chaos of this big city of a personal God holding his hands over the world, as there is in Herwig's own novels: "An die Stelle Gottes tritt die Totalität der kosmischen und unterbewußten Kräfte, etwas schicksalhaftes Natur-Mystisches, in dem die Sterne leuchten und die Gräser wurzeln": God is replaced by the totality of the cosmic and unconscious forces (265–66). But is the metropolis really "durchwaltet" or controlled by pantheistic forces à la Spinoza, or is it inappropriate to use the word "nature"? In any event, it was a religious message, even more than a political one, that critics (and readers) seemed to expect from this book.

The Frontal Attack of the Linkskurve

Bernhard von Brentano, another fellow novelist who would later change his convictions and return to Hitler's Germany from exile in Switzerland, had faulted Döblin for writing a novel that pretended to be proletarian but was really a bourgeois novel in disguise. According to Brentano, the novel's disguise fooled the bourgeois press and readership, and this was the primary reason for its enthusiastic acceptance. This huge success bothered Brentano, as Döblin's novel would stand in the way of real proletarian literature, which was then just beginning to appear. Brentano seems to defend Döblin against some negative criticism from left-wing writers who decried *Alexanderplatz* as a failed attempt, an example of the decay of the bourgeois novel as a form. But they are barking up the wrong tree, says Brentano: this criticism does not apply, since what Döblin has written is not a novel but a depiction of the life of a man (214). There is a generic difference, or so we must understand, between a biography and a novel. However, Brentano parts ways with Döblin at the end when Biberkopf dies and is resurrected. Biberkopf is still alone, a loner, and that means, for Brentano, that he cannot be a proletarian. Biberkopf, after what he has been through, cannot be as "apolitical" as Döblin (who is or was a socialist) represents him to be. Something does not add up.

Die Rote Fahne of 17 December 1929 attacks not so much Döblin himself, but the label of his novel: "der erste proletarische Roman Berlins!"[5] What Döblin offers as the proletariat is in reality "Lumpenproletariat" (70). There are serious flaws in accuracy: for instance, although the Communist Party (Kommunistische Partei Deutschlands, or KPD) was by far the strongest party in the district around the Alexanderplatz, not one communist worker appears in the text. And the "Alex" is shown without "Zörgiebel," meaning without the Polizeipräsidium — which is indeed a glaring and surprising omission, especially when one thinks of its later significance in *November 1918*. The reviewer recounts the action and concludes that the meaning is not to be determined ("Nicht festzustellen") (71). He asks who will write the novel of proletarian Berlin, for there is not one (71). Döblin's brilliant style comes to nothing. What he tells is not what the workers, the real proletarians, need and want.

The criticism of Döblin's novel heated up after the newly formed Bund proletarisch-revolutionärer Schriftsteller (BPRS, League of Proletarian-Revolutionary Writers) decided that it considered the left-leaning bourgeois writers to be their enemies, just as the KPD considered the SPD (Sozialdemokratische Partei Deutschlands) their worst enemies, before they understood that the Nazis were the more urgent threat. The BPRS journal *Die Linkskurve* launched an offensive against *Berlin Alexanderplatz*. Its reviewer, Klaus Neukrantz, begins by charging that the novel had no connection whatsoever with Berlin or the Alexanderplatz (228), and then goes on to charge him with open hostility toward the organized working class (229). Döblin is a self-declared enemy of the KPD, which is in its own understanding the carrier of the class struggle of the proletariat. And consequently, the novel is reactionary, hiding a counter-revolutionary attack on the idea of the organized class struggle beneath a skillfully crafted mask. But it is only one example for many: all "bourgeois-leftist" (linksbürgerlichen) writers are enemies that need to be exposed, a political danger for the proletariat that deserves keen attention (229). Neukrantz is speaking to his own comrades who might harbor ideas of a "popular front," as it would be called in the thirties, and do not understand the need for the purity of the party line. Neukrantz and other communists considered writers they saw as "bourgeois-leftist" to be much more dangerous than conservatives or liberals, as their ideas could be seductive: they were socialists who opposed the doctrinaire orthodoxy of the communist parties.

In a 1930 article in *Die Linkskurve* titled "Einen Schritt weiter!," Johannes R. Becher uses Döblin as an example of the need to clarify the revolutionary position. Becher had taken part in the "Gruppe 1925," and his personal relations with Döblin remained cordial in spite of their ideological conflicts, to the very end of their lives. But here he draws the line, writing that proletarian-revolutionary literature has made enormous progress in the past two years, and that books have shown themselves to be weapons in the class struggle (Pr 88). Becher's statements followed the party line of the Komintern and must be seen in the context of the total Soviet Stalinist reorientation, but in our context it will suffice to note the effects of these struggles on the German literary scene. Because books are seen as weapons in a struggle or war, there arises the possibility of "Literarischer Hochverrat," or literary treason (89). Becher demands that literature be taken seriously by the party, so that it would come under the same kind of party control as any other political activity (89–90). All comrades must now make the decisive "Ruck nach links," or move to the left (90). This means "Abgrenzung," a clear dividing line, first of all between the proletarian writers and the so-called "Arbeiterdichter" (90) who were usually affiliated with the SPD if they belonged to any party, and second, and even more urgently, from the "Sympathisierenden," the sympathizers, the writers of what Becher calls "Linksleuteliteratur" (90). This literature is the real enemy. Becher sets against this bourgeois-left literature proletarian literature, which he defines as being a new form of realism, usually biographical or autobiographical, and which would soon receive its programmatic name "socialist realism." Proletarian literature, in contrast to bourgeois-left literature, says Becher, does not aim at or need aesthetic refinement: it is not high-minded ("edel") or polished crystal-clear, not designed for the recognition of a silly *Dichterakademie* or ready for a Nobel Prize (and here Becher contrasts it with the works of Döblin, which were thought by many at the time to be "Nobelpreisreif"). Instead, says Becher, ironically employing metaphors that are highly literary, it has an aggressive toughness that grows out of the storm that blows through history. The proletarian writers of the future will not find it necessary, as Döblin has, to use a wholly unrealistic method despite their ultrarealism (93). For Becher,

Döblin's book is a product of the decadent bourgeoisie, but it may take some time before the bourgeoisie and its literature will come to an end. Until then, there must be war: literature is not a neutral zone, but a war zone, and Becher says that he and his fellow writers are there to make war: "Zum Kriegführen sind wir da!" (94).

After Döblin had replied in *Das Tagebuch* with a very sarcastic review of *Die Linkskurve* and their pretensions, Otto Biha replied in another long article in the same publication titled "Herr Döblin verunglückt in einer "Linkskurve." At this point, it was not so much *Berlin Alexanderplatz* that Biha wanted to "exorcise," but Döblin the writer. Whereas Becher is the true poet of the workers, Döblin's audience is made up of thousands of society-eligible ladies and clever stock-market speculators who delved into the Buddhist mysticism of *Manas* and by way of this detour have embarked on the plebeian pilgrimage to *Berlin Alexanderplatz* (Pr 95–96). But who is this Döblin anyway? For Biha Döblin's intellectuality, which he casts in the crude metaphorical terms of "ein Wasserkopf" (a hydrocephalus), means he is without roots in German society (96). Biha also has a new definition: "*Berlin Alexanderplatz* ist ein witziger Narrenführer in eine sagenhafte *Unterwelt des Proletariats*, die nur in Dichterhirnen existiert" (98), a humorous idiot's guide to a mythical underworld of the proletariat that only exists in the poet's mind. Döblin's analysis of the decadent society is anything but original, as his predecessors from Strindberg to Dostoyevsky have done this much better (99). What does the book say about its author Döblin? It is the confession of a cultural nihilist, a labile, disoriented, resigned bourgeois who has finally found the outer form (his style) for his inner disunity ("Zerrissenheit"). It is a symptomatic, but not even a representative bourgeois novel (99). And its author? "A spiteful *Literat* with Freudian complexes and a melancholy soul: a Biberkopf" (100). The *Linkskurve* was able to announce triumphantly that the planned publication of *Berlin Alexanderplatz* in the Soviet Union had been prevented.

Franz Carl Weiskopf wrote his review in *Berlin am Morgen*, published 2 February 1930, under the heading "Die Pleite des großen deutschen Romans, Döblin, der deutsche Normaleinheits-Joyce." He characterized all of Döblin's work as bourgeois, but saw differences in quality; for instance, he praised *Wang-lun* for its collectivistic perspective. *Berlin Alexanderplatz*, however, is full of "zersetzenden Elementen," decadent corroding elements (Pr 101). It has been ruined by Döblin's mania for originality, his need to be different, and then, paradoxically, by his imitation of Joyce's *Ulysses*. Everything in the book is artificial, including Biberkopf: even though Döblin strives hard to achieve realism, Biberkopf remains a construct with an intellectual ingredient, and even the huge dose of Berlin dialect does not succeed in coloring him as a proletarian (102). Yet for all the book's faults, it is nevertheless an important work, an interesting if unsuccessful attempt (102).

Döblin's novel provoked the Communist Party and its cultural strategist at a crucial juncture, when in their estimation, the advancement of true proletarian literature of party loyalists needed separation from bourgeois literature, and when the influence of the "fellow travelers" seemed too strong for the emerging socialist realism. Attacking such an enormously popular work and its prominent author was a good way to separate the party loyalists and the "others." Whereas the style and form of *Berlin Alexanderplatz* were usually mentioned last in Communist reviews, the message was clear: neither the content nor the form of this work should in any way be used as a model. One can say that the controversy about *Berlin Alexanderplatz* was a prelude to the conflict of Stalinists vs. anti-Stalinists in the late thirties, and also to the Expressionism debate of the exiles. In this light the "popular front" tactics of the 1930s, prominent in Spain and France, in which the communists and socialists temporarily cooperated, look like nothing but a temporary diversion from this inevitable formation of hostile fronts.

Wissen und Verändern!

While the political controversy around *Berlin Alexanderplatz* was still going on, Döblin was prompted to write his political confession. In 1930, a student by the name of Gustav René Hocke, who was to become a well-known essayist and book author after 1945, asked Döblin for guidance in the confusing chaos and crisis of the Weimar Republic. Döblin's "Offene Briefe an einen Jungen Menschen" appeared in book form in 1931 under the title *Wissen und Verändern,* and aroused a good deal of attention and controversy. Döblin's positive message was less than clear, but it was evident that he opposed organized class struggle, meaning the political parties on the left, the SPD and especially the KPD. With the belligerent attitudes of his communist fellow writers in mind, Döblin charged that violence and war, including class warfare, can never lead to harmony and peace. The solution of the German crisis could only come through the abolition of political parties.

Döblin formed his own political discussion group, which disbanded in 1933. Most of the reviewers of *Wissen und Verändern!* disagreed with Döblin, and focused mainly on one point: was any part of his advice practical or useful for the purpose — would Hocke now know what to think and what to do? The reviewers' answer was mostly no. Döblin's ideas reflected the fragmentation of the cultural scene, and of the help-lessness of the intellectuals during the breakdown of the parliamentary system. Unless they consented to be propagandists for specific political parties, usually radical ones, they had no voice, no place in the momen-tous conflicts and decisions that changed German society forever. *Wissen und Verändern!* and the responses to it look futile, like a preview of the coming exile.

Translations of Berlin Alexanderplatz

Berlin Alexanderplatz was translated into twelve languages. The English translation by Eugene Jolas appeared in 1931. The American reviews were mixed, as the following excerpts, all from the fall of that year, show. F. H. Britten, writing in the *New York Herald Tribune Books*, 13 Sep-tember, calls it "a tale of the underworld of Berlin, in the manner of James Joyce's *Ulysses*. . . . The range and grotesqueness of the materials which Döblin uses makes *Alexanderplatz* a sort of evil smelling, Gar-gantuan stew . . ." (Pr 114). Fanny Butcher, in the *Chicago Daily Trib-une* of 12 September finds "the color, the cruelty, the savagery, the passionate rhythm of the underworld. . . . *Alexanderplatz, Berlin* is a remarkable, an unforgettable book, but also, like *Ulysses*, it's almost a life's work to read!" (114). Louis Kronenberger, writing in *Forum*, vol. 86, writes that "Herr Döblin pushes the realistic toward the grotesque, and gives the book, at rare moments, the ironic, pathetic, ominous, hallucinated touches of good grotesquerie" (115). K. F. Geiser, in *The Nation*, on 23 September, concludes that "there is no selection and there are no evaluations . . . which grips the reader and depresses this reviewer" (115). Percy Hutchison, *New York Times*, 13 September, calls Döblin's book ". . . an audacious adventure, . . . on the whole, weakened rather than strengthened by the multiplicity of devices employed in the expectation of increasing the effect" (115). A. W. Porterfield, in the *Outlook and Independent* on 23 September, criticizes the translation: ". . . there was really no need of perfect indecency. Comparison with the original makes this evident" (115). Arthur Ruhl, in *The Saturday Review of Literature* of 12 September sounds a more laudatory note: "whatever your incidental quarrels with it, *Alexanderplatz* gets under the skin, gets through to the real thing" (116). The *Springfield Republican* of 11 October, however, is less enthusiastic: "*Alexanderplatz, Berlin* was hailed in Germany with considerable enthusiasm. Possibly the work has lost something in translation. At all events, as an epic of the Berlin under-world it does not quite come off" (116).

Berlin Alexanderplatz or, as the English translation read, *Alexander-platz, Berlin,* was something like Joyce's *Ulysses,* a tale of the Berlin underworld, with the use of modern narrative devices, hard to read, "evil smelling," but somehow gripping, a problematic production — not unusual for German literature — but the reviewers wondered why the Germans were so enthusiastic about it. There seems to be no mention of John Dos Passos, and the similarities between Berlin and New York did not seem to be evident. There is no mention of Biberkopf's quest or of the "new man." The reviews, while respectful, were definitely not an invitation to read the book.

Notes

[1] *Alfred Döblin im Spiegel der zeitgenössischen Kritik,* ed. Ingrid Schuster and Ingrid Bode (Bern/Munich: Francke Verlag, 1973). This will be cited subsequently in the text with the abbreviation "Sch."

[2] Remarkably, Döblin's tales had already been diagnosed as *Legenden,* a word that is not adequately translated by English "legend," since "legend" is closer to the German *Sage. Legenden* are stories of saints and martyrs, and a crucial element in them is the miracle. Such miracle motifs existed in many oriental tales and from there found their way into the tales about Christian saints. The last two hundred years have seen a revival of the *Legende* as a poetic genre, often laced with irony and agnosticism. That Döblin formed the fate of the Emperor Ferdinand in *Wallenstein* into a *Legende* beyond historical documents and probabilities seems indicative of the hoped-for religious revival after 1918.

[3] In 1931 the conflict led to the rightists' resignation from the Academy and the election of Heinrich Mann as the president of the Literary Section. Eventually, of course, in 1933 the Literary Section was transformed in the Nazi image, with the return of Kolbenheyer and his cohorts and the expulsion of Heinrich Mann and his partisans.

[4] The volume *Erläuterungen und Dokumente, Alfred Döblin: Berlin Alexanderplatz,* by Gabriele Sander (Stuttgart: Reclam, 1998) contains a list of the contemporary reviews of the novel and of the film of 1931 by Phil Jutzi (269–74) and a bibliography of scholarly studies (276–85); she also gives an overview of the early reviews with excerpts (137–64) and a summary of significant scholarship (164–256).

[5] Matthias Prangel, ed., *Materialien zu Alfred Döblins "Berlin Alexanderplatz,"* Suhrkamp Taschenbuch 268 (Frankfurt: Suhrkamp, 1975), 70. Hereafter cited as "Pr" with page number in parentheses.

2: Contemporary Reviews after 1933: Döblin in Exile

Asylum in Paris

AFTER THE BURNING of the Reichstag on 27 February 1933, Döblin was warned that his life was in danger. He left for Switzerland and crossed the border on 2 March 1933. After months of hesitation, the family settled in Paris in early September 1933, and stayed in and around the city until the German offensive of May 1940. In October 1936 the family obtained French citizenship, due to the special protection it afforded and the fact that Döblin's sons would be able to do military service. Döblin missed the work in his medical practice, and moreover, he was forced to concentrate on his writing as his only source of income. Between 1933 and 1940, when he was forced to flee from the advancing German troops, he had produced the novels *Babylonische Wandrung, Pardon wird nicht gegeben,* the trilogy *Amazonas,* and was working on his tetralogy *November 1918.* From 1933 to 1935 Döblin was actively engaged in the Jewish "Freiland" movement, the non-Zionist movement for a national Jewish territory. He also took part in German writers' activities in Paris, and in 1938 he became close to Willy Münzenberg, Arthur Koestler, and Manès Sperber, who were active in a socialist movement against Stalinism, a position voiced in the short-lived journal *Die Zukunft.*

Although the exile publishers in Amsterdam, Querido and Allert de Lange, were unexpectedly successful, it is evident that the critical response to the publications of exiled writers was much reduced compared to the time before 1933, and that reviews from fellow exiles tended to be friendly rather than incisive. Still, there was a range of critical responses indicating differences in the reception of the various works. Döblin remained a prominent and respected writer, but none of his new publications was particularly successful. The market in Britain and the United States was commercially all important then as now, but the only contemporary English translation of one of his exile works was that of *Pardon wird nicht gegeben* (as *Men without Mercy*) in 1937, the year when Italian, Russian, and Polish translations of the work also appeared, along with a French translation of *Babylonische Wandrung* published as *Voyage babylonien* by Gallimard of Paris. One of the factors for Döblin's failure on the American market was that before 1933, he had not been able to establish a stable relationship with a publisher in England and America, although *Berlin Alexanderplatz* was published by Viking in 1931 and was widely reviewed. Writers like Thomas Mann, Lion Feuchtwanger, Franz Werfel, and Stefan Zweig were able to continue their longstanding contacts and contracts with Knopf or Viking after 1933 and did not have to beg for acceptance.

No Second *Berlin Alexanderplatz: Babylonische Wandrung*

When Döblin went into exile, he had already begun work on *Babylonische Wandrung, oder Hochmut kommt vor dem Fall*, which would appear in 1934 with Querido in Amsterdam. Döblin continued to work on it in Switzerland and in Paris. From Paris, he returned once more to Zurich for a short time to advance his work. The story reflects both his stations of exile, Switzerland and France. The French parts of the text may explain Gallimard's interest in the work.

The response to *Babylonische Wandrung* was practically restricted to the journals of the exiles themselves. There were still echoes of the ideological conflicts of the pre-1933 years, although the "popular fronts" were coming in France and Spain. Albin Stübs, who had already chastized *Berlin Alexanderplatz* as pre-fascist, writes in the Prague *Neue Deutsche Blätter* in 1933/34 that Döblin considers a failed and reborn pimp more valuable than the fighting workers organizations. Doorkeepers ("Portiers") go through a mystical transformation in a new guise: they are turned into heroes ("Heldenseelen") akin to those named by Hitler to be house-block leaders ("Häuserblockwarte") (Sch 266). That is, National Socialism is the transformation of the "Lumpenproletariat" into political gangsters, and Döblin does not denounce it, but rather affirms the mentality of these "Portiers" such as Biberkopf, who become little Nazis and enemies of the working class.

The *Babylonische Wandrung* offered even more weak spots to be attacked than did *Alexanderplatz*, as Stübs pointed out. The main thrust of the criticism is that, once the false legend of Döblin as the friend of the poor and downtrodden has been exposed, it is time to show that he is only concerned with his own inflated self. This novel, even more than the most insipid Nazi texts, is the expression of the deepest, the final crisis of bourgeois culture. It is comparable to a "delirium tremens, . . . the galloping consumption of bourgeois culture" (Sch 332). Again, after a sarcastic overview of the text, the denunciation: it was short-sighted of the Nazis to chase Döblin away; he would have supplied them with suitable texts (333). In his hateful commentary, Stübs comes up with real insights: he says that on occasions Döblin's style rises to the pathos and dignity of a real poet, for instance when he addresses Christ as "Mann aus meinem geschlagenen Volk," though he accuses Döblin at the same time of having a new "Jewish mission" (334). But above all, it is the narcissistic Döblin that Stübs wants to unmask: Döblin's text is a "Spiegelkabinett," in which he reflects on his own inflated ego, offering in Stübs's phrase "the literary St. Vitus dance of a narcissist" (334). Is Döblin a fool? By no means; rather, an abstruse book mirrors an abstruse society.

Ludwig Marcuse, in a 1934 review in *Das Neue Tagebuch,* has familiar problems with this text: he cannot stomach it; it is hard to find one's orientation in this encyclopedic offering. But then, at the end, rereading parts of it, one is suddenly attracted, and feels that in the end a close friendship will develop with this book (336). (Interestingly, Marcuse and Döblin also developed a personal friendship, especially while both were living in exile in Los Angeles.) But on the way to Marcuse's friendship with *Babylonische Wandrung,* there were some hurdles. He saw the novel's beginning as a less than original parody of the "Vorspiel im Himmel" of Goethe's *Faust* (334). Marcuse is also critical of the overabundance of encyclopedic knowledge and data in the book. But then, strangely enough, he comes to see the extraneous data as part of the narrative flow. At first the reader wants to tell Döblin he should not go on like a talkative old woman, but then suddenly feels himself carried away ("hineingerissen") into a narrative stream of a power unheard of in the era of the "Kunstroman" (335). The tumult of emotions the reader feels for this extraordinary novel is equal in intensity to the tumult of the world Döblin describes in it (336). Marcuse uses the word "humor" without emphasis, and seems to avoid the word "grotesque." He is evidently intent on conveying to the reader that there is a serious purpose to Döblin's seemingly chaotic multiplicity of facts, figures, locations, and characters. This purpose must have escaped the "simpler" minds of other reviewers. E. Horbach, in a 1934 review in *De Weegschaal,* looks in vain for such a purpose. In view of Döblin's subtitle, "Hochmut kommt vor dem Fall," Horbach thinks that the protagonist Konrad's insight, "Er erkennt seine Laster: Größenwahn und Eitelkeit," is a pitiful result for the tiresome wanderings through the 700 pages of Döblin's difficult novel (337).

It was Hermann Kesten, writing in Klaus Mann's journal *Die Sammlung* in 1934, who rose as Döblin's real defender and champion. One can get the impression that he discovered an unknown great writer.

Döblin, Kesten says, "fabuliert"; he has the imagination of a born story-teller, and masters the German language to such a high degree that he sometimes seems possessed by it (339). Being the true epic tale-teller, Döblin is interested in everything and anything: the novel is satirical, ironic, often humorous, with not one but a hundred tendencies (339). Döblin criticizes the modern world, but at the same time he is enamored with its chaotic and vibrant hustle and bustle, and celebrates, praises it: "Viel lieber besingt er die Welt" (339). This is no realism; the narrator takes any license that he wants: he is a Romantic who speaks with a thousand tongues and tells the bittersweet tales ("Märchen") of our world (339). Kesten ranks this book very highly — especially at this juncture, when Europe is still numb from the shock of Hitler's takeover in Germany — among the very rare and extraordinary comic novels of this age (340). And he does not consider *Babylonische Wandrung* politically escapist, pointing out that Döblin depicts Europe falling into the arms of the stupidest dictators in its history, and shows how much Europeans are fallen gods, sharing in guilt for the rise of the "Halbkreaturen," the fascists, who lust for beatings, lies, and the chains of slavery (340). Kesten sees "Halbheit" (halfness) as Döblin's diagnosis of the fatal ills of the time: "Halbwissende, Halbgebildete, Halbnarren, Halbmörder, Halbverbrecher, Halbteufel, Halbmenschen" (340). Kesten counts himself among these fallen gods of Europe, who are guilty of thinking they were above such dangers as that of National Socialism: and as Döblin's subtitle reminds us: pride goeth before the fall. Döblin, says Kesten, "deutet an, wie sehr wir wahren Europäer gestürzte Götter sind, wie schuldig an der Heraufkunft der Halbkreaturen" (340). When Döblin writes about the ex-god Konrad, he means himself and his fellow intellectuals; but, equally, when he alludes to the Babylonian exile of the Jews, he refers to the present — an association which, however, the reviewers did not pick up. The main reasons this book was not received more positively may have been that it went into too many directions, and that the later parts were somewhat baffling.

Günther Anders wrote his essay, "Der letzte Roman. Gebrauchsanweisung für Döblins Buch *Babylonische Wandrung oder Hochmut kommt vor dem Fall*" in 1935.[1] His recipe for the bewildered reader, his key to the book, was to read backwards (32). He draws a parallel between the novel and the present: the well-to-do fall, and the rest is left to chance (32). Konrad's life remains "in statu nascendi": it is a novel of birth ("Geburtsroman") (34). In other words, we could think of Laurence Sterne's *Tristram Shandy*. But Konrad does not really enter the world, he remains nowhere ("nirgendwo") and in no specific time period (36).

It is a "last" novel about a non-person, that ends as a non-novel, negating itself (40). But Konrad makes his defeatedness his life's work and its meaning: "Sein Besiegtsein ist schließlich seine Beschäftigung und seine Moral" (41). Döblin would arrive at a similarly verdict on the novel in later years, but for very different reasons than those of Anders.

No Mercy: *Pardon wird nicht gegeben*

Döblin's shorter novel *Pardon wird nicht gegeben*, published in 1935, is an anomaly in his oeuvre, as it offers a clear plot told in a straightforward or traditional fashion; a traditional novel about individuals, with obvious autobiographical elements. It has been suggested that Döblin wrote *Pardon wird nicht gegeben* for commercial purposes, and it was more reader-friendly and more successful on the market than the other exile works. It was even picked up by the Büchergilde Gutenberg, the German book club in Zurich, in 1938. There was, however, little critical attention. It seemed superfluous to comment on this apparently plain tale. While the plainness of the story is deceptive, and there are many interesting aspects, especially the ending, the direct political connections between the protagonist's dilemmas and the situation of 1935 did not make much of an impact. Thus the work has largely remained neglected by critics, just as *Babylonische Wandrung*, albeit for quite different reasons.

Writing in *Die Sammlung* in 1935, Heinrich Schütz welcomed *Pardon* as a real novel, a story of simple human events, told in a straightforward manner (Sch 341). Schütz misses what other shortsighted critics also failed to see: the traces of Döblin's first exile experiences from 1933 to 1935. But should one not wonder that the story is so ordinary ("landläufig")? The novel's plot is so commonplace that it hardly even involves invention (342). So what makes the book remarkable? Not the story as such, not the way to find general meaning in an individual destiny, not the structure and the style, but the point of view of the narrator. The "Blick" or view of the author, his special way of seeing, does not mean simply taking in facts; instead his gaze gives "selbst Licht," a peculiar light that illuminates people and objects in a particular way (342). The "Dichter" is transformed into a "Forscher," and what this researcher uncovers is the difference between real and unreal, the typical existence of an empty society, the insufficient, the half-real ("Halbwirkliche") in it all (343). The author has used a merciless light like X-rays (343), he is not moralizing, but judges his characters by their actions. The story takes place inside a family, whose characters are called by their first names; their public, official existence in which they go by their family name is omitted. They live in an inner space. Also the name of the location, the city, is omitted, it becomes simply *the* metropolis (344) Even the time is unspecified — although all indications are that the novel takes place in the twenties and the following Depression — and the author speaks "von dem *Wesen* einer Zeit" (of the essence of a period of time) (344). Döblin has extracted the essence from the data of reality, the mark of great art (344). Schütz praises Döblin, who was always accused of cluttering his stories with too many details, which made it impossible to find the essence, for a vision that elevates a story of everyday life to the level of human fate. Schütz does not inquire into the psychological intricacies and the political aspects, both of which leave many unanswered questions. Some of these are treated by Robert Minder, the French Germanist who would later become one of Döblin's closest friends, in "Marxisme et Psychoanalyse chez Alfred Döblin. A propos de son dernier roman: Pardon wird nicht gegeben," in *Revue de l'enseignement des langues vivantes* in 1937. Minder found in this tale both a case of Freudian family entanglement and an example of the dead-end situation of capitalism and the bourgeois class.

Europe's Rape of South America: *Amazonas*

Döblin's next exploration brought him once more to foreign lands and a previous age. His epic tale of the colonization of South America, *Amazonas*, grew into two volumes. The first volume, *Die Fahrt ins Land ohne Tod* appeared in 1937; the second volume, *Der blaue Tiger*, in 1938. *Die Fahrt ins Land ohne Tod* focused on the exploration of South America and the original encounters between Europeans and Indians. A large part of the second volume is devoted to the attempt of the Jesuits to create a Christian state in Paraguay and peaceful relations with the Indians. Then, rather abruptly, Döblin takes the action into present-day Europe, with a story whose political and philosophical implications and connections with the previous parts become clear only at the very end. In 1947 and 1948, Döblin republished the book in three parts, the third part being named *Der neue Urwald*. The edition of *Amazonas* in Döblin's *Ausgewählte Werke*, published in 1963, omitted this third part altogether. This was finally corrected in 1988 by Werner Stauffacher's new edition of *Amazonas* in the *Ausgewählte Werke*. Such a twisted edition history is typical for Döblin's delayed reception after 1945; it also indicates that the book did not have a chance to make its mark in 1937/38 and did not seem directly relevant to the immediate postwar situation in Germany either. It was for all practical purposes engulfed by the Second World War.

Ferdinand Lion, editor of the journal *Maß und Wert*, published in Switzerland under the guidance of Thomas Mann, had published Döblin's programmatic essay "Prometheus und das Primitive" in early 1938. He also wrote a long review of *Die Fahrt ins Land ohne Tod.* Lion considers the central question in all of Döblin's oeuvre to be that of "Tun oder Nichttun": action or inaction (345). The new epic moves in wide spaces, a setting the likes of which Döblin had never before operated in: "Urwald, Urstrom, Urnatur" (345–46). Lion sees the colonial invasion and the conflict it brings about in the context of Döblin's previous works, and locates an ironic contrast in the incursion of Nietzschean supermen into the Rousseauian world of the Amazon (346). He asks which side Döblin's heart is on, and finds that it is on both, sympathetic to the Indians but understanding the need for progress as well; similarly mixed is his depiction of events, swinging as a pendulum from the monstrous to the idyllic, and this is contrasted with what the reviewer calls "Thomas Mann'schen Menschenmaß" (346). It cannot have pleased Döblin to be set against the standard of Mann as the judge of the "Menschenmaß." Lion sees Döblin as at his best when depicting encounters between the two worlds, their mutual impact, and a figure like Las Casas.

Lion believes in the relevance of Döblin's critique, but not in its radicalism, for, according to him, much of what Döblin represents much more openly and radically in this novel than before was being debated in the new European states or even being implemented experimentally (348). In the end, Lion elevates Döblin to the highest literary level by comparing him favorably to Thomas Mann and his novel tetralogy *Joseph und seine Brüder:* both Döblin's novel and Mann's are created from the same crisis of need as are Germany's internal politics, but whereas those politics degrade everything to the point of unrecognizability, the two works of art are worthy of the "Erkenntnis- und Gestaltungskraft" of the former Germany. But the works of Mann and Döblin must provoke great hatred in those in power in Germany, Lion says, because they are artworks that portray a politics of possibility that, while based on the same premises as the current policies of Germany, is diametrically opposed to those policies (348). Ferdinand Lion sees a common mythical ground for the opposing irrational movements, and he calls Döblin with his own words "ein Primitiver," a primitive. This brings Lion to his final resumé: "Bei Döblin wird der Urzeit die Tat entgegengestellt, die in sie eingreift": in Döblin the primitive age is confronted with the action that invades it (349).

Döblin was by no means pleased with his "elevation" to the rank of Thomas Mann (neither was Mann!), and Döblin wrote several angry letters to Lion (on 18 January 38, 27 May 1938 and once more, date unknown).[2] More important is Lion's insinuation that both authors had "mythical" foundations in common with National Socialism. Whatever Thomas Mann's and Döblin's doubts were about the virtues of rationalism, they had abhorred totalitarian state power and the racist ideology of the Nazis even before Hitler's regime was established. Ferdinand Lion's hesitance to condemn the Hitler regime perhaps reflected his native Swiss diplomacy, and seemed to justify what the Nazis pretended to do: find a way out of the crisis of the failed democracy in the name of a "true" Germany, objecting only that they used the wrong means, and seemed to be the wrong people for the right task. It is incongruous to bring Döblin's radical critique of colonialism and Eurocentrism into this context — as it is incongruous to drag Mann's *Joseph* into it, even if Lion could not foresee the orientation of the last volume of Mann's tetralogy, *Joseph der Ernährer.*

Lion also reviewed the second volume of *Amazonas, Der blaue Tiger,* in *Maß und Wert* in 1938/39. This time he avoided any reference to Mann. The review clearly takes pains to be "objective," neutral, and does not enter into the fundamental questions raised by the book, although Lion mentions Oswald Spengler and Keyserling and their radical critique of the West. He notes the two disparate halves of the text and tries to cope with the more difficult second part. His discussion of the Jesuit state in Paraguay is brief and centers not on its internal problems, but on the "Doppelbühne," the changing perspectives of Europe and South America, and on the advancement of the European sciences, the "Prometheisch-Tätige" (357). The Jesuit idyll is followed, for Lion, by an abrupt change, a new satirical narrative voice. Lion understands this second part as novellas following rapidly on one another (358) and is particularly interested in the two "Ingenieurdeutschen" — the Germans of the future, in the eyes of Spengler. One of them makes his peace with National Socialism — which both had originally rejected as too "sentimental-patriotisch" (358) — whereas the other remains opposed to it, as he is transformed by love. The ending, the voyage to the penal colony in South America and the escape into the primeval forest, is, for Lion, "nochmals höchster epischer Ton" (358). The Europeans are sucked up by the jungle; the snake goddess of the Amazonas basin triumphs in the end. Whereas Lion was correct in applying the categories of "Prometheus und das Primitive" to *Amazonas,* he should have realized, however, as Döblin did himself, that the epic history contained so much more, and was clearly intent on pointing to a direction beyond that dichotomy. It is remarkable that Lion did not even address the crucial question of *Gewalt*, of violence in nature and in human societies.

Kurt Kersten, writing in 1938 in Moscow's *Das Wort*, looks at the first volume of *Amazonas* from another side. He polemicizes against Döblin's recent essay on the historical novel, "Der historische Roman und wir," which had appeared in *Das Wort* in October 1936, and then applies his criticism to the text of *Amazonas*. It is well written, he says, but has no breadth, merely offering well-known facts in an exciting manner (351). Kersten sees the figure of Las Casas as a self-portrait of Döblin; he knows what is right and is unable to stand up for it. The novel is not only useless, it is harmful. Before reading the second volume, readers should exhort themselves to resist the temptations of Döblin's irresponsible ambivalence, Las Casas's escapism, and the novel's seductive style; as Kersten says, to "Widerstehe dem Übel!" (351).

In contrast to Kersten's harsh but sincere words, the long review of Julius Hay in *Internationale Literatur*, published in Moscow in 1938, is definitely politically motivated. It has to be seen in the context of the popular front movement and the festivities in Paris for Döblin's sixtieth birthday that year. The Moscow-based Communist orthodoxy, which had condemned Döblin as a dangerous and pre-fascist "sympathizer," now praises his great contributions on the side of the working class. Hay makes a clever and valid point when he argues that not all anti-fascist literature has to be topical: fascism aims at destroying the whole human being; anti-fascism seeks to save it, rescuing it from new attacks of destruction (351). Hay offers as evidence the "Indianerrepublik" of the Jesuits, which he considers a more timely and relevant example than Döblin's direct analysis of the twentieth century; and he draws an unexpected but important insight from the tale, a terrible truth and insight: ". . . Völker können jäh sterben" — peoples can die; and they can commit suicide. Yet in the same vein they can be saved: "Völker können gerettet werden" (352). Hay might have said more precisely, "peoples can save themselves," because he considers the basic reason for the downfall of the Jesuit republic the separation of the two classes, with the Jesuits as the guardians, and the Indians as childlike (slave) workers in a benevolent tutelage, with no chance nor any effort to liberate themselves. It was a "künstliches Gebilde" (355), similar to those erected in the present to preserve and prolong the life of the capitalistic system.

Döblin, according to Hay, has learned more about history in these last years, and readers of this historical novel will be helped to understand the present as Döblin does. Döblin's progress toward realism and humanism, his finding of the will to fulfill his own demand for a humanization of literature, make him to a higher degree than before the poet of the German people (356). Biberkopf was already proof of Döblin's "Volksverbundenheit," and this is confirmed and strengthened by the later work.

Döblin's Isolation

In 1939, just before the demise of exile publishing in Amsterdam, Döblin brought out the first volume of his *November 1918* trilogy or tetralogy, *Bürger und Soldaten 1918*. A few reviews appeared, among them Alexander Moritz Frey's in *Maß und Wert* of 1939/40 and Hermann Kesten's in *Das Neue Tagebuch* of 1940. These were the last echoes Döblin would hear from his writings for a long time. In September 1939, the outbreak of the Second World War radically changed the situation of the exiles for the worse.

Döblin continued working on the second part of the trilogy, which then grew so large that it had to be divided into halves for the later publication. He had just completed a draft of this part in May 1940 when German troops advanced on Paris, and he had to embark on a traumatic escape through France, with a fortuitous ending: the reunion with his family and their voyage to the United States.

From 1940 to 1945 Döblin lived in California, in and around Santa Monica. He never achieved a presence on the American book market. He could not place his autobiographical account of his 1940 flight, "Robinson in Frankreich," which then became the first part of his 1949 autobiography *Schicksalsreise*, nor did he find a publisher for *November 1918*, whose last part, *Karl und Rosa*, was written in Los Angeles. Only two short excerpts were published in German, in limited editions.

Döblin, his wife, and their youngest son converted to Catholicism in November 1941. He began to write stories and essays reflecting his conversion and had started work on his last novel *Hamlet* when the war ended in 1945. Isolated and unhappy as he was in the United States, Döblin welcomed the chance to be active in the rebuilding of Germany. As a French citizen, he was invited to work for the cultural section of the military administration of the French Occupation Zone in Germany, which included parts of southwest Germany. Whereas the Soviet Union promoted the return of (mostly communist) German exiles to their occupation zone, with the goal of the reconstruction of Germany and its society, the Western Allies were reluctant to do so. They had used emigrants for military intelligence and psychological warfare, but only rarely did exiles participate in the organization of cultural life in the Western zones. Trade unions and the Social Democratic Party were more effective channels.

Döblin was one of the exceptions, due to his French citizenship. However, it is evident that at the age of 67 he had limited energy, and he remained an outsider in the French administration. Still, he was able to get some of his works published in Germany. It is doubtful whether his strategy of giving priority to the new works written during the exile period was effective in reacquainting the German public with his name and style. But in any event, his return was problematic for a variety of reasons: in Germany, he was still remembered as the author of *Berlin Alexanderplatz*, but his political and philosophical positions had changed radically. He did not fit into the socialist and "humanistic" literature advocated in East Berlin, but he also could not align himself with "Christian" writers in the West such as Reinhold Schneider, Edzard Schaper, and Gertrud von le Fort. And although he established friendly relations with some of the representatives of the "inner emigration," he was not one of them either. His radical-sounding faith in Jesus Christ and divine grace distanced him from more moderate writers who were intent on re-establishing the pre-1933 conservative literary scene. The reception of Döblin's exile and post-exile works in postwar Germany has to be seen in this complex and unfavorable context.

Although Döblin had shown his good will by returning to Germany in 1945, the alienation between exiles and those who had remained in Germany, typical for the postwar years, did not spare him either. Those who had remained in Germany, among them the writers, declared with few dissenting voices that the exiles had become foreigners who could no longer understand Germany and the Germans. The majority of the exiles had expected some feelings of guilt and shame among the Germans and were angered to find only denial and self-pity, as they saw it. Especially the typical excuse "Ich habe nichts gewußt" sounded dishonest from the point of view of the anti-fascists. In this climate of mutual suspicion, it did not help that Döblin was wearing a French officer's uniform when he visited Berlin for the first time. In spite of the resurgence of the Christian faith at the time, Döblin's Christian message did not reach his audience. Thus the critics tended to treat him with distant respect, condemning his works with faint praise, and readers largely ignored his books. Therefore, when the monetary reform of 1948 caused a crisis on the book market, Döblin's publishers withdrew. Finally, his *Hamlet* novel did not find a publisher until East German friends and publishers picked it up in 1956 — the publication made quite a stir, but came too late for the dying Döblin.

Reassessing 1918: *November 1918*

Döblin published the trilogy *November 1918* in three volumes, in 1948, 1949, and 1950. Only short sections of the original first volume, *Bürger und Soldaten 1918,* could be included, since the main part of the action takes place in Alsace, and the French censors objected to such a critical depiction of the 1918 French occupation.

When *November 1918* was published, the critics had already formed certain expectations of the "new" Döblin. In 1946, he had published two dialogues on the Christian religion, *Der unsterbliche Mensch: Ein Religionsgespräch,* and *Der Oberst und der Dichter,* both of which were taken very seriously and widely and positively reviewed. This was followed in 1947 by *Die literarische Situation,* a new version of Döblin's 1938 essay *Die deutsche Literatur im Ausland seit 1933.* It was a bad omen, however, that *Amazonas* published in 1946/47 in three volumes, did not find a friendly reception, and was considered to be rather insignificant. While Döblin the Christian was initially accepted in Germany, Döblin the exile novelist found the doors closed, and that would be the fate of *November 1918.*

The first part of the trilogy, *Verratenes Volk,* appeared in 1948. A number of reviewers commented on this volume. The very well-informed review by Peter Bor in the Göppingen *Neue Württembergische Zeitung* of 18 August 1949 first orients the reader about the author and his fate after 1933. Bor had read *Bürger und Soldaten 1918* when it appeared in 1939, and regrets that most of it has been sacrificed in this edition, surmising correctly that the reason is its setting, Alsace-Lorraine. Yet the new first volume of the novel offers enough material (Sch 403). Bor characterizes Döblin's approach as typical for him, with little reflection and reasoning, instead action, concrete, bursting reality, a multitude of tragic, grotesque, and sad characters. There is a good reason for calling it an "Erzählwerk" and not a novel: Döblin never wanted to be a novelist, and all his major novels are in reality "Epen," epic works. He is the most important, most powerful exponent of the modern prose epic in Germany (404). The only comparable author that comes to Bor's mind is Hans Henny Jahnn with his *Perrudja.*

Döblin, Bor says, lets the reader find his own way through his confusing multiplicity of scenes and characters. But the reviewer senses that in this vast panorama there must be an "Ariadne thread" that will show the reader the way through the narrative. He expects from the Catholic convert Döblin a different type of revolution, embodied in Oberleutnant Becker, and it looks as if within this man another revolution is in preparation, a revolution on a different level from that of the empirical facts (404). *November 1918* was going to be analyzed either as the account of the failed German revolution or as the path of Becker to his final destiny — it is, of course, both, and there are considerable tensions between the two accounts.

Robert Haerdter, in a 1949 review in *Die Gegenwart,* does not mention Becker. He tries to do justice to Döblin's harsh criticisms by mentioning that the book was written before and during and not after the Second World War. Still, it has an uncomfortable aftertaste of "Rechthaberei," of righteousness (405). The defensive German attitude toward outsiders who proclaim the collective guilt of the Germans is unmistakable. This "failed" revolution can only be evaluated in its own context and in accord with its goals. But if a picture reveals so many blemishes, is it the fault of the object or perhaps that of the reflecting mirror? (405). Is it Döblin who projects so many blemishes onto German history, or was the time of 1918/19 really so bad? Haerdter tends to the first alternative. This becomes evident in his second review in *Die Gegenwart* in 1950, in which he assesses the entire trilogy, finding that the whole work is saturated with "Ressentiment" against the course of German history after the collapse of 1918 and against the political character of the Germans (401). He also objects that the novel's concentration on Becker's story moves the question out of the realm of history: Becker's is a *personal,* not a political solution, and his remorse about what he has done and failed to do before, during, and since the war exists in the realm of faith, and is irrelevant in terms of the political arena (401–2). Haerdter first refuses to accept Döblin's view of the events of 1918/19, attributing them to the resentments of an exile, and secondly considers Becker's way out of the conflict to be an escapist non-solution. Haerdter's criticism of Döblin based on this second point can perhaps be considered legitimate only if Becker's perspective is conflated with that of the author/narrator, which indicates the intricacies of this seemingly simple "chronicle."

Horst Krüger, writing in Freiburg's *Badische Zeitung* on 15 September 1949, takes his clue from the work's subtitle *Eine deutsche Revolution.* Linking *November 1918* with Döblin's great first success *Berlin Alexanderplatz,* which, he says, was written by a "young doctor" (although Döblin was around fifty years old at the time!) Krüger says that the subtitle indicates the direction and the goal is to go beyond documentary and historical facts to a higher, timeless truth. "Eine deutsche Revolution" is an ironic misnomer, because it is a grotesque story with tragic overtones, accusation and confession. It is the self-revelation of a German in exile, almost another Heine, who gives a laughing and painful testimony on the political incompetence of his people (406). Later, after mentioning Hindenburg and those around him, Krüger calls the book "eine tragisch-komische Schaubühne der Zeit" (407). The review ends with the point that Döblin's assessment of German history should not be seen in terms of the ideologies of political parties, but from a standpoint of a "christlichen Humanismus" (408) — an assumption based less on this volume than on Döblin's biography and on the religious dialogue *Der unsterbliche Mensch*. Krüger reviewed the third volume of the trilogy, *Karl und Rosa*, in the *Badische Zeitung* on 5 October 1950, and took the previous points to their conclusion.

Peter Lahnstein, in a *Stuttgarter Zeitung* review on 3 August 1949, sees little value in *Verratenes Volk* except as a panorama of the period. The only virtue of the many naturalistic portrayals is that they entertain the reader (409). The private love stories are "Kintopp von der billigen Sorte" (409). And politically, Döblin does not have much to say; it is highly questionable whether the political substance is more significant than the literary quality (409).

Robert Haerdter had questioned the wisdom of bringing out the trilogy volume by volume rather than at the same time. Indeed, this may have harmed the reception; but, on the other hand, the arrival on the market of a massive three-volume opus would not have been too inviting either. After the publication of the last volume, *Karl und Rosa*, there were a number of reviews and reassessments, but interest was not high: *November 1918* was anything but an "event" on the German book market. The significance of the work would not be recognized either in West or East Germany until more than thirty years later.

Joseph Baur, in a review in *Wetzlarer Neue Zeitung* published on 23 September 1950, belongs to those who find the central point of the work in Friedrich Becker, whom he calls "ein faustischer Mensch unseres Jahrhunderts" (399). But the analogy with Faust, especially Goethe's *Faust*, is tenuous, as it is the "Passionsweg" rather than a compact with the devil and eternal striving that Baur has in mind. Baur is convinced of what he calls the Döblinesque religious-rational synthesis (400) and the religious message of the book. He also acknowledges Döblin's place in the history of literature and mentions that it should not be necessary to stress Döblin's rank as one of the great German novelists — which he nevertheless proceeds to do (400). In the end he abruptly prophesies that Döblin's trilogy may end up belonging among those books that still matter when most of the books of the present day are forgotten (400).

Felix Stößinger, writing in Zurich's *Die Tat* on 9 December 1950, focuses on the revolution and the opposition of "Idee" and "Verrat," idea and treason: "Die 'Idee' und der 'Verrat' sind das Thema des Gesamtwerks, das dort gipfelt, wo die Idee ihre Irrealität enthüllt und daher dem Verrat wehrlos ausgeliefert ist" (402). Stößinger is not convinced by Döblin's religious antidotes. He considers the depiction of the "Verrat" the strongest part of the work, also from a literary point of view. And the essential weakness is that the novel does not offer a constructive political counter-program (403). This argument had already been voiced against *Wissen und Verändern!* Whether the reviewers want to talk about the revolution or take Becker as their focal point, they demand extra-literary dimensions, political or religious solutions (or both).

Reviewing this and other critical statements, it comes to mind that Döblin's *November 1918*, a monumental achievement with all its faults and weaknesses, was largely ignored by the major daily papers and weeklies and by the literary journals. It is not far-fetched to use once more the comparison with Thomas Mann, whose *Doktor Faustus*, although most controversial and reviewed with many reservations and polemical attacks, could not be ignored as a major event in German literature. Mann's visit to East and West Germany in 1949 was the occasion of countless commentaries. Meanwhile, Döblin, like Mann's brother Heinrich, was virtually ignored.

Return to the Devastated Self: Döblin's Last Novel, *Hamlet oder Die lange Nacht nimmt ein Ende*

Döblin would not again be present on the German book market with a new novel until shortly before his death in 1957, with *Hamlet oder Die lange Nacht nimmt ein Ende*. In 1949, between the volumes of *November 1918*, he had published his "Bericht und Bekenntnis" *Schicksalsreise*, the account of his flight through France during the summer of 1940, where he turned to Christianity during his forced stay in the small town of Mende in the Auvergne. This "Robinson in Frankreich" had been rejected for publication in the United States. Döblin added a short second part, on his experiences in the United States and his return to Germany. The reviewers at the time focused mostly on Döblin's conversion to Catholicism, and noted that the added second part did not have much life and color, whereas the first part gave a vivid picture of the French débâcle in 1940 and Döblin's disorientation and feeling of having arrived at a dead-end street. Whereas Christian reviewers lauded his conversion, secularists deplored his rejection of reason in favor of mysticism. Carl Seelig, writing in Zurich's *Das Bücherblatt* on 28 August 1953, considered Döblin's conversion to be another attempt at an escape, a flight away from Judaism. The erstwhile fighter has turned into a penitent, and this last spiritual transformation will always remain a curiosity (424). Indeed, while Döblin was shunned as a traitor in some Jewish circles, he was by no means accepted with open arms on the "other side." He was once more, as many times before, "zwischen den Stühlen."

An anonymous reviewer in Munich's *Echo der Woche*, on 3 March 1950, brought up a very significant point when he doubted that it was correct or meaningful to speak of Döblin's (or Ernst Jünger's or Stefan Andres's) "Wandlung," a ubiquitous catchword at the time (420). "Geistig-konsequente Menschen gehen ihren Weg," and all their productions are documents of their development (420). Instead of the "proteus" Döblin or the Döblin of the radical turn-about or of an inner transformation, the reviewer sees a consistent and continuous development. The statement is remarkable not only as an assessment of Döblin, but also of German cultural history before and after 1945.

In 1945, before leaving California, Döblin began work on his last novel, *Hamlet oder Die lange Nacht nimmt ein Ende*. He completed the manuscript in Baden-Baden in 1946, but he did not want to present himself to the German reading public with this newest text before they had a chance to get acquainted with previous works from his exile, notably *Amazonas* and especially *November 1918*. Therefore, he rejected offers from publishers for *Hamlet*. However, by the time Döblin was ready to release the book, conditions had changed radically. The *Währungsreform* had a deep impact on publishing, and the initial curiosity of the Germans for works by the exiles had vanished. *November 1918* was a dismal failure on the book market, especially the last volume of 1950, *Karl und Rosa*. After 1950, a number of West German publishers went out of business, and the survivors rejected Döblin's works. The old connection with S. Fischer seemed long forgotten. Döblin was embittered and left Germany in 1953 to live in Paris, but he had to spend most of his four remaining years in hospitals and sanatoriums in Baden. On 7 September 1954, he received the visit of Peter Huchel, Hans Mayer, and Eberhard Meckel. Huchel, then editor of *Sinn und Form*, asked Döblin about new unpublished manuscripts and was given the typescript of the novel, which he in turn offered to the East Berlin publisher Rütten & Loening. The publisher accepted, but asked for a more "positive" ending. (In Döblin's text, Edward Allison, the protagonist, was to enter a monastery at the end.) Döblin complied, and the book appeared in 1956. Following its widespread acclaim in East and West, a West German edition by Langen-Müller of Munich followed in 1957.

Döblin's difficulty in finding and staying with publishers after his exile and the war was partially of his own making and partially a result of the climate of restoration and repression of the past during the Adenauer years. It needs to be noted that one of the major East German publishers did not hesitate at the height of the Cold War to publish a decidedly Christian book by an author who, although famous, could easily be considered a member of an anti-communist front. In 1954, Huchel had pre-printed a chapter from the book in *Sinn und Form*. It is an intriguing conjecture to imagine how the German readers would have reacted in 1946, when *Hamlet* was completed, to this very personal and "psycho-analytic" novel about a seriously wounded soldier returning from the war.

Hamlet after the Second World War

Any new version of the Hamlet story is sure to arouse curiosity in Germany. The 1945/46 programs of most German theaters included Shakespeare's *Hamlet*, together with Goethe's *Iphigenie*, Lessing's *Nathan der Weise*, and topical plays like Friedrich Wolf's *Professor Mamlock*. *Hamlet* is undoubtedly at the top of the German Shakespeare canon, and there is a specifically German view of Hamlet — both the character and the play — that can be traced back to the eighteenth century, most visibly in Goethe's *Wilhelm Meisters Lehrjahre* (1794). Edward, Döblin's Hamlet, a seriously wounded British soldier returning from the Second World War, needs to uncover the dark secrets of his family in order to heal himself and try to begin a new life. However, in the course of his investigation, his family is torn apart, and his parents meet a tragic fate.

Ludwig Marcuse, Döblin's old friend, hailed the publication of the novel in the *Frankfurter Allgemeine Zeitung* of 5 April 1957, lamenting that at a time when every greenhorn writer is being praised as the harbinger of a new era, Germany's greatest living novelist must wait ten years for the publication of a book that is weightier than many of the tons of paper that is boasted about in the statistics of the Frankfurt book fair (Sch 434). Marcuse had a point, although he should have said "six years," since the first four years of the delay were of Döblin's own making. Marcuse's initial characterization of the book is surprising: he says that this masterwork is "heiter, bunt und wahr" — but that it also has the heavy pathos of life (434). Döblin is "ein Aschenbrödel der literarischen Welt," a neglected Cinderella. As a writer, he has never come back home, and he remains an exile after twenty-four years. In the postwar years he has been published but largely ignored: in a time enamored of the awarding of prizes Döblin is the least-crowned among the princes of literature ("der ungekrönteste Dichterfürst") (434).

Döblin's novels arise from two impulses: he is a "Fabulierer," spinning tales, and a "Forscher" with a scientific mind. He does not describe characters as much as he opens them up (434). Döblin tends to overload his texts with ideas and information; every novels feeds the reader to the fullest, who may perish from overindulgence ("Völlerei"), but certainly not from lack of nourishment ("Unterernährung") (435). Marcuse believes that with *Hamlet,* Döblin has set himself the question: How does someone who has been torn to pieces make himself whole again? — a question he had already dealt with in *Berlin Alexanderplatz.* In Marcuse's view, Döblin shows the direction in *Hamlet,* but is unable to follow it through: the subtitle *Die lange Nacht nimmt ein Ende* sounds very optimistic, he says, but it is the only thing wrong with this book (435). Marcuse parodies Goethe's *Faust:* "Wer immer strebend sich bemüht, wie Edward Allison, hat viele Labyrinthe zu durchwandern, sie sind übervölkert mit Ungeheuern. Die lange Nacht nimmt — kein Ende; jedenfalls nicht, solange wir dabei sind" (435–36). Marcuse does not believe the novel's last sentence: "Ein neues Leben begann." Skeptical as he is, he makes predictions as to the durability of this work. He predicts that the narrative technique will be imitated as soon as it is discovered (436–37).

For Marcuse, Döblin is the model writer, and avoids the two pitfalls of the age: that of the "militante Friedenstaube" as well as the "Elfenbeinturm" (437). Militant peacenik refers to Eastern bloc propaganda and socialist realism; the ivory tower to the academism of the West. Döblin, says Marcuse, was able to capture so much of the essence of the universe exactly because he did not think that he could define it.

Although Marcuse's review was a spirited defense of his friend Döblin — the last Marcuse would carry out during Döblin's lifetime — and of the cause of the German exiles, it pales in comparison with Walter Muschg's enthusiastic praise in *Texte und Zeichen* in 1957, in which he calls *Hamlet* Döblin's testament, his "dichterisches Vermächtnis" (437). That *Hamlet* was being ignored by West German publishers and critics (according to Muschg) was another sign of the destruction of German literature, because the novel is a masterpiece, the gripping human testimony of a great author, one that all who believe in German "Dichtung" have been waiting for (437–38). Muschg associates this work with great Christian texts like Jeremias Gotthelf's *Geld und Geist* and the last works of Tolstoy. Döblin differs from them in his sense for unconscious processes and his "Tiefblick," his deep intuition concerning the human psyche, sharpened by his years as a psychiatrist. His familiarity with the dark abysses of the age yields an approach that is much more radical than that of his literary forebears. This is combined with the wisdom of old age, gained through long suffering, which features newly in the late works

(438). While Döblin opens up what he himself had called "die Tiefen-schicht," the deep level, this time in psychological dimensions, Muschg praises the artistic achievement equally. He defines *Hamlet* as a "Novel-lenzyklus," a cycle of novellas of a perfection unparalleled in the German language (438). This is a bold statement, especially from a Swiss critic, who had to be mindful of Gottfried Keller. But Muschg backs up his claim, pointing out not only the aesthetic perfection and understanding ("Kunstverstand") with which the novellas are interwoven with the main plot, but also that the reader's resulting aesthetic pleasure is balanced by an emotional involvement in fundamental themes of these variations: those of the guilt and responsibility of humans for the present condition of the world, the nature of evil, and the possibilities of overcoming it. This is what links the family story with the crisis of the Second World War and its aftermath (440). Even as a "fromme[r] Christ" Döblin has remained like the author of *Wang-lun*: playful, with a liking for improvi-sation, and there is nothing of "berechnender Absichtlichkeit" (calcu-lated intentionality) in this text (441). There is a full scale of stylistic forms and levels, from sloppy slang to rhapsodic singing. For those who see possibilities for the genre of the novel only in formal experiments as a response to a total crisis, *Hamlet* provides an alternative (441). Muschg reminds his audience indirectly of the non-return of the exiles, hailing Döblin as a voice of the exile generation, whose surviving representatives have a message that only they can tell, but who are almost unknown to the youth of the day. He asks how those who care about the fate of German literature can be content with the fact that such a wonderful book is read only outside Germany's borders (442).

Muschg's enthusiasm for Döblin as well as his decided opinions on the "Zerstörung" of German literature have a special significance for Döblin's reception, as he became the first editor of Döblin's collected works. In this role Muschg did not consider it his responsibility to offer accurate reprints of the published texts and extant typescripts, but to improve on them, so that he could present aesthetically perfect texts. The "definitive version" of a literary text is often hard to determine; Döblin presents an extreme case of a writer who continually revised and rewrote. This is in keeping with his procedure: he never presents an end result, or closure, but always a thinking process, and his texts are an invitation to his readers to think for themselves. Muschg's idea of aesthetic perfection could not do justice to this open form of the epic narrative.

Generally speaking, the critics of *Hamlet* focused on one or two of the following aspects: Döblin's stature as a writer; the family conflict and its psychoanalysis; the connection between the personal and the historical situation; Döblin's baffling language and style. Negative criticism attacked particularly the last aspect. Wolfgang Grözinger, writing in *Hochland* 49 (1956/57), calls *Hamlet* an important, bold work, and identifies the central theme as initially that of guilt for the war, widening rapidly into the question of evil in the world and in human beings (425). He is full of admiration for the exposition and the development of the plot until the moment of acute crisis, to which point he considers the novel a masterwork. He finds the novel's revelation that the guilt of causing the war cannot be isolated from human guilt in general or from original sin aesthetically and ethically convincing (426). But he is dismayed by what he sees as a breakdown of stylistic unity in the book's denouement, where it simply falls apart, as the characters lose their contours and the main idea dissolves. Here Grözinger finds not only a failure of art, but of thought (427). He goes on to surmise that the first, the good part had been written in America, and that the failure of the second part is connected with Döblin's return to Germany: he writes that Döblin appears in this novel as "ein umgekehrter Antäus" (a reverse Antaeus), who after his return to his homeland fell victim once more to the "Ungestalten" (monstrosities) of the German character he had seemed to overcome during his exile (427).

In a review in Stuttgart's *Deutsche Zeitung und Wirtschaftszeitung* on 17 July 1957, Hans Daiber classifies *Hamlet* as a "Heimkehrerroman" (novel of return to one's homeland) and immediately defends it against the bad reputation of the genre, calling it a "masterful composition." Daiber praises the richness of the material offered, saying it would supply half a dozen presentable books, and excusing minor stylistic deficiencies as immaterial in comparison. Ironically, Daiber considers the novel's conclusion, which Döblin had only recently changed at the demand of the East German publisher, to be typical for what he sees as the "optimistic" mood after 1945 (428). In fact, the mood was anything but optimistic. The ending that Döblin wrote after the war was not hopeful either. The optimistic conclusion was supposed to reflect the East German will to transform society.

Karl August Horst, writing in *Merkur* 11 (1957), uses the opportunity to review *Hamlet* for a general assessment and historical placement of Döblin's work, before he analyzes the text itself. He attempts to come to grips with the broken continuity of German literature by reclaiming Expressionism and the other literature of the Weimar Republic. For him, Döblin is the foremost representative of this literature, and he claims that Döblin's works after 1933 never changed: even *Hamlet* remains typical of his texts of the 1920s.

According to Horst, when Döblin returned to Germany and published *Der Oberst und der Dichter* and *Amazonas*, it seemed as if the connection ("Rückverbindung") to the 1920s had been established. But in retrospect, as seen from 1957, this was not so, as Horst realizes that postwar literature in general is very different from the literature of the twenties. He concludes that a real coming-to-terms with the literature of the interwar period has not taken place, so that its most prominent representatives have escaped attention since the war (429). One of these representatives is Döblin, and although it is good to have *Berlin Alexanderplatz* available in a cheap edition, it would be equally important, writes Horst, to reacquaint oneself with *Wang-lun* and *Berge Meere und Giganten*.

Although *Hamlet* is not written in the Expressionist style, one would associate it with the Döblin of the twenties; the fundamentals have not changed, according to Horst, though the manner of their execution has (430). Döblin's *Hamlet* is especially suited as a bridge to the literature of the twenties and its basic elements. This is particularly due to the pathological nature of the main character Edward's experiences, his "Schicksalserfahrung." The protagonists of the twenties succumbed to a pathological fatalism (430). Horst's examples reach from Hesse's Harry Haller and Thomas Mann's Hans Castorp to Musil's Ulrich, in *Der Mann ohne Eigenschaften,* and to Broch's Vergil, once more connecting exile literature with that of the twenties. Moreover, he connects Döblin's *Hamlet* not with Shakespeare, but with what the Germans of the twenties made of Shakespeare's *Hamlet.* The mother-son relationship is at the center of both (432). The hatred between son and father also points back to the literature of the twenties, but Horst sees the father in Döblin's book as being placed in a different historical context: as a "Mitläufer" and a nihilist: he embodies the "feuilletonistischen Zeitgeist," the mindset of the journalistic age that can be pressed into any form without losing its brutal egotism (432). In addition to echoing Hesse's *Glasperlenspiel,* this definition of the father as a typical Nazi *Mitläufer* is obviously a very German perspective from the generation of the returning soldiers, the *Heimkehrer.* Through his unending probing, Edward destroys the foundations of the house that sheltered him after his return (433). Horst is not fooled by the optimistic tone of the conclusion, which is actually at a deeper level very thought-provoking: has one witnessed a tragedy or a dialectical process that exposes an ultimate incompatibility? Has one seen "Urbilder" or gotten a glimpse of a mystic "coincidentia oppositorum" (433–34)? Maybe all of the above. In any event, the obvious contradictions contribute to Horst's point: that the work can be seen as a kind of summary of the trends of the twenties (434).

Typical for a new trend opposed to the ideology of the new begin-
ning-point or "Stunde Null" at the end of the war, Horst insists on continuity. He finds this continuity with the twenties among the exiles, and he
wants to bring it (and them) back to Germany; but he wants to find them
unchanged, fundamentally as they were in 1933 when they left Germany,
although neither Germany nor the exiles could possibly be the same. His
perceptive look at *Hamlet* finds many familiar features, however, and
together with *November 1918, Hamlet* could be called a work of self-
reflection and reckoning both in a personal and in a historical sense.

Piero Rismondo, in his 12 January 1957 review in Vienna's *Die
Presse,* reinforces basic points of other reviewers. He, too, admires the
unique structure, "die Eigenart der Form" (442). While this is not new
in Döblin's work, *Hamlet* reaches a new level of mastery: Döblin's play
with the various epic forms, his montage technique, the weaving together of the different strands has achieved a new perfection, a "Selbst-
verständlichkeit" (442). The action moves to the catastrophe with a
causal logic, and when one looks back from the ending, one admires the
antithetical structure (443). And yet the ending seems too short, too
fragmentary to provide closure. This novel will remain "einem gewalti-
gen Torso gleich" (like a mighty torso) (444) above the flood of forget-
table novels of the period.

Reinhard Federmann, writing in Vienna's *Forum* (5, 1958), does not
waste many words on what he sees as a senseless compilation of heterogeneous material. So much knowledge, know-how, and imagination has
been wasted on this useless text that the reader must despair (444). The
combination of history with family conflict does not make sense, and the
solution offered, to get rid of old problems and complexes first, leaves an
aftertaste of despair ("Trostlosigkeit") (445). Ludwig Pesch, in *Frankfurter Hefte* (13, 1958), offers a much more serious analysis before he reaches
his negative verdict. His strategy is to verify or falsify Muschg's enthusiastic
recommendation. Pesch cannot believe, if the book is as extraordinary as
Muschg had claimed, that no West German publisher would have accepted
it, because there are, after all, unconventional publishers who have a sense
for the unusual and extraordinary. Yet Pesch concludes that the book has
a certain greatness and relevance to the present time and its people (446).
Döblin, he says, is a physician who is confronted with the "Geschwür der
Zeit" (abscessed wound of the time). He has to cut it open, and do it in
a clean and honest and competent way. But the quotes from the text are
damning. The contrast between the monumental project and the awful
style is literally painful ("peinlich"), not just embarrassing: the style becomes a caricature of itself (448). The worst aspects of Expressionism have

returned: "Zu viel Absicht und zu wenig Kunst" ("Too much intention and too little artfulness") (449). Pesch contradicts Muschg and other reviewers here. The coming-to-terms with ("Bewältigung") the war has not even begun. But the world we live in, says Pesch, the world that rushes from one hell to the next, will have to find a different savior than this *Hamlet* (450). With this last word, Pesch makes clear that he expects from *Hamlet* and from an author like Döblin much more than just a novel, but a statement that will provide an orientation and have an impact on the time and its people.

Döblin has come full circle. The reviewers of his last novel rediscover in *Hamlet* the Döblin of the early short stories and of *Wang-lun*. *Hamlet* appeared at a time when German critics were beginning to investigate Expressionism and to look for traces of a cultural continuity beyond the Nazi years. It is doubtful whether *Hamlet* was a suitable object for this search. Yet it is revealing to discover so many features in this book, albeit in a modified form, that were typical for Döblin's earlier texts. Previously, critics had always felt compelled to confront every new book by Döblin as something radically different, as a new departure. Every one of Döblin's narrative texts was a surprise, a new adventure, both in content and in form. It was impossible to get familiar and comfortable with this writer. If you liked *Wallenstein,* you would shake your head about *Manas;* if you were an enthusiast for *Berlin Alexanderplatz,* you would totally reject *Babylonische Wandrung.* Surprisingly, it was *Hamlet,* another very different text, and the unexpected departure after *Amazonas* and *November 1918,* that made critics think of the underlying continuity in Döblin's works. He had indeed remained true to himself until the very end.

Notes

[1] Quoted from Anders's volume of essays on literature, *Mensch ohne Welt: Schriften zur Kunst und Literatur* (Munich: C. H. Beck, 1984), 31–41.

[2] Alfred Döblin, *Briefe,* ed. Heinz Graber (Olten/Freiburg: Walter-Verlag, 1970), 221–22, 224–25, 229.

Part Two:
Döblin Scholarship

3: Döblin Scholarship: The First Approaches

Texts and Editions

DÖBLIN'S TEXTS were never unequivocal and easy to grasp; but the often contradictory opinions on his work were also caused by faulty, or at least differing, editions. Döblin's editors are faced with multiple problems. First and foremost, it is never easy to determine the definitive, final text. If an editor follows the principle of establishing and publishing the text that the author considered final, he is confronted with the fact that Döblin never stopped changing his works, and did not consider any of his texts to be "final." Döblin wrote his works in longhand, in Gothic script and his hard-to-read doctor's handwriting. There are usually several stages and versions. His "final" manuscripts have many deletions and additions, so that his typists, even his wife, made mistakes or were unable to read some words. The typescripts show numerous handwritten corrections, and Döblin kept on making changes at the proof stage. Therefore, it is by no means easy to assess his true intentions.

The problems multiply with the works written during the exile period. Together with the obvious problems of geographical distance from the publisher and non-native typesetters and proofreaders, Döblin's eyesight worsened, and he had less patience for the painstaking work of proofreading. With some works published or re-published after 1945, problems of censorship arose as well, especially with *November 1918*.

In 1960, Walter Muschg began a first edition of Döblin's collected works, modestly called "Ausgewählte Werke in Einzelausgaben," with the Walter-Verlag, then in Olten and Freiburg. Döblin's sons and heirs had declined the offer of Döblin's friend, the French Germanist Robert Minder, to undertake a historical-critical edition of his works that would have been underwritten by the Academy of Literature and Sciences in Mainz. Instead, the intention was to make the major texts available for a general readership in "Leseausgaben." Muschg, moreover, did not feel obliged to respect the texts as Döblin had left them, but in order to popularize the works and make them more readable, he made numerous changes, from small ones such as changing paragraphs, to some rewriting and even deletion of smaller or larger portions — in the case of *Amazonas*, the entire third part.[1]

After Muschg's death in 1965, subsequent editors, especially Heinz Graber, began to rethink these editing methods. With the assumption of the editorship by Anthony W. Riley, the collection assumed the character of a critical edition, although the apparatus does not contain all of the variants from manuscript and typescript versions. The aim of the edition now became the publication of Döblin's entire oeuvre, which included the reworking of Muschg's volumes. As of this writing, the edition is nearing completion; it offers reliable texts of all major and most of the minor works, and has proved to be the foundation for wide-ranging scholarly work. The renewed work on this critical edition helped scholarly work on Döblin begin on a larger scale in the later 1960s.

The Work of Döblin's Friends, Colleagues, Early Admirers, and Detractors

The time of Döblin's death coincided with renewed interest in Expressionism and the Weimar period in general. This interest brought back Döblin's name as a "forgotten writer" of considerable stature who had been excluded from the canon of German literature. Most eulogies contained the complaint that Döblin's work had been neglected. Therefore the first scholarly studies usually included an affirmation of Döblin's rank and significance and tried to give an idea and a survey of his entire work. Those German histories of literature before 1933 that devoted attention to contemporary literature had not failed to mention Döblin, albeit usually in fairly short passages.[2] This was also the case in the histories of literature published after 1945, although the works of the exile period were not mentioned.[3]

Remarkably, there had been a fair amount of scholarly attention paid to Döblin's work in the United States beginning in the thirties, in the form of dissertations and journal articles,[4] and this continued in the fifties.[5] A typical example for the continuity and the renewed interest is the 1960 article in *German Quarterly* by Joseph Strelka, "Der Erzähler Alfred Döblin,"[6] which is a survey of Döblin's narrative works. Strelka sees Döblin's career as an ascending curve, climaxing in *Berlin Alexanderplatz*, with an abrupt descent, a "Sturz" (206), during the emigration, as Strelka laments the "wirklich ziemlich tiefe Niveau der Romane der Emigrationszeit" (207). Strelka notes the lack of closure in Döblin's novels, and says Döblin "never found a solution without discovering at the same time or soon after its contradiction" (197). In *Wang-lun* he sees a "Durchbruch" to a "Großform," as a kind of realism, and, most importantly, a breakthrough to the "Ost-West-Problematik" (198), which he considers one of the constants in Döblin's oeuvre.

The three prominent scholars in Europe who come to mind among those who drew attention to Döblin's oeuvre in the fifties and early sixties are Fritz Martini, Walter Muschg, and Robert Minder.

Martini included a chapter on *Berlin Alexanderplatz* in his widely used 1954 book *Das Wagnis der Sprache*.[7] Martini focuses on Franz Biberkopf, contending that Döblin's intention is to follow his character from his return to life after his time in prison until his complete outer and inner breakdown, which, along with the accompanying realization that he is on the wrong path, leads to a mental healing and thus the restoration of meaning ("Sinnerfüllung") to an existence that had been driven into meaninglessness through his own guilt and the coercing conditions of life (339). Martini believes that the success of *Berlin Alexanderplatz* may have been due to "Irrtümer," misperceptions among critics and readers who understood the novel as a naturalistic picture of Berlin, a socialist story of the proletariat, a novel of the proletarian milieu. For Martini the experimental daring of the epic form, the innovation in terms of narrative point of view and technique, are more important than the novel's subject-matter, even if that subject-matter had not previously been dealt with so unconditionally (339). Martini finds Naturalism and Expressionism, usually considered opposites, to have found their synthesis in Döblin's novel, and its style and technique are due to this synthesis (340). The aesthetic ideal is replaced by a new ethos, as the ideal of "das Schöne" had to give way to the radical search for truth and authenticity, which implies the intensity of the attempt to portray life. It is this intensity of style that replaces beauty (341). Döblin strives for precision, as well as for the depiction of an unlimited totality of existence, and this last quality is what makes him "ein geborener Epiker," a born writer of epic works (344). Martini sees this epic quality first exemplified in *Wang-lun*, which he analyzes briefly before he turns to *Berlin Alexanderplatz*. What Martini really wants to work out is the realization that language in Döblin becomes self-creating, "Sprache als Schöpfung aus sich selbst heraus" (352), which brings him into the line of writers from Nietzsche to Benn, including Arno Holz, Rilke, Thomas Mann, Kafka, and Broch, among others. Thus Martini speaks of the "ins Unerschöpfliche entgrenzenden Sprachstrom" (353) that carries Döblin beyond literature; he wants to overcome forcibly everything that is mere "literature" (354). In Döblin's new form of epic, close to the immediacy of life, congruence of content and form is achieved, but in a seeming chaos (359). Martini goes so far as to call this "an almost programmatic nihilism toward the traditional laws of structuring and presenting narration" (365) and finds a "Weitung der Erzählraumes in die irrationale Dimension des Welt-Seins," an enlargement of the narrative space into the irrational dimension of being in this world (366). Martini considers *Berlin Alexanderplatz* to be the fulfillment of Döblin's own theoretical demands, and the only German novel of the big city that speaks poetically ("der einzige dichterisch sprechende Großstadtroman . . ., den die deutsche Literatur aufzuweisen hat") (372). Martini thus stresses the novel's immediacy of life, "Unmittelbarkeit des Lebens," together with its self-creating language, which achieve a new form that depicts the chaos of the metropolis, but leads Biberkopf eventually to a meaningful life.

Walter Muschg, whose chief impact on Döblin scholarship came through his editions and their "Nachworte," had staked out his general positions on modern German literature in his *Tragische Literaturgeschichte* of 1948.[8] This survey of Western literature and of the virtues and deficits of German literature did not reach into the present, and ignored most of the exile writers, including Döblin; among them, it only mentions Thomas Mann. Stressing the fundamental difference between the "Dichter" and the "Literat" (who produces "Literatur" rather than "Dichtung"), Muschg condemns Heinrich Heine, and turns Mann's *Betrachtungen eines Unpolitischen* against its author, describing Mann as the prototype of the *Literat,* the chief representative of what Muschg calls "das bastardierte Dichtertum" (254). Mann, Muschg says, joked about or mocked ("witzelte") the calling of the *Dichter* by characterizing the writer and artist as a morally dubious character who wondered why society would honor him so much. But after what Muschg calls "jenes bodenlose Deutschland der Republik," the groundless Germany of Weimar, the Germans had suddenly understood that a writer of Mann's type was a contemptible creature, and had chased him out (255). Since that time, Mann has not wanted to be a German writer anymore, but claims to be an American. In Muschg's terms, Mann is proud to play the role of the prima donna in the "Totentanz," the *danse macabre* of literature. All that Mann produces is fluff; he transforms all that was sacred into the "glitzernden Schaum," the glittering foam, of his novels (255). Muschg sees Mann as a mere epigonal follower of Wagner and Nietzsche, and says that his worst work of all was his portrayal of Goethe, especially in *Lotte in Weimar.* Mann had turned Goethe, the great *Dichter,* into a mere *Literat,* thus achieving the absolute denial of true "Dichtertum" (256).

It is evident from his attack on Mann that Muschg lacked the sensibility to understand the German "tragedy" and the meaning and impact of the Nazis' destruction of "Literatur." With his anti-modern standards and criteria and his firm religious beliefs, it comes as a surprise that he valued Döblin so highly. He saw Döblin as the antithesis of Thomas Mann — as Döblin himself did, but in a different way. With Muschg's criteria of "Dichtung" derived from Goethe and nineteenth-century writers like Stifter and Keller, it makes sense that he wanted to "correct" Döblin's texts according to his own preferences. In his long essay of 1956, "Die Zerstörung der deutschen Literatur,"[9] Muschg underscores both his moral condemnation of "mere" literature and his categorical separation of "Dichtung" and "Literatur," "Dichter" and "Literaten." While he describes the individual fates of the exiles of 1933 with empathy, he stresses that, except in the case of acute danger to one's own life, it is immoral to leave one's country for political reasons. It appears that he has more respect for the writers of the "inner emigration," who suffered persecution and hardship within Germany. He finds redeeming features in the exile of religious Jews who found their true home in Palestine/Israel, and, to a point, for Jews like Karl Wolfskehl who found their way back to the Jewish faith during their exile. Most of all, he praises the resistance of Christian writers like Reinhold Schneider, and he counts Döblin among the Christian writers. Döblin had left Germany as a writer of great works of a pagan reverence for nature, "Naturanbetung," and had his encounter with Jesus Christ on his erring way to California, a religious conversion that is demonstrated by his book *Der unsterbliche Mensch* (44).

Muschg contends that the political events of 1933 did not destroy German culture and literature, but only revealed the destruction that had already taken place through what Adorno and Horkheimer would call the "culture industry." Modern culture had been built on sand (22). When the German writers were forced into exile in 1933, they faced harsh living conditions. But in a way, says Muschg, they got what they deserved: their life before 1933 had been wrong and immoral. Exile became a test of one's worth, of the dignity and the real talent of a writer. Very few of them, we have to conclude, passed that test, according to Muschg's criteria. While he praises Hermann Broch's *Der Tod des Vergil* as rightfully indicting the poet/writer for offering beauty instead of truth, he faults Broch's novel as an aestheticist artifice that contradicts the message (20). Muschg sees a continuity from the year 1945 to the present — the year 1956 — a total decline of literature that reflects the conditions of present society. The writer has lost his place in society (32). The most dangerous enemy of the *Dichter* is not political dictatorship, but the satisfaction or diversion ("Vergnügen") of the masses through technology, so that they desire a comfortable life rather than freedom (32). In this situation, which Muschg compares to a total deforestation or clearcut of literature, it is necessary to make a new start with short pieces, fragments, rather than long and perfected masterworks. Muschg refers to Döblin's statement of 1948: "Dies ist nicht die Zeit für 'Gesammelte Werke'" (33). Here we can see the source of Muschg's aversion to the plan to edit Döblin's works as "collected works." In the conclusion of his essay, Muschg rejects what he sees as the two dominant alternatives of literature at that time: commercialism and aestheticism. By implication, he opts for a religiously based literature of positive values. Döblin, we understand, is Muschg's example of the great writer who was an erring pagan, but who finally saw the light.

For the 1966 Döblin volume of *text & kritik*, Muschg wrote a few pages, his testament, as it were (1–4). He fears that Döblin will never occupy the place that he deserves. He classifies him as one of the writers who were awoken or stimulated by Expressionism (1) and insists on Döblin's "double face," which he defines as "naturalistic-mystical" (2). *Wang-lun*, he says, had caused a storm of enthusiasm and rejection (1–2), a statement that distorts the recorded facts. But Muschg likes to be categorical in his judgment: *Pardon wird nicht gegeben*, for instance, is for him nothing but a product of the total confusion of the first years of Döblin's exile (1). Most of Muschg's evaluations are close to Döblin's own in his late essay "Epilog," where he passes judgment on his entire oeuvre from the perspective of the Catholic convert. An intriguing statement by Muschg is that Döblin had never overcome the German defeat of 1945 (3). Does he mean that Döblin never found the way back to his homeland and his people, or could it be that Döblin himself suffered from this defeat? It is true that Döblin felt isolated in Germany and never regained the audience that he had had before 1933.

Robert Minder had a radically different view of his friend Döblin, although he knew Döblin precisely during the years when he was on the way to his conversion, as well as after 1945 when he had become a professing Christian. In his contribution to the *text & kritik* volume, "Begegnungen mit Alfred Döblin in Frankreich" (57–64), Minder alludes to Döblin's marriage, which he calls a true "Strindberg-Ehe" (57), to Döblin's "Schwesterseele" Yolla Niclas (59), and most of all to Döblin's unending search for the truth. Even Döblin's Christianity is, for Minder, of a very free and searching kind (64). While the focus of the article is primarily biographical, Minder repeatedly characterizes Döblin's writing and attitudes as "humoristic." With reference to *Babylonische Wandrung,* he speaks of a "Jean-Paul-Humor" (60), and he relates that during Döblin's last years in Paris he read Jean Paul's works (at Minder's suggestion) and was baffled that it had taken him so long to find a German writer who was so close to his heart (64).

In his essay "Döblin zwischen Osten und Westen,"[10] Minder summarized his overall view of Döblin, also expressed in several other studies and essays.[11] According to Minder, Döblin is marked by his upbringing in authoritarian Prussia, but even more by his origins in a Jewish family migrating from East to West, from an orthodox faith to liberal secularism. The social and economic rise of this Jewish middle class was at the cost of "Wurzellosigkeit" and "seelische Entleerung" (161). But this rootlessness was not just a Jewish problem: the majority of the German people had migrated from the rural areas to the industrial cities, where the reactionary nostalgia for romantic village life was born.

Minder finds the traces of the idols of Döblin's youth, Hölderlin and Kleist, in his first attempts at writing novels, *Jagende Rosse* and *Der schwarze Vorhang* (163). *Wang-lun* was the breakthrough from the narrow straits of the short volumes of stories into the dimensions of the thousand-page novels, where all the barriers have been removed and cataracts thunder into the ocean (164–65). Döblin presents the case of the weak who are oppressed by fate and become exemplary human beings, and searches for a solution, opting for a transformation of the world through this "Selbstopfer" (165). *Wadzek*, an "ins grotesk-phantastische spielende Geschichte eines Einzelnen" (166), is a retreat from German reality, whereas *Wallenstein* reaches right into the panorama of war, the disoriented masses, and "das große Anonyme," nature (167), which takes the isolated individual back into its lap, as in the death of Emperor Ferdinand. In *Berge Meere und Giganten,* Minder sees a migration or progression from East to West, in the hubristic struggle of the human race to dominate nature that ends in the acceptance of nature as nurturing power.

Minder sees a decisive change in Döblin's thinking after 1924, the date of the publication of *Berge Meere und Giganten:* a new emphasis on the individual, and the majority of Döblin scholars have concurred. Minder points to crucial events in Döblin's private life: his relationship with Yolla Niclas and his decision not to leave his wife and children. In any event, the transformation is visible in the new figure of the woman in *Manas,* an epic poem steeped in metaphysics. Metaphysical concerns carry over into *Berlin Alexanderplatz,* which Minder calls a "religiöses Lehrgedicht," a religious didactic poem, rather than an example for the new novel exemplified by Dos Passos and Joyce (170). But in the character Biberkopf we also have something else: he is an embodiment of the "German Michel," the little man who closes his eyes to all social concerns (173). The sinister aspect of this national type of twisted personality is his belief in authority that goes beyond "law and order." *Berlin Alexanderplatz* demonstrates "die erotische Wurzel einer solchen Machthörigkeit" (174). The homoerotic dimension of Döblin's novels is unmistakable.

Minder, who witnessed the genesis of *November 1918* firsthand, draws a line from Döblin's experiences of and immediate reactions to the events of 1918/19 to his political pronouncements, his activities in the Prussian Academy for the Fine Arts, his book *Wissen und Verändern*, and even to his philosophy of nature as expressed in *Unser Dasein*. *Babylonische Wandrung* and the deposed god Konrad appear to Minder as a grotesque counterpart to Biberkopf and *Berlin Alexanderplatz*, except that later in the novel, serious events intrude and some stories slip off into the darkness ("gleiten ins Finstere ab") (179). As Döblin himself did later in his *Epilog*, Minder sees a continuity from the *Babylonische Wandrung* to Döblin's later faith in Christ. In *Amazonas*, Minder stresses the history of the Jesuit republic in Paraguay, and, in *November 1918*, Friedrich Becker's visions of Tauler. The latter, Minder says, was written in a dry documentary style, as Döblin the exile was deprived of contact with the setting of the work, Germany, the fertile soil ("Nahrboden") that had enriched *Berlin Alexanderplatz*. Döblin's last novel, *Hamlet*, according to Minder, receives its "metallisch dunklen Glanz" from the devastating experiences of the death of Döblin's son Wolfgang and the tensions in his marriage (184).

Minder characterizes the basis for Döblin's creativity as "eine tief im Vegetativen verwurzelte Mitschwingungsfähigkeit, All-Sympathie von ungewöhnlicher Ausstrahlungs- und Umklammerungsbreite" (185). When a person with these qualities is thrown into a period of radical historical changes as Döblin was, it is not surprising, says Minder, to find contradictions and seeming extremes in his nature. Even the last dictated meditations of the suffering author struggling with his acquired faith are perfused with pantheistic strains ("pantheistisch durchströmt") (188).

Döblin's "Gesamterscheinung," his complete picture, has yet to be recognized (190); there is no acceptable biography of him. In spite of the calls of Günter Grass and others, the public at large continued to ignore him. Döblin, however, remains connected to larger (historical) contexts, as a bridge between East and West (190). East and West stand for the political fronts of the Cold War, but more than that, they stand for larger cultural traditions. For Minder, Döblin points a way out of the Decline of the West, the Untergang des Abendlandes, to which Minder had alluded before (186). Minder's approach, influenced by both psychoanalysis and sociology, with the clear eyes of a Frenchman who had critical distance but was too close to the Germans for comfort, has had its impact on a then-young generation of German scholars critical of their country's past. They did not dare, however, to approach the problems of Döblin criticism in such sweeping generalizations as Minder felt empowered to do.

In 1970, one of Robert Minder's students, Louis Huguet, wrote his voluminous thesis *L'Oeuvre d'Alfred Döblin ou la Dialectique de l'Exode 1878–1918: Essai de psycho-critique*, which was not published until 1978.[12] The book includes a discussion of the early stories and essays, of *Der schwarze Vorhang*, *Wang-lun*, and *Wadzek*. Huguet uses primarily a psychoanalytic approach, emphasizing the mother-son relations and the missing father, as well as the various aspects of early child development and their later consequences, as reflected in these texts. Huguet stresses rightfully the crucial importance of the "exode," the exile from a place believed to be a safe home, for Döblin's life and work: beginning with the forced departure from Stettin to Berlin as a child, with the many later repetitions of exile. Huguet's approach reflects the ideas of C. G. Jung, and analyzes the mythical images and symbols with a particular thoroughness. Huguet's work is very detailed, using all the sources available at the time. His research resulted also in the first comprehensive biblio-biography, *Alfred Döblin: Eléments de biographie suivis d'une bibliographie systematique*, published in German as *Bibliographie Alfred Döblin*.[13] While Huguet's work may be seen in the context of the new interest in Döblin around 1970, to be discussed presently, it stands out as a thorough and interesting approach that has found few successors. Huguet's thesis is listed in the bibliographies of many subsequent studies, yet it is evident that few scholars have used it or even read it. This is a unique case of a fairly complete non-reception, at least until very recently.[14] There was limited attention paid to Huguet's later studies, as they were mostly published in unusual venues, such as the *Annales de l'Université d'Abidjan*.[15] Still, Huguet's merits as a researcher of biographical and historical sources, details, and connections have been acknowledged, while his psychoanalytic approach remains largely unexamined.

There were two early dissertations produced in Munich. Helmut Schwimmer's 1960 study, "Erlebnis und Gestaltung der Wirklichkeit bei Alfred Döblin,"[16] deals with Döblin's works before 1933, stating that there was a radical change afterwards. Schwimmer characterizes Döblin's experience of reality as that of a big-city dweller who witnessed the increasing mechanization, the velocity of the new modes of transportation, dissociation from nature and its rhythm, the artificiality of the environment, and the general perception of chaos, discontinuity, and disruption. In this environment, the "I" and the world, "Ich und Welt," cannot remain in a stable interacting polarity; the ego appropriates reality, and reality, in turn, devours the ego. They cannot be separated: they are intermingled, and these phenomena lead to a new style and structure of narration. Schwimmer enumerates inner monologue, associative narration, and the montage technique as the main elements of Döblin's response, and notes their similarity with filmmaking techniques. His prime example remains *Berlin Alexanderplatz*, and as others before him he refers to its similarities with Joyce's *Ulysses* and Dos Passos's *Manhattan Transfer*. Schwimmer focuses mostly on the montage elements taken from documents and current events in Berlin, but also mentions the significance of biblical and literary allusions. Although a rather short dissertation (79 pages of text), Schwimmer's study contains many valid observations. It is remarkable for its almost complete omission of social and political issues.

In 1964, Hansjörg Elshorst wrote his dissertation, *Mensch und Umwelt im Werk Alfred Döblins*,[17] in which he surveyed the entire novelistic oeuvre with regard to the relation between man and environment, with particular attention to the evolution of the collectivist and individualistic phases in Döblin's work. Elshorst calls Döblin a *Zoon politikon* (Greek for political being), and divides his works into four phases: 1) "Powerlessness of the human being against fate and the collective forces," including the novels from *Wang-lun* to *Berge Meere und Giganten*; 2) "The individual and his way into the world," including *Manas, Berlin Alexanderplatz,* and *Babylonische Wandrung*; 3) "The human being in a confused, dead-end world," including *Pardon wird nicht gegeben, Amazonas,* and part of *November 1918*; and 4) "Experience of the religious dimension: the fullness of human existence," dealing with the religious aspects of *November 1918* and *Hamlet*. Elshorst posits a general mutual dependency of human beings and their environment, and of individuals and their socio-political environment; he follows this thread and arrives at interesting evaluations, as he finds more value in *Wadzek, Babylonische Wandrung* and *Hamlet* than do most critics. Elshorst also arrives at the clear opinion that there is a gradual shift of emphasis in Döblin's worldview over time, rather than a radical break. He defends more vigorously than most critics the significance of primary human relations, especially the family, whereas other critics focus on the oppositions of the masses vs. the individual and man vs. nature. Döblin's oeuvre offers the paradox of a work of intense social engagement without a specific purpose or political partisanship, but rather with the attempt to penetrate deeper into psychological and sociological reality and demonstrate their complex relationships and contradictions.

In the years before 1966, German scholars had conducted an extensive discussion about Expressionism, a discussion that included Döblin's early work, especially his short stories, and it became apparent how little was known about this great writer. In the late sixties and early seventies, a surprising number of dissertations appeared, mostly focusing on the earlier works. These dissertations have remained orientation points for subsequent studies, and will be cited again in the following chapters. Typically, they included Döblin's entire work at a particular period of his life. Some of the best-known of these studies are Karl Herbert Blessing, *Die Problematik des modernen Epos im Frühwerk Alfred Döblins* (Meisenheim am Glan, 1972); Leo Kreutzer, *Alfred Döblin: Sein Werk bis 1933* (Stuttgart: Kohlhammer, 1970); Roland Links, *Alfred Döblin: Leben und Werk* (Berlin [East]: Volk und Wissen, 1965); Klaus Müller-Salget, *Alfred Döblin: Werk und Entwicklung* (Bonn: Bouvier, 1972); Ernst Ribbat, *Die Wahrheit des Lebens im frühen Werk Alfred Döblins* (Münster: Aschendorff, 1970); Monique Weyembergh-Boussart, *Alfred Döblin: Seine Religiosität in Persönlichkeit und Werk* (Bonn: Bouvier, 1970).

Studies focusing on *Berlin Alexanderplatz* abound. Among the earlier influential essays are Albrecht Schöne's contribution to Benno von Wiese's collection *Der deutsche Roman: Vom Barock bis zur Gegenwart* (Düsseldorf: August Bagel, 1963), vol. 2, 291–325, the Döblin chapter in Volker Klotz's *Die erzählte Stadt* (Munich: Carl Hanser, 1969), and Theodore Ziolkowski's *Dimensions of the Modern Novel: German Texts and European Contexts* (Princeton, NJ: Princeton UP, 1969).

In the seventies, attention shifted to studies on individual works other than *Berlin Alexanderplatz*. Under the editorship of Anthony W. Riley, more texts from Döblin's exile and late periods became available. The hundredth anniversary of Döblin's birth in 1978 saw the Deutscher Taschenbuch Verlag paperback edition of *November 1918*, which brought the work to the attention of a wider audience. Riley contributed several studies to the investigation of the late works, especially *Hamlet*.[18] In 1977, Manfred Auer's dissertation *Das Exil vor der Vertreibung: Motivkontinuität und Quellenproblematik im späten Werk Alfred Döblins* (Bonn: Bouvier) initiated a more text-oriented and less prejudiced examination of Döblin's late works, leading to the comprehensive book by Helmuth Kiesel, *Literarische Trauerarbeit: Das Exil- und Spätwerk Alfred Döblins* (Tübingen: Niemeyer, 1986).

An important impetus for study came with the organizing of the Alfred Döblin Symposia, beginning in Basel in 1980, and the subsequent founding of the International Alfred Döblin Society, which continues to hold international symposia, usually every other year. The publication of the papers of these conferences constitutes an essential step in the academic reception and acceptance of Döblin.

As this books limits itself to the reception of the individual works, we will now discuss their scholarly reception one by one.

Notes

[1] Cf. Klaus Müller-Salget, "Neue Tendenzen in der Döblin-Forschung," *Zeitschrift für deutsche Philologie* 103 (1984): 263–77, and the preface to the second edition of his book, *Alfred Döblin: Werk und Entwicklung* (Bonn: Bouvier, 1973; 2nd rev. ed. 1988), xv-xxv.

[2] Three examples: Albert Soergel, *Dichtung und Dichter der Zeit* (Leipzig: Voigtländer, 1928); Alfred Biese, *Deutsche Literaturgeschichte*, 3 vols. (Munich: C. H. Beck, 1930); Arthur Eloesser, *Die deutsche Literatur*, 2 vols. (Berlin: Bruno Cassirer, 1930).

[3] The prominent examples are Gerhard Fricke, *Geschichte der deutschen Dichtung*, and Fritz Martini, *Deutsche Literaturgeschichte*, both 1949 and in many subsequent editions.

[4] Godfrey Ehrlich (1934), Harry Slochower (1934), Martha Fried, *Der dreißigjährige Krieg in der modernen deutschen Literatur, dargestellt an einer vergleichenden Analyse des Werkes von Ricarda Huch und Alfred Döblin* (New York, 1936).

[5] For example: Henry Regensteiner, "Die Bedeutung der Romane Alfred Döblins von *Die drei Sprünge des Wang-lun* bis *Berlin Alexanderplatz*" (Diss. New York University, 1954), and Anne Liard Jennings, "Alfred Döblin's Quest for Spiritual Orientation, with Special Reference to the Novels *Die drei Sprünge des Wang-lun*, *Berlin Alexanderplatz* and *Babylonische Wandrung*" (Diss. U. of Illinois, Urbana, 1959).

[6] Joseph Strelka, "Der Erzähler Alfred Döblin," *German Quarterly* 33 (1960): 197–210. Actually, although this study was published in an American journal, Joseph Strelka was at that time still in Vienna.

[7] Fritz Martini, "*Berlin Alexanderplatz*," in *Das Wagnis der Sprache: Interpretationen deutscher Prosa von Nietzsche bis Benn* (Stuttgart: Ernst Klett Verlag, 1954), 336–72. Martini, operating similarly to Erich Auerbach's method in *Mimesis*, offers sample passages of the texts with his interpretations.

[8] Walter Muschg, *Tragische Literaturgeschichte* (Bern: Francke Verlag, 1948.)

[9] "Die Zerstörung der deutschen Literatur," in Walter Muschg, *Die Zerstörung der deutschen Literatur* (Bern: Francke Verlag, 1956), 9–46.

[10] Robert Minder, "Döblin zwischen Osten und Westen," *Dichter in der Gesellschaft: Erfahrungen mit deutscher und französischer Literatur* (Frankfurt: Insel, 1966), 155–90, expanded and revised version of a contribution to *Deutsche Literatur im XX.*

Jahrhundert, eds. H. Friedmann and O. Mann (Heidelberg: Wolfgang Rothe, 1954), 249–68.

[11] Robert Minder, "Döblin en France," *L'Allemagne d'aujourd'hui* (1957, No. 3): 5–19; "Begegnungen mit Döblin in Frankreich," in *text & kritik: Sonderheft Alfred Döblin* (Munich: text & kritik, 1966), 57–64; "'Die Segelfahrt' von Alfred Döblin. Struktur und Erlebnis. Mit unbekanntem biographischen Material," in Helmut Kreuzer, ed., *Gestaltungsgeschichte und Gesellschaftsgeschichte: Literatur-, kunst- und musikwissenchaftliche Studien: Festschrift für Fritz Martini* (Stuttgart: Klett, 1969), 461–86.

[12] Louis Huguet, *L'Oeuvre d'Alfred Döblin ou la Dialectique de l'Exode 1878–1918* (Université de Paris, Faculté des Lettres et Sciences Humaines, Paris-Nanterre, 1970) published by Lille/Paris, 1978.

[13] Louis Huguet, *Bibliographie Alfred Döblin* (Berlin/Weimar: Aufbau-Verlag, 1972).

[14] Luca Renzi, "Alfred Döblins Dampfturbine. Symbol, Gleichnis, Mythos, Realität." *Internationales Alfred-Döblin-Kolloquium Bergamo 1999,* ed. Torsten Hahn (*Jahrbuch für Internationale Germanistik,* series A, vol. 51, Bern etc.: Peter Lang, 2002), 55–74, makes extensive use of Huguet's work; references also in Ira Lorf, "'Hier war man im echten Urwald.' Zur Verarbeitung ethnographischen Wissens in einem 'nicht-exotistischen' Text Alfred Döblins," *Internationales Alfred-Döblin-Kolloquium Paris 1993,* ed. Michel Grunewald (*Jahrbuch für Internationale Germanistik* series A, vol. 41, Bern etc.: Peter Lang, 1995), 113–25.

[15] For instance: "Alfred Döblin et le judaïsme," *Annales de l'Université d'Abidjan,* series D, vol. 9 (1976), 47–115; and "Pour un centenaire (1878–1978). Chronologie Alfred Döblin." *Annales de l'Université d'Abidjan,* series D, vol. 11 (1978), 7–197, the second being a book-length study with useful information and references that has been used by a number of scholars.

[16] Helmut Schwimmer, "Erlebnis und Gestaltung der Wirklichkeit bei Alfred Döblin," Diss. Munich, 1960 (typescript).

[17] Hansjörg Elshorst, *Mensch und Umwelt im Werk Alfred Döblins* (Munich 1966) (Diss. Munich, 1964)

[18] For instance, "Zum umstrittenen Schluß von Alfred Döblins *Hamlet oder Die lange Nacht nicht ein Ende,*" *Literaturwissenschaftliches Jahrbuch* NF, 13 (1972): 331–358); "Jaufré Rudel und die Prinzessin von Tripoli. Zur Entstehung einer Erzählung und zur Metamorphose einer Legende in Alfred Döblins Hamlet-Roman," *Festschrift Friedrich Beißner,* eds. Ulrich Gaier and Werner Volke (Bebenhausen, 1974, 341–358); "Ein deutscher Lear? Zu einigen Quellen in Alfred Döblins "Erzählung vom König Lear" in seinem Hamlet-Roman," *Akten des V. Internationalen Germanisten-Kongresses,* eds. Leonard Forster and Hans-Gert Roloff (=*Jahrbuch für Internationale Germanistik,* series A, vol. 2, Bern/Frankfurt: Peter Lang, 1978, 475–82).

4: *Die drei Sprünge des Wang-lun*

WANG-LUN'S PUBLICATION in 1915 not only introduced Döblin as a new novelist to a wider audience, but also impressed many of his fellow writers and gave him an immediate standing in the literary community.[1] However, it was later overshadowed by *Wallenstein* and *Berlin Alexanderplatz*, so that scholarly attention to *Wang-lun* was directed predominantly to a few areas: its depiction of the masses; the question of religion, specifically mysticism; the political meaning of "Wu-Wei," non-violent resistance; and the image and idea of China and the question of exoticism.

Werner Falk published his article "Der erste moderne deutsche Roman: *Die drei Sprünge des Wang-lun* von Alfred Döblin," in 1970.[2] In it, he states that *Wang-lun* has been largely neglected up to that point in time. Modernity for him is the result of a deep-reaching change in history that asks for new responses. One of the features of modernity is that nature is no longer depicted for its own sake, but to reveal "Extranaturales" (515). Falk considers the primary quality of *Wang-lun* to be its entrancing rhythm, which carries the reader away (518). It is not a story of an individual, but of a collective, and this is a crucial feature of modernity (522). Collective forces have become the preoccupation of the age, and in this connection Falk reminds the reader of Heidegger and C. G. Jung. In *Wang-lun*, the conflict is between "Kollektivität und Egozentrik" (528).

Leo Kreutzer, in his 1970 book *Alfred Döblin: Sein Werk bis 1933*,[3] stresses both the socio-political dimension of Döblin's oeuvre and its psychological or even pathological aspects. He considers *Wang-lun* an "Übergang . . . zu einer Epik des Monumentalen und Brutalen, des Heftigen und Häßlichen," a transition to an epic literature of monumental and brutal, violent and ugly dimensions (38). In his analysis of the novel (46–54), Kreutzer underlines the political aspects: Wang-lun is a political leader (50). Kreutzer sees the originally planned and then omitted first scene of the novel as a key to its message and its problematics. This episode, "Der Überfall auf Chao-Lao-Sü," first published in *Genius* 3 (Munich 1921): 275–85, brings the story of Wang-lun from the beginning into the context of the socio-political upheavals in eighteenth-century China and puts an emphasis on the revolutionary fervor of the masses. The ending leaves everything open: "Keine Lösung also: ein offener Schluß." It is a story that relativizes its own message. This is a pattern that Kreutzer sees repeated throughout Döblin's oeuvre.

In Roland Links's remarkable book published in the German Democratic Republic in 1976,[4] *Wang-lun* is seen as an expression of an unsolvable ambivalence between subjectivity and objectivity:

> Selbst jenes Schillern zwischen Objektivität und Subjektivität, das sich ohnehin aus der Gesamthaltung Döblins ergibt, ist noch verstärkt. Daß man nie genau sagen kann, ob ein Bild für sich steht, ob es als Zeichen für innere Vorgänge gemeint oder solchen Vorgängen parallelgeschaltet ist, liegt in der Absicht des Autors. Gerade dadurch erweckt er den halluzinatorischen Eindruck, der dieses Werk kennzeichnet. (51–52)

Politically speaking, the novel is the lament of a bourgeois intellectual who is opposed to the existing social order, but has no alternative for it (53). This seems to be an apt summary of the communist/socialist criticism of Döblin's work as a whole. Still, Links concedes, with reference to a review by F. C. Weiskopf from the year 1931, that while Döblin does not offer solutions, the events represented conceal a hidden desire, which can easily be thought through in the process of reception to a vision of a classless society (58).

Wolfgang Kort, in his 1970 book on Döblin,[5] treats *Wang-lun* as an exemplary presentation of human dialectics, specifically, one that is contained in the opposite terms of "Nicht-Widerstreben" and "Widerstreben" (7). Kort refers to Döblin's later *Das Ich über der Natur* (1927) for an explanation of these polarities. For Kort, the alternatives are "Auflehnung" and "Unterwerfung," referring to the "Nicht-Widerstreben," but both extremes are impossible to achieve (16). People rebel against "Zwang und Vergewaltigung durch das Schicksal," yet they should stay in harmony with the "allgemeinen Weltlauf" (16). Kort argues against the view that Döblin's hero is the collective, the masses. Instead, individuals like Wang-lun, Ma-noh, and the emperor remain the true protagonists. Thus the human condition is characterized by "die Antithetik von individueller Bestimmtheit und anonymem Geschehen," the antithesis of individual determination and anonymous events (18). For Kort, Döblin does not give solutions; he postpones a possible harmony to a future time.

A dialectics of a different kind is affirmed by Louis Huguet in his long chapter on *Wang-lun*.[6] *Wang-lun* is an exotic and esoteric story of initiation into secret worlds and secret societies, yet it is equally a political novel dealing with the actual situation just before the First World War, and the restless masses, revolting against the tyranny of the ruling class. These political conflicts are at the same time family conflicts of a sado-masochistic kind, of repression and resistance or "non-resistance," on a psychological and a societal plain. The revolt of Wang-lun, the "son," and Wang-lun as leader of the poor masses, as it ends in a massive slaughter of the poor, has an ambiguous outcome that affirms the right-eousness of non-resistance but also shows its inner contradictions. Huguet pays special attention to the mythical dimensions of the text, and finds close correspondences between the Taoist, Buddhist, and classical Greek myths, as he detects many "masks" for psychological constellations and conflicts in the mythological as well as in the political events.

Huguet underlines that while *Wang-lun* was seen by a number of critics as a prime example of an Expressionist novel, it is anything but "Wortkunst" (695), or l'art pour l'art, but the representation of an inner universe that corresponds to the "outer" forces active in society. However, it is definitely a work of non-closure, carrying over its unsolved problems into Döblin's next works. All in all, *Wang-lun* is a very contemporary European story with a historical and mythical Chinese "mask."

Klaus Müller-Salget, in *Alfred Döblin: Werk und Entwicklung* (116–64) gives examples for the dynamic language that transforms descriptions into motion and action. The structure of the novel is dominated by repetition. Müller-Salget demonstrates that the (seeming) elimination of a narrator in the later novels is by no means valid for *Wang-lun*. Of special interest are two partially polemic points.[7] First, *Wang-lun* is not a direct commentary on Europe in the years before 1914 and its moral/intellectual crisis; it is the depiction of an alternative, with all its problematic sides. It takes seriously Chinese Taoism's humility and re-fusal to resist violence, and if it is a commentary on Western civilization, it attacks such behavior and violence — when the novel was published during the First World War, the armies had become faceless masses instead of individual heroes, and the civilian masses at home began to strike and to riot.

The second point Müller-Salget makes is that, despite all the novelty of Döblin's representation of mass behavior, *Wang-lun* is, after all, also about individuals within their social contexts; they are not faceless, mere names or numbers, as later in *Berge Meere und Giganten,* but instead figures like Wang-lun, Ma-noh, and the emperor have their individual profiles and fates. Even in the description of mass scenes, Döblin always builds up the big picture from individual elements. Also, in spite of

Döblin's own theories, both the narrator and the individual characters are central to the novel, and instead of a novel on mob behavior it makes better sense to see in it the search for harmony between the individual and the crowd. Nevertheless, there are impressive and climactic scenes of crowd hysteria that stay in the reader's mind.

Two more of Müller-Salget's observations are reinforced by Ernst Ribbat's interpretation in *Die Wahrheit des Lebens* (117–70). First, the predominance of parataxis, emphasized by the striking usage of the word "und," especially at the beginning of sentences and paragraphs, even chapters. Second, the predominance of nature over history. Müller-Salget points to the importance of the seasons as a structural element, while Ribbat analyzes the "Aufhebung der Geschichte," the transformation of the historical into the cyclical, into repetition, and the longing for the eternal. *Wang-lun*, a historical novel in generic terms, does not comply with the usual demands made on such novels, and de-emphasizes time in a radical manner. The author abandons the safe distance of the historian and enters into the inner life of the characters and world that he has created.

The topic of orientalism or exoticism as a form of escapism was taken up by Wolfgang Reif in his 1975 dissertation, *Zivilisationsflucht und literarische Wunschräume.*[8] His long section on *Wang-lun* (101–14) takes its orientation from his overall thesis of apolitical escapism. He diagnoses a trend toward escapism in Döblin's biography, and considers *Wang-lun*, although it is an example, or possibly a prototype, of the long Expressionist novel (105), as an inconclusive story that conjures up a China of the imagination and for the imagination, beyond social and political concerns either in terms of eighteenth-century China or of twentieth-century Germany. This attitude of helplessness and political non-engagement is reflected in the protagonists of the novel itself, specifically Wang-lun and the emperor, who retreat before the tasks and responsibilities of real life into a dream world. As China and the eighteenth century serve as escape routes from the ugly and restricted existence of the petite bourgeoisie — the proletarian middle-class — of Berlin, the immersion into nature mysticism and Taoism and the escape from Confucian ethics and responsibilities build up a dream world: the vicarious satisfaction ("Ersatzbefriedigung") that occurs in this text functions such that the alienating experiences of restriction, complexity, and uniformity are reversed into their opposites (114). This has transparent autobiographical reasons and consequences:

> Was Döblin abzubilden vermag, ist lediglich das eigene gestörte Verhältnis zu dieser Realität und die daraus resultierende Labilität seiner

weltanschaulichen Positionen. Das Verlangen nach dem Außergewöhn-
lichen erfüllt sich in den häßlich-monströsen und ästhetisch-sublimen
Akzentuierungen eines Phantasie-China. (114)

It is understandable that the Chinese perspective on Döblin's novel
is quite different. Fang-hsiung Dscheng, writing in 1979, places *Wang-
lun* in the context of other German literary images of China.[9] The first
half of Dscheng's book is devoted to German translations of Chinese
literature and philosophy, and the changing images of China in Germany
between the discovery of Buddhism and Taoism following Schopenhauer
and Nietzsche, interest in East Asian art, and the contradictory political
images of the Chinese as threatening and as victims of Western colonial
exploitation. The German literary response reaches from the many attempts to translate Chinese poetry (Hans Bethge, Richard Dehmel,
Albert Ehrenstein, Klabund, Paul Zech), especially that of Li Tai-pe, and
to render Chinese philosophy (Richard Wilhelm), from Chinese elements
in stories and plays (Hofmannsthal, Max Dauthendey, Hermann Hesse,
Klabund), to the preoccupation with the Chalk Circle parable (Klabund,
Brecht), and to a long general preoccupation with Chinese culture, as in
the case of Klabund, Paul Zech, and especially Bertolt Brecht, with
whom it culminated in his plays *Der gute Mensch von Sezuan* and *Der
Kaukasische Kreidekreis* and in his remarkable, very personal ballad of
1938 "Legende von der Entstehung des Buches Taoteking auf dem Weg
des Laotse in die Emigration."

Döblin's *Wang-lun* emerges as one of the most significant literary
documents — perhaps *the* most significant — of the German pre-First-
World-War interest in China and Taoism, and in the confrontation between Western activism and Eastern passivity, or "Nichthandeln." Fang-
hsiung Dscheng demonstrates that Döblin stayed as close to historical
events as his German sources permitted; equally, he had achieved a real
understanding of the Taoist texts, and indeed a deeper understanding of
the Chinese mentality than the reader is able to perceive in his text
(142). Döblin's own views on social ethics and the relationship of the
individual to the collective were deepened and clarified by his Chinese
studies, according to Dscheng:

> Döblin sieht im Rad des Schicksals die Verkörperung des Kollektiv-
> wesen der Gesellschaft und gelangt zu einer sozialethischen Einsicht,
> daß der einzelne Mensch innerhalb des Kollektivs nicht nur seine eige-
> ne Bedeutung als Individuum zu verlieren droht, sondern auch nur in
> ihm als Teil des Ganzen mächtig ist. (146)

Döblin's views in this respect did not change during the twenties, says Dscheng, as Döblins Biberkopf in *Berlin Alexanderplatz* is in his view not a biblical figure, but instead a positive model for the contemplative, calm "Wu-wei" man (148). And the novel's last scene, the mass scene marked by the brotherhood and love for humanity that is emphasized in Döblin's entire oeuvre, becomes a symbol of an ethic that stems from Buddhist-Taoist pessimism and pity ("Mitleid"), the same ethical attitude of "Nächstenliebe" as in Schopenhauer and Nietzsche (148). The name Nietzsche may surprise in connection with love for one's neighbor, but the connection Schopenhauer-Nietzsche-Taoism in Döblin's thinking is undeniable.

Dscheng offers a Buddhist version of the "Three Leaps" to counter the misunderstandings of Western scholars beginning with Muschg. These Buddhist leaps are leaps across the river separating the world from the underworld, and Wang-lun's final leap brings him into the attitude of non-resistance and harmony with the universe, which is consonant with Döblin's own natural philosophy, or as Dscheng puts it, "Wu-wei in Döblins naturphilosophischer Anschauung" (206ff).

Ultimately, Dscheng sees parallels between the social-ethical ideal of Taoist wisdom (209) and Döblin's attitude as pacifist and committed socialist: Wu-wei, the lingering in weakness and softness, became the expression of the strength of wisdom and humanity (212). Döblin's empathy with Taoism is proven by many direct quotes, but also by his adaptation of phrases, idioms, similes, and metaphors. For Dscheng, Döblin's epic theory and practice in *Wang-lun* owes a good deal to his knowledge of Chinese novels. Thus, his holistic view of the universe was amalgamated with Taoist universalism: art, like Zen Buddhist religion, becomes the recognition of the connection of the human being with nature, of the individual with the anonymous society, a new art that Döblin wanted to liberate from the one-sidedness of bourgeois art (224). Dscheng's analysis indicates the differences between the Western and Far Eastern views of the individual and individualization, and the impact of the Eastern view on Döblin's epic narrations and his idea of nature and history.

Two more dissertations by Chinese scholars appeared in 1991, Zhonghua Luo's *Alfred Döblins "Die drei Sprünge des Wang-lun," ein chinesischer Roman?* and Zheng Fee's *Alfred Döblins "Die drei Sprünge des Wang-lun": Eine Untersuchung zu den Quellen und zum geistigen Gehalt.*[10] Both of these were dissertations at the University of Regensburg, with Leo Kreutzer as their advisor, and both criticize Dscheng's book and disagree with major points of his findings. Zhonghua Luo denies the evidence of any impact of Chinese novels on Wang-lun. Since

Döblin was restricted to Western sources for his knowledge of China, his view of China and its history had to be biased, and his familiarity with Chinese life is more apparent than real. Moreover, his sources gave only minimal information on the events of 1774, the uprising led by the historical Wang Lun, and they did not provide much help for the characterization of the main figures. In fact, Döblin's portrayal of the emperor Khien-lung contradicts the historical accounts, and indicates that Döblin was much more concerned with universal human problems than with writing a historical novel. Another indication of this is that the very important visit of the Tashi-Lama in Beijing did not take place in 1774, but in 1779. Döblin had an important non-historical reason for inserting it into the context of this story: he wanted to confront the emperor with a higher authority.

However, Döblin was surprisingly familiar with Taoism. Zhonghua Luo points out that Taoism evolved from the time of Lao-tzu on to later centuries, and that Döblin's main reference point was the philosophy of Lieh-tzu. The differences among the Taoist classics include very diverse ideas on the meaning of "Wu-Wei," the non-resistance concept central to the novel. Lao-tzu and later followers were also social, even political philosophers whose ideas responded to major moral and political issues of their time. Wu-Wei was by no means just a religious movement of the poor striving for redemption in another, better life. Wang-lun's uprising was a political rebellion with religious overtones, but the ethical and political issues were decisive. Zhonghua Luo agrees with Roland Links and Leo Kreutzer on this point, but sees the need to differentiate which type of Taoism and which conception of Wu-wei Döblin actually portrayed. The main point is that different ideas of Wu-wei are personified by the major characters, all of them agreeing that Wu-Wei means acting or non-acting in accordance with the laws of the Tao, whereas "You-Wei" means acting out of the subjective will of the individual. Thus the non-resistance of Wu-Wei does not at all mean non-action.

The success or failure of Wang-lun's movement, which was brought into being by the disorder of the empire and its society, depends largely on the response of the worldly powers, that is, the emperor, and when the emperor fails the recognize the movement and make peace, mass slaughter and violence ensues.

Ernst Ribbat, in his chapter on *Wang-lun* in *Die Wahrheit des Lebens im frühen Werk Alfred Döblins* (117–70), had pointed out the parallels between Döblin's natural philosophy and Taoism; Zhonghua Luo takes this further. Even 1933's *Unser Dasein*, he says, shows the same convictions, a statement that may be debatable.

Zheng Fee pursues similar goals. She wants to clarify how "Chinese" this novel is, what Döblin actually means by Wu-wei, how typical *Wang-lun* is for German Expressionism, and how Döblin's understanding of Taoism compares to that of other contemporary German writers, specifically Klabund, Brecht, and Hesse. In Zheng Fee's view, the Chinese "realia" in the novel are nothing but decoration, extraneous elements for a novel that is really concerned with European, and specifically German, problems before the First World War. The emperor Khiem-lung even looks like a caricature of Kaiser Wilhelm II. Indeed, compared to the very laconic historical sources, the characterization of the main figures is not only much more complex, and thus more human, but they exhibit contradictory and sometimes pathological traits; they are ambivalent, they are unsure of themselves. This is not the aggressive, autocratic, even brutal emperor Khiem-lung of history, nor is it the radical revolutionary Wang Lun. Döblin may have intended initially to write a "historical" novel with a clear plot and closure, as the original first chapter, later eliminated, indicates, but the novel as written is centered around the contrasting, yet mutually dependent characters and their search for the right way to live and the true meaning of life. Zheng Fee agrees on the close connection between Döblin's philosophy of nature and his view of Taoism, and she analyzes some of the nature images, especially water, the forest (or trees), and the emperor's giant turtle. The conceptions that other German writers like Klabund, Brecht, and Hesse had of Wu-wei are much less ambiguous than Döblin's, whose basic ambivalence about the idea is reflected in the different, even contradictory Wu-wei attitudes of the main characters. From Zheng Fee's analysis, Döblin's *Wang-lun* emerges as a very complex, very non-Chinese novel without a clear message, very much a work of an author who is still on his way to a position of clarity. Somewhat surprisingly, Zheng Fee regards *Wang-lun* as a big-city novel, a forerunner to *Berlin Alexanderplatz* with elements of the Berlin environment, not simply because of the emphasis on the masses, but also because of the inner dynamics of the novel, which she contrasts with the poetry of Expressionism.

Whereas these Chinese dissertations clarify aspects of the novel relating to Taoism and Chinese history, and place Döblin in the context of the preoccupation of German authors with China and specifically Taoism in the very early years of the twentieth century, the basic points about Döblin and Taoism had already been made by Ingrid Schuster in her article of 1970, "Alfred Döblins 'Chinesischer Roman,'"[11] expanded in her 1977 book *China und Japan in der deutschen Literatur 1890–1925,*[12] and summarized in her contribution to her own edited volume of 1980 *Zu Alfred Döblin.*[13]

Schuster locates Döblin's motivation in his empathy with the suffering masses, pointing out that at one time he had planned a second novel on Russia, which, like China, was ruled by a repressive regime close to collapse. Wang-lun's rebellion was in part a rebellion against the "foreign" Manchu dynasty, which finally ended in 1912 just at the time when Döblin was writing the novel. Schuster links Wang-lun with other secret societies that fought foreign influences, including that of the Boxers, whose rebellion was brutally crushed by European troops in 1900. The Boxer secret society apparently goes back to the time around 1770.

Most scholars agree with Schuster that Döblin's main source for his views on Taoism in the book was Lieh-tzu; the German translation by Richard Wilhelm had just been published in 1911. From the perspective of 1912, and in connection with Taoist views on the transitory nature of history, the long reign of the emperor Khien-lung (1735–96), which is commonly considered to be a high point of the Manchu dynasty's power and glory, begins to look like a turning point and the beginning of its downfall. All historical events, like all human beings, "tragen ein doppeltes Gesicht" (90–91), that is, contain good and evil, as long as they are not in total harmony with the Tao — which is apparently unattainable in this society. Döblin's depiction of an eternal repetition and of unsolvable conflicts follows Taoist pessimism more closely than the originally planned circular structure that would have made the slaughter of Wang-lun's Wu-wei movement into a one-time and final tragic event. It is only one episode in the endless flow of events.

Schuster adds a short demonstration of the impact of *Wang-lun* on young writers during the decade between 1915 and 1925. She mentions in particular Ernst Toller, Oskar Maria Graf, Ludwig Rubiner, and Bertolt Brecht. Brecht's reception of *Wang-lun* and Wu-wei meant a decided rejection of "non-resistance," whereas Toller and Graf saw in the novel an affirmation of their pacifism.[14] *Wang-lun*, though later overshadowed by *Berlin Alexanderplatz*, remained for these writers and other readers of their generation the first experience of an overwhelming, disturbing, and provoking Döblin text.

In his article "Bemerkungen zu Alfred Döblins Roman 'Die drei Sprünge des Wang-lun'"[15] Hajime Kojima agrees largely with Fang-hsiung Dscheng on the "Three Leaps," but the outstanding point of his contribution is his differentiation between Taoism and Buddhism proper. According to Kojima, a "Verquickung zweier Lehren" (13), a conflation or confusion of the two doctrines, is rather common in Chinese history. Whereas in

Taoism the goal is "Erlösung" (redemption), the characteristic point of Buddhism is the repetition of the same: The human being is caught in the circle of the San-shih (three worlds: former, present, and future reincarnation), and it must be his goal to get out of this cycle, to be able to enter into the "Westliche Paradies" (13). Kojima also points out that Döblin tried to rethink the Taoist concept of Wu-wei; Wu-wei refers to a personal, individual attitude, and Döblin tried to transfer it to a group, a crowd, a collective entity (12). This "Idee vom Wu-wei als Erlösungsweg für die Gruppe" (15) remains a dream in the novel, an unrealized idea, with a final question mark, but it continued to preoccupy Döblin in subsequent works like *Wallenstein* and *Berge Meere und Giganten*.

In Roderich Gathge's study "Die Naturphilosophie Alfred Döblins: Begegnung mit östlicher Weisheit und Mystik,"[16] the point of orientation is *Das Ich über der Natur* of 1927 and its Eastern sources. Gathge finds that Döblin expresses in *Wang-lun* the acceptance of an anonymous power immanent in this world, a power that is the foundation and predetermination of all being (18). He also draws a direct line from *Wang-lun* to *Das Ich über der Natur* and from there to the priority of "Wissen" over "Handeln," of knowledge over action.

Besides the questions how authentic Döblin's depiction of China was and whether *Wang-lun* is a historical novel or a novel about contemporary German problems, scholars have predominantly focused on the connections between Taoist thinking and Döblin's philosophy of nature and on phenomena of the masses: on crowds and their behavior and on the relationship between individuals and the masses. While opinions differ sharply on the political/social content and meaning of the novel and the concept of Wu-wei, there is agreement on Döblin's fatalistic and thus pessimistic outlook. There is no agreement on the possible religious meaning of the novel, other than the idea of a "religion of nature" without a personal God. Scholars agree that the complex and antithetic structure of the novel underscores its ambiguous or tentative message, ending with a question mark.

Notes

[1] Ingrid Schuster, "Die Wirkungen des *Wang-lun* in der Weimarer Republik," *Internationale Alfred-Döblin-Kolloquien 1980–1983*, ed. Werner Stauffacher (Bern: Peter Lang, 1986), 45–53; she mentions Ernst Toller's *Die Wandlung*, Oskar Maria Graf's *Die Heimsuchung*, works of Lion Feuchtwanger, especially *Warren Hastings*, Ludwig Rubiner, Bertolt Brecht's *Im Dickicht der Städte*, and Arthur Koestler's *Die Gladiatoren*.

[2] Werner Falk, "Der erste moderne deutsche Roman: *Die drei Sprünge des Wang-lun* von Alfred Döblin," *Zeitschrift für deutsche Philologie* 89 (1970): 510–31.

[3] Leo Kreutzer, *Alfred Döblin: Sein Werk bis 1933* (Stuttgart: W. Kohlhammer, 1970).

[4] Roland Links, *Alfred Döblin,* Schriftsteller der Gegenwart 16 (Berlin: Volk und Wissen, 1976).

[5] Wolfgang Kort, *Alfred Döblin: Das Bild des Menschen in seinen Romanen* (Bonn: H. Bouvier, 1970); on *Wang-lun,* 7–18.

[6] Louis Huguet, *L'Oeuvre d'Alfred Döblin ou la Dialectique de l'Exode, 1878–1918* (Thèse pour le doctorat, Université de Paris-Nanterre, 1970, quoted from the typewritten thesis), 523–695.

[7] Klaus Müller-Salget, *Alfred Döblin: Werk und Entwicklung* (Bonn: Bouvier, 1973; 2nd rev. ed. 1988), 116–64.

[8] Wolfgang Reif, *Zivilisationsflucht und literarische Wunschräume: Der exotistische Roman im ersten Viertel des 20. Jahrhunderts* (Stuttgart: J. B. Metzler, 1975). Reif focuses his attention primarily on German-language novels and stories. Although he has a comparatistic perspective and points out the interconnections between the different European literatures, he rarely considers the knowledge European authors might have of Oriental literature, for instance, Chinese and Indian literature.

[9] Fang-hsiung Dscheng, *"Die drei Sprünge des Wang-lun" als Spiegel des Interesses moderner deutscher Autoren an China,* Europäische Hochschulschriften Reihe I, Deutsche Literatur und Germanistik, vol. 305 (Frankfurt am Main: Peter Lang, 1979).

[10] Zhonghua Luo, *Alfred Döblins "Die drei Sprünge des Wang-lun," ein chinesischer Roman?,* Europäische Hochschulschriften, Reihe I, Deutsche Sprache und Literatur, vol. 1282 (Frankfurt am Main: Peter Lang, 1991); and Zheng Fee, *Alfred Döblins Roman "Die drei Sprünge des Wang-lun": Eine Untersuchung zu den Quellen und zum geistigen Gehalt,* Regensburger Beiträge zur deutschen Sprach- und Literaturwissenschaft, Reihe B, Untersuchungen, vol. 49 (Frankfurt am Main: Peter Lang, 1991).

[11] Ingrid Schuster, "Alfred Döblins 'Chinesischer Roman,'" *Wirkendes Wort* 20 (1970): 339–46.

[12] Ingrid Schuster, *China und Japan in der deutschen Literatur 1890–1925* (Munich/ Bern: Francke, 1977).

[13] Ingrid Schuster, "Die drei Sprünge des Wang-lun," *Zu Alfred Döblin,* ed. Schuster, LWG-Interpretationen, vol. 48 (Stuttgart: Ernst Klett, 1980), 82–97. Most of the other articles in the volume are reprints.

[14] Schuster mentions Ernst Toller's *Masse-Mensch,* Oskar Maria Graf's *Die Heimsuchung,* Ludwig Rubiner's *Die Gewaltlosen,* and Brecht's *Im Dickicht der Städte* and *Mann ist Mann.* As noted above in note 1, in her article "Die Wirkungen des 'Wang-lun' in der Weimarer Republik" (*Internationale Alfred-Döblin-Kolloquien 1980– 1983,* ed. Werner Stauffacher, 45–53), she also mentions in connection with Brecht's attitude Lion Feuchtwanger's play *Warren Hastings,* and especially Arthur Koestler's

The Gladiators, written during Koestler's period of growing disenchantment with the communist parties.

[15] Hajime Kojima, "Bemerkungen zu Alfred Döblins Roman 'Die drei Sprünge des Wang-lun,'" *Internationale Alfred Döblin-Kolloquien 1984–1985,* ed. Werner Stauffacher (Bern: Peter Lang, 1988), 10–15.

[16] Roderich Gathge, "Die Naturphilosophie Alfred Döblins: Begegnung mit östlicher Weisheit und Mystik," *Internationale Alfred Döblin-Kolloquien 1984–1985,* ed. Werner Stauffacher, 16–29.

5: *Wadzeks Kampf mit der Dampfturbine*

THE INITIAL DISAPPOINTMENT and bewilderment after the publication of *Wadzek* has had visible consequences for scholarship. Very few scholars have considered the novel worthy of a special study. Müller-Salget skips it altogether. Among the studies on Döblin and Berlin, David Dollenmayer alone devotes an entire chapter of his book *The Berlin Novels of Alfred Döblin* to the text,[1] in addition to his 1983 paper, "Heroismuskritik in einem Frühwerk von Döblin: 'Wadzeks Kampf mit der Dampfturbine.'"[2] In this paper, beginning with the usual statement that *Wadzek* has caused bewilderment and attracted little scholarly attention, Dollenmayer points out the fact that the title does not agree with the text: the struggle of man and machine is not at all Wadzek's real problem — which may be one of the reasons why the novel has been misunderstood. Dollenmeyer's point is reinforced by Anthony Riley's afterword to his new edition, which indicates how much the conception of the book changed during the period of gestation and writing, so that, in a way, the title represents an earlier stage of the work.[3] Dollenmayer follows the lead of earlier readers, for instance Bertolt Brecht,[4] that *Wadzek* represents a potential tragedy that is turned into a grotesque or an absurd comedy. One essential feature of this is the mock-heroic pathos and the Don Quixote-like misperception of reality by the characters, specifically by Wadzek himself. From this perspective, the ending, Wadzek's escape with Gaby to America, seems more comprehensible in its total lack of logical sequence with the text. Dollenmayer admits that even his perspective does not entirely clarify a text that seems to defy interpretations based on consistency.

In his book, Dollenmayer is more concerned with the image of the big city Berlin, which figures only sporadically in the text, which is surprising for a "big city novel." Reinickendorf, the location of the second book, is described as rural, beyond the city limits proper. There is only one memorable description of a street scene, toward the end of the novel, seen from Wadzek's and Gaby's perspective as they are riding in a horse-cab through the Friedrichstraße, that foreshadows Döblin's technique in *Berlin Alexanderplatz* (Dollenmayer 51). *Wadzek* is primarily concerned with domination and submission, human relationships, specifically sexuality of a rather abnormal kind; interwoven is the theme of illusions, wishful dreams, and inaccurate perceptions that are defeated by reality. The reader cannot be sure whether these Don Quixote-like illusions are just escapist and somewhat deranged, or whether they are meant to be idealistic.

The chapter on *Wadzek* in Louis Huguet's *L'Oeuvre d'Alfred Döblin ou la Dialectique de l'Exode, 1878–1918* (Thèse pour le Doctorat Université Paris-Nanterre, 1970, 696–757) is noteworthy on several accounts. Huguet demonstrates the continuation of the unsolved problems in *Wang-lun*. He shows from a psychoanalytic point of view that problems that were treated in a veiled manner in *Wang-lun* come into the open in *Wadzek*, such as the deracination, the absent father, and the mother-problem. According to Huguet, *Wadzek* is (among other things) a parody on the tragedy of the Atrides in Greek mythology. There are also traces of the main character of Heinrich von Kleist's novella *Michael Kohlhaas*. Huguet notes a trend of inserting stories that would point toward the form of a cycle of novellas, a form that Döblin modified in his last novel *Hamlet*.

According to Huguet, every critic of *Wadzek* is faced with the fact of its largely negative reception by the reviewers when it appeared in 1918, beginning even before that, with Döblin's 1915 correspondence with Martin Buber, who had praised *Wang-lun* but was very disappointed by *Wadzek* (753–55). Huguet, who has high regard for *Wadzek*, maintains that the critics were put off by its burlesque tone and failed to see the serious problems below the seemingly farcical and sometimes incoherent surface. These problems are both personal (deracination; isolation; escape; the urge to free oneself from the oppressive burdens of family, business competition, and the repressive society) and universal (the critique of competitive capitalism and technology run wild). *Wadzek* does not only articulate major concerns of Döblin's entire career, but also should be taken seriously, says Huguet, as a critique of Western civilization at the beginning of the twentieth century.

Werner Stauffacher, in his 1983 paper, "'Komisches Grundgefühl' und 'Scheinbare Tragik.' Zu 'Wadzeks Kampf mit der Dampfurbine'"[5] takes his departure from the contrast between the apparent tragic conflict and the comic mood of the story. Döblin himself in his commentaries on the work had stressed the comic or humoristic elements. Stauffacher finds comic techniques at work that resemble techniques of the silent movies, and specifically the early Charlie Chaplin films. He struggles with the central problem when he says that *Wadzek* may be neither a very funny nor an entertaining book, but that the comic aspects of the text are nevertheless evident (173). It is easier to describe the details of the comic techniques than to convince an unamused reader that the text should make him laugh. The parallels with silent movies offer an indication that an often grotesque distortion of reality is at work, and that the text cannot be seen as a realistic picture of Berlin or of characters in a milieu of entrepreneurs and engineers. These are caricatures reminding us of George Grosz. Moreover, the course of events are mere "Abläufe," as Leo Kreutzer has defined them, defying any reasonable expectations of cause and effect. Each event is an entity unto itself and does not lead to a next event, an attitude in keeping with Döblin's epic theories, which Stauffacher defines as "behaviouristisch" (179). Finally, Stauffacher addresses a point that would gain fundamental significance in *Berlin Alexanderplatz*: Wadzek's "Verstümmelung," his mutilation (179). Stauffacher asks the question whether, after all, there is significance in the fact that *Wadzek* was written in the early part of the First World War.

In two papers delivered at the 1993 and 1995 Döblin colloquia, Ira Lorf illuminates an essential aspect of one major scene of the novel: the exoticism of the costume party Pauline Wadzek arranges for her women friends. In "'Hier war man im echten Urwald.' Zur Verarbeitung ethnographischen Wissens in einem 'nicht-exotistischen' Text Döblins,"[6] she describes the sources for Döblin's knowledge of African and American Indian works of art, customs and objects, and analyzes the pervasive colonial attitude and irony with which they are presented. It is not always clear whether the exoticist attitudes exhibited are solely those of the characters or also those of the author. In her second article, "Wissen — Text — kulturelle Muster. Zur literarischen Verarbeitung gesellschaftlicher Wissenbestände in Alfred Döblins Roman *Wadzeks Kampf mit der Dampfturbine*,"[7] Lorf places this problem of understanding an alien culture in a larger and somewhat different context, still referring to the same scene. Her first point is how closely Döblin followed his sources, books on Africa and the artifacts in the Völkerkundemuseum in Berlin. The boy Philipp uses a "negro language" that seems to be Döblin's own invention; but on closer inspection, it is taken from the examples of West African languages in the books he used. Döblin develops a sophisticated game of authenticity and pretense, truth and falsehood. The costume party may be a satirical reflection of the Wilhelminian culture of costume and façade, but here, as in his *Wang-lun* and elsewhere, Döblin comes close to the fascination of the modernists in the visual arts with "primitive art," specifically African art, exemplified by Ernst Ludwig Kirchner, who illustrated Döblin's texts and also painted his portrait. Wadzek flees from the party into a hotel, is haunted by visions of his "African" wife, and tries in vain to "distort" her image back into a civilized face. There are both Freudian and political implications of this menacing — but still funny, and therefore grotesque — jungle scene, of which Döblin must have been aware. In her subsequent book *Maskenspiele: Wissen und kulturelle Muster in Alfred Döblins "Wadzeks Kampf mit der Dampfturbine" und "Die drei Sprünge des Wang-lun"*[8] Lorf places these problems in a larger context. After a discussion of the concepts of masks, of *Karneval,* and of fashion, as well as exoticism, she analyzes the two novels from that perspective and arrives at the conclusion that *Wadzek* exhibits non-functional masks; it is a response to the well-functioning "masquerade" of *Wang-lun,* a demasking of the German colonial craze and the disguises that try to cover a disagreeable truth. Thus *Wadzek* and *Wang-lun* can be and should be seen together, calling into question a real evocation of a foreign culture and parodying the German longing for exotic lands and costumes.

The issue of "exoticism" in Döblin's works had already been raised by Wolfgang Reif in his provocative book of 1975, *Zivilisationsflucht und literarische Wunschräume,* which discusses *Wang-lun* and *Berge Meere und Giganten* along with works by other authors, and by Winfried Georg Sebald, in his no less provocative *Der Mythos der Zerstörung im Werk Döblins* of 1980.[9] Sebald attacks Döblin scholarship in general since Muschg and Minder, which he sees solely as an attempt to rehabilitate an author whose fundamental contradictions and flaws should not be denied. *Hamlet,* for example, although praised by some critics, is "objectively" nothing but the confusions of an old man, "die Verwirrungen eines alten Mannes" (6). Sebald condemns the purely academic studies for a lack of intellectual curiosity and as an expression of "déformation professionelle" (8). Sebald sees the absence of a "materialistische Analyse" as one of the reasons for this blindness; this is a verdict based on Adorno from which Sebald excludes only some passages of Leo Kreutzer, Klaus Schröter, and Roland Links. Sebald advances as his fundamental thesis that the later works of Döblin, especially those of the exile period, are less an expression of "Souveränität" than "Verstörtheit" on the part of the author (9). Sebald himself offers a "historisch orientierte materialistische Bedeutungsanalyse" of Döblin's life and work (10). Since Sebald levels a fundamental attack on Döblin's entire oeuvre and raises general issues, especially that of violence, in addition to that of exoticism, it is necessary to discuss his thesis, although it does not pertain specifically to an analysis of *Wadzek.*

According to Sebald, Döblin, undoubtedly critical of his time and society, has a tendency toward exotic and alien worlds in his novels, and while this might be expected to result in critical distance, any such distancing is negated by the Döblin's suggestive, descriptive style, which leads one to the assumption that the author is more society's medium than its critic (15). Thus Sebald diagnoses for instance Döblin's intense interest in the concept of "Räte," the workers' and soldiers' councils, as expressing political wishful thinking rather than the need for real political involvement (27). Döblin's contradictory political views are a symptom of an attitude that refuses to be engaged. Sebald pursues his thesis of the author incapable of rational reflection and clarity through its various dimensions of messianism, eschatology, apocalyptic images, nature mysticism, and reactionary politics, all of which reveal themselves to be fascist, as Döblin does not describe the violence and senseless aggression of humanity as horrors to be overcome, but as the prevailing and necessary condition, and even seems to relish destruction and ugliness. With his suggestive style, Döblin draws the reader into a similar enjoyment of violence and destruction, instead of a sane enlightenment. His characters are medical cases: he writes "Pathographien" (14). The characters look like comic-book figures in their pure two-dimensionality (70). Döblin and authors like him did their part to entice the masses into fascist mass behavior, and his works share not only Nazism's teleology but also its apocalyptic desires:

> Was in Döblins Werken an Apokalypsen und anderen Bildern der Zerstörung des Lebens rhetorisch heraufgezaubert wird, gehorcht der selben Teleologie wie die Sehnsucht der Faschisten, die trotz des Traums vom tausendjährigen Reich auf ein baldiges Ende gerichtet war, wie an Formeln wie "Endziel," "Endsieg," "Schlußziel" und "Endlösung" ablesbar ist. (160)

The apocalyptic images in Döblin's rhetoric follow the same teleology as the fascist dreams of a thousand-year Reich that was in reality geared toward a short-term goal, as can be seen in formulas like *Endziel* and *Endlösung*. The denunciatory tone of the last part of Sebald's statement was one of the major reasons for the many angry reactions to his book.

Part of the problem, according to Sebald, is Döblin's inability to cope with his rootless Jewish existence and his loneliness in the big city. Furthermore, once cut off from Berlin, the nourishing soil that inspired his one great work, *Berlin Alexanderplatz*,[10] his creativity withered away. Sebald agrees with Klaus Schröter (and some others) that Döblin's exile works are inferior,[11] and insists on the insincerity of his involvement after 1933 in Jewish organizations, just as he doubts the sincerity of Döblin's convictions, political or otherwise.

Sebald's polemic thesis, especially his moral condemnation of Döblin as a pre-fascist writer whose "Monumentalismus" reminds of Wagner's operas (140, 144) drew strong protests, and his insistence on the gratuitousness of Döblin's depictions of violence generated responses that pointed out his one-sided and distorting use of quotations.[12] Sebald has remained a thorn in the flesh for Döblin scholarship, and Döblin detractors continue to find in his book a good source for their arguments.[13]

Ernst Ribbat took up the issues of exoticism, regressive tendencies, and gratuitous violence once more in 1990, trying to trace the broad contours of the phenomenon for Döblin in his article "Ein globales Erzählwerk. Alfred Döblins Exotismus."[14] Seen from the perspective of "das Fremde," the theme of the Eighth International Germanists Congress, at which Ribbat presented the paper, Döblin's oeuvre has two distinct parts: the "Heimatromane" located in Berlin, from *Wadzek* to *November 1918*, and the exotic narratives from *Wang-lun* to *Amazonas*, even some of the novellas of *Hamlet* take place in the Orient. It is soon evident that this dichotomy is more apparent than real, but Ribbat's thrust leads elsewhere: after noting the surprising fact that Döblin — who loved to travel through space and time in books, pictures, maps, and museums — was a most reluctant traveler in real life, and definitely a non-tourist, Ribbat analyzes the functions and intentions of Döblin's imaginary travels that cannot be called exoticist either in the sense of the stories of "real" travelers, like Joseph Conrad, nor escapist in the sense of Karl May. Döblin aims at a global perspective, culminating in the visions of *Berge Meere und Giganten*, texts presenting and representing a total reality that "real" life can never yield. Döblin's imaginary voyages are Columbus expeditions into new territories. Each book is designed to expand the vision of the world and of history.

Luca Renzi, in the study "Alfred Döblin's Dampfturbine: Symbol, Gleichnis, Mythos, Realität. Gesellschafts- und Zukunftskritik im Roman *Wadzeks Kampf mit der Dampfturbine* (1918),"[15] underscores the point that Döblin's emphasis changed from the original conception while he was writing the book, and that, consequently, several interpretations of the text are possible. The original theme of man versus technology seems submerged and crowded out by the psychological or even psychoanalytical problematics of Wadzek and his family, although it is still a major point, meaning: can man dominate and control technology, or has it become a savage beast that threatens humanity's existence? Renzi points out that in *Wadzek*, as before in *Wang-lun*, the alternatives of resistance ("Widerstand") and adaptation, acquiescence, non-resistance ("Anpassung") are outlined, without a clear decision. *Anpassung* refers also to man's adaptation to nature; therefore, it seems to imply an anti-technological attitude. It is not clear from the final text whether the positive evaluation of technology that was part of the original conception is maintained or whether "Zivilisationskritik" has taken over.

In a second contribution to the same symposium on *Wadzek*, "Döblin's Reflexionen zur technischen Zivilisation. Das Beispiel des *Wadzek*-Roman,"[16] by Pierre Nenguie Kodjio, the emphasis is on the movement within the novel from an enthusiastic affirmation of technology to a critical attitude. Wadzek is at first an engineer who sees his inventions as progress for humanity. But later he realizes that the technological civilization needs an ethical basis. However, this growing critique of technological progress is expressed in the form of a grotesque parody, and Wadzek himself turns from a hero of civilization who struggles to retain dominance over his machines into a laughable victim of technology and capitalistic competition. It is this aesthetic weapon of parody that Döblin uses to call into question the beneficial nature of technological progress and to demonstrate the powerlessness of human beings in their attempt to control their machines.

Notes

[1] David B. Dollenmayer, *The Berlin Novels of Alfred Döblin* (Berkeley/Los Angeles/London: U of California P, 1988), 33–53.

[2] David B. Dollenmayer, "Heroismuskritik in einem Frühwerk von Döblin: 'Wadzeks Kampf mit der Dampfturbine,'" *Internationale Alfred-Döblin-Kolloquien 1980–1983*, ed. Werner Stauffacher, 270–79.

[3] Anthony W. Riley, "Nachwort" in Alfred Döblin, *Wadzeks Kampf mit der Dampfturbine, Ausgewählte Werke in Einzelbänden*, ed. Riley (Olten/Freiburg: Walter-Verlag, 1982), 365–93.

[4] Bertolt Brecht, *Tagebücher 1920–1922* (Frankfurt: Suhrkamp, 1975), 48.

[5] Werner Stauffacher, "'Komisches Grundgefühl' und 'Scheinbare Tragik'. Zu 'Wadzeks Kampf mit der Dampfurbine,'" *Internationale Alfred-Döblin-Kolloquien 1980–1983*, ed. Stauffacher, 168–83.

[6] Ira Lorf, "'Hier war man im echten Urwald.' Zur Verarbeitung ethnographischen Wissens in einem 'nicht-exotistischen' Text Döblins," *Internationales Alfred-Döblin-Kolloquium Paris 1993*, ed. Michel Grunewald (Bern: Peter Lang, 1995), 113–25.

[7] Ira Lorf, "Wissen — Text — kulturelle Muster. Zur literarischen Verarbeitung gesellschaftlicher Wissenbestände in Alfred Döblins Roman *Wadzeks Kampf mit der Dampfturbine*," *Internationales Alfred-Döblin-Kolloquium Leiden 1995*, ed. Gabriele Sander (Bern: Peter Lang, 1997), 83–94.

[8] Ira Lorf, *Maskenspiele: Wissen und kulturelle Muster in Alfred Döblins "Wadzeks Kampf mit der Dampfturbine" und "Die drei Sprünge des Wang-lun* (Bielefeld: Aisthesis Verlag, 1999).

[9] Winfried Georg Sebald, *Der Mythos der Zerstörung im Werk Döblins*, Literaturwissenschaft–Gesellschaftswissenschaft vol. 45 (Stuttgart: Klett, 1980); he expanded on his thesis in "Alfred Döblin oder Die politische Unzuverlässigkeit des bürgerlichen Literaten," *Internationale Alfred-Döblin-Kolloquien 1980–1983*, 133–39, and "Preussische Perversionen. Anmerkungen zum Thema Literatur und Gewalt, ausgehend vom Frühwerk Alfred Döblins," ibid, 231–38.

[10] Sebald does not fail to note and to repeat that he considers the ending of *Berlin Alexanderplatz* "mißraten" (92).

[11] This was also Klaus Müller-Salget's initial position, which he relativized later; see the preface to the second (1988) edition of his book, *Alfred Döblin: Werk und Entwicklung* (xvii).

[12] See for instance the dissertation by Otto Klein, *Das Thema Gewalt im Werk Alfred Döblins: Ästhetische, ethische und religiöse Sichtweise* (Hamburg: Verlag Dr. Kovac, 1995), which offers a detailed analysis of all Döblin's major works.

[13] One good example is Ulrich Dronske's *Tödliche Präsens/zen: Über die Philosophie des Literarischen bei Alfred Döblin* (Würzburg: Königshausen & Neumann, 1998). Dronske's real project is the radical deconstruction of Döblin's philosophy of nature and his literary theory, with some relatively positive pages on *Berlin Alexanderplatz*.

[14] Ernst Ribbat, "Ein globales Erzählwerk. Alfred Döblins Exotismus," in *Begegnung mit dem 'Fremden': Grenzen — Traditionen — Vergleiche*, Akten des VIII. Internationalen Germanisten-Kongresses Tokyo 1990, vol. 7 (Munich: Iudicium Verlag, 1991), 426–33.

[15] Luca Renzi, "Alfred Döblins Dampfturbine: Symbol, Gleichnis, Mythos, Realität. Gesellschafts- und Zukunftskritik im Roman *Wadzeks Kampf mit der Dampfturbine* (1918)," in *Internationales Alfred-Döblin-Kolloquium Bergamo 1999*, edited by Torsten Hahn (Bern: Peter Lang, 2002), 55–74.

[16] Pierre Nenguie Kodjio, "Döblin's Reflexionen zur technischen Zivilisation. Das Beispiel des *Wadzek*-Romans," *Internationales Alfred-Döblin-Kolloquium Bergamo 1999*, 75–85.

6: *Wallenstein*

DÖBLIN'S *WALLENSTEIN*, written during the First World War and dealing with another catastrophic event, the Thirty Years' War of 1618–48, has always been considered a commentary on war, violence, and possible ways to achieve peace. Above all, it was a historical novel, but one of a very peculiar kind. This is where the emphasis of scholarship has been so far.

Wolfdietrich Rasch, in his article "Döblins *Wallenstein* und die Geschichte," first published in the Festschrift for Döblin's seventieth birthday,[1] begins with the global statement that *Wallenstein* is the great historical novel of the postwar period. It is the first work that reveals the entire span of Döblin's narrative art (228). It is wrong to consider Döblin's oeuvre only from the perspective of *Berlin Alexanderplatz*. There is in fact a unity among the first four great novels, *Wang-lun*, *Wallenstein*, *Berge Meere und Giganten* and *Berlin Alexanderplatz*, and it is mandatory to see the "Gleichberechtigung," the equal stature, of these four novels (228).

It is also a falsehood, writes Rasch, that Döblin found his true topic and setting only in *Berlin Alexanderplatz* (228). Döblin's work is based on an extraordinary power of imagination, presented with optimal precision and fullness of detail (229). It is the opposite of "Geschichtsschreibung mit literarischen Mitteln" (230), but just because Döblin does not dwell on facts and figures, does not keep the reality of past ages from coming to the surface. Rasch compares *Wallenstein* to Flaubert's *Salammbô* in its use of realism. With *Wallenstein* the German historical novel gains a European standing (231). It is "ein *Geschichtsroman jenseits des Historismus*" (233). Döblin is able to transcend historicism, which is an offspring of Romanticism, and leaves the entire nineteenth century behind. Rasch goes so far as to say that Döblin's standpoint is beyond history: "Sein Standpunkt ist jenseits der Geschichte" (235). This became evident already in *Wang-lun*, where the victory of the emperor over Wang-lun and his followers is clearly marked as hollow. So are the victories of Wallenstein. In this novel Döblin signals the farewell from the history-obsessed nineteenth century, which was destroyed in the First World War, only for the idea of "history" that characterized it to be revived after its time, with the catastrophe of the Second World War as its consequence (241). Döblin's *Wallenstein* is a novel anticipating the awareness, which is now so common, of the departure from previous history ("Abschied von der bisherigen Geschichte") (242).

This leap to the time after 1945 is crucial for Günter Grass's lecture "Über meinen Lehrer Döblin," presented for the tenth anniversary of Döblin's death in June 1967 and first published in *Akzente*.[2] Whereas Grass's emphatic eulogy and declaration of his indebtedness to Döblin, above all to *Wallenstein*, has been used as an argument by Döblin's defenders ever since it was first presented, the content of his speech has received much less scrutiny. Grass's purpose was to speak about Döblin the man and his work, and to use a perspective other than *Berlin Alexanderplatz*. Thomas Mann and Brecht, he says, built their work on a solid foundation, stone by stone, and became classics, with shelves full of secondary literature and congresses in their honor; even Kafka reached that status. Döblin, however, seemed to discard what he had built at any juncture, and start from somewhere else. His work is not a monument. For Grass, the late Döblin, who followed Kierkegaard instead of de Coster's *Ulenspiegel*, is not the man from whom he learned to write; it is the earlier writer, and especially the author of *Wallenstein*, closest to *Ulenspiegel*. *Wallenstein* should be called "Ferdinand der Andere," Grass thinks (8), and later scholarship agreed with him. Döblin knew that "ein Buch mehr sein muß als der Autor, daß der Autor nur Mittel zum Zweck eines Buches ist" (9). Döblin writes about history, but he knows the difference between conventional history-telling and real history. All the facts are narrated, "betont achtlos, weil es nun mal dazu gehört; aber Geschichte, und das heißt die Vielzahl widersinniger und gleichzeitiger Abläufe, Geschichte, wie Döblin sie bloßstellen will, ist das nicht" (13). The real history is not told by facts. Döblin himself spoke later of a "Tiefenschicht," a deep level, of history. The Thirty Years' War has left many traces in German literature, from Grimmelshausen to Brecht. One point of orientation is Schiller, both his *Geschichte des Dreißigjährigen Krieges* and his *Wallenstein* trilogy. Schiller wants to make sense and order out of chaos: "Seine ordnende Hand knüpft Bezüge, will Sinn geben. Das alles zerschlägt Döblin mehrmals und bewußt zu Scherben, damit Wirklichkeit entsteht" (14). Grass is fascinated by Döblin's image of Wallenstein the financier whose real purpose is power through money and not victories in battle, and he draws parallels with Hitler and German industry, a German "military-industrial complex" reaching in unbroken tradition from the seventeenth to the twentieth century. Grass understands that he cannot call *Wallenstein* "einen geschlossenen, wohlausgewogenen Roman," but only an "epische[n] Aufriß," which ends with a scene that transcends all historical facts — the emperor is "ins Fabelreich enthoben" (21).

Grass offers further perspectives on *Berge Meere und Giganten* and *Berlin Alexanderplatz*, fascinated by Döblin's vision of the tree trunks that inspired the last scene of *Wallenstein*. Döblin, says Grass, dared to live with his contradictions (25). *Wallenstein* is for Grass an example of a futuristic technique of the novel (26), and with his lecture, he wants to repay a debt to a teacher. Read Döblin, he urges, but be prepared to be disquieted; Döblin wants to change you, and he may not be easy to digest. If you want to have sweet dreams, he is not for you.

Leo Kreutzer, who considers *Wallenstein* Döblin's most important novel after *Berlin Alexanderplatz* (67), analyzes Döblin's view of the figure of Wallenstein and of his period as a turning point in German history: "Döblins Wallenstein ist im Begriff, für Deutschland das zu leisten, was Richelieu für Frankreich tatsächlich geleistet hat, nämlich die Ablösung des Mittelalters, der Feudalität, das Bündnis zwischen König- tum und Bürgertum — Absolutismus als notwendige Durchgangsstufe zur bürgerlichen Revolution" (58). This view of necessary change, of historical teleology, seems however not quite consistent with the even- tual outcome of the novel: Kreutzer sees Döblin's interpretation of Wallenstein as a declaration of his will for political, revolutionary action, and historical change, but a declaration that is expressed in an ambiguous manner (61). Indeed, most other interpretations focus much less on Wallenstein than on the Emperor Ferdinand, less on the historical dy- namics than on the cycles of death and renewal.

The dissertation of Dieter Mayer, *Alfred Döblins Wallenstein,*[3] em- phasizes Döblin's "Geschichtsauffassung," his view of history, not so much Döblin's view of the Thirty Years' War as his ideas on history in general. Mayer sees Döblin's views on human history as derived from his philosophy of nature, and acknowledges the impact of the Taoist world- view on Döblin. The author himself had declared the Emperor Ferdi- nand II to be the work's true protagonist, and Mayer concurs, and then goes on to and defends the ending of the novel as consistent with the entire action and with Döblin's conceptions of the epic narration of history. Mayer explains the work in light of Döblin's own pronounce- ments on the philosophy of nature, on politics, and on poetics. Although he admits that most of Döblin's theoretical pronouncements came after the writing of *Wallenstein*, Mayer nevertheless uses them to elucidate the novel, positing the fundamental continuity of Döblin's thinking and writing, even after his conversion and up until his death, just as he also proposes a unity of natural and human history.

Whereas the larger part of Mayer's book is devoted to the philosophy of history and Döblin's theory of the epic, Mayer offers an analysis of the structure of *Wallenstein* that shows that while Döblin deemphasizes dates and "major" events, he adheres rather closely to the historical chronology of the years from 1621 to 1634 (the year of the assassination of Wallenstein) with an appendix reaching to the death of the emperor in 1637. Despite Döblin's theory of eliminating the narrator and letting the events speaks for themselves, the intrusion of a narrator is noticeable in many ways, such as the selection of the episodes, the relative emphasis, and the perspective on the characters and the masses. Although commentaries by a "personal" author may be absent, this is by no means an "objective" history telling itself.

Mayer analyzes the crucial significance of images of nature, above all of flowing water, trees, and forests (the latter of which are the locale for many of the deaths of Döblin's characters — from the Emperor Ferdinand to Mieze in *Berlin Alexanderplatz* and Las Casas and the escaping Europeans in *Amazonas*). Finally, in spite of the powerful images of the end of human life, returning to the anonymity of mother nature, there is still a fundamental ambiguity: the non-resistance of the Wu-wei is balanced by an activism that springs from an empathy with the downtrodden and the suffering poor whose lot needs to be improved should the world ever come into a meaningful order.

Klaus Müller-Salget, in his *Wallenstein* chapter, stresses the structural principle of repetition, which entails variation and intensification, reaching from key words, motifs, and metaphors to key scenes.[4] This is connected with a pessimistic outlook on history that sees a way out from the senseless repetition of violence only in an immersion in nature, which means the annihilation of what is human. The Emperor Ferdinand, who, as Müller-Salget agrees, is the real protagonist, offers the prime example of this path from power and glory through to a self-abandonment and decomposition into the elements. Müller-Salget pays little attention to Ferdinand's antagonists, Wallenstein, Maximilian of Bavaria, and Gustav Adolf.

Karl Herbert Blessing, in his 1972 publication *Die Problematik des "modernen Epos" im Frühwerk Alfred Döblins*[5] recognizes the "Mehrsträngigkeit," the multiple-strandedness, of the action and the absence of a real protagonist. He argues that even though Emperor Ferdinand is the one who is most easily understood, he does not provide the "backbone" for the work, which is to be found elsewhere, in the theme of war, which, he says, is portrayed as the fundamental situation ("Ursituation") of human action (35). The many scenes and details are not causally connected, but have their own substance in themselves. The result is an "Erzählstruktur des Nebeneinander" (narrative structure of juxtaposition) (37). There is, however, a structure of variation and correlation that connects the individual scenes with the entire work. In fact, the expected direct links of cause and effect are replaced by more indirect "Verweisungen," indications of repetitions or connections, which, however, can never replace the dominant impression of a mere "Nebeneinander."

The fact that Döblin neglects to mention dates in a historical novel seems to Blessing to indicate a more than historical meaning. The action in the book is not restricted to a specific time in the past and so becomes valid also for other periods of history (168). De-emphasizing the temporal specificity of the historical events has another consequence as well: time in *Wallenstein* is indifferent, it shows no effects; nothing is changed by it (170). Historical events do not change anything, they just repeat themselves. On the other hand, there are spaces that are correlated with particular characters, and the entire space of the action is well defined. This does not mean mere topography, but space in the relation of man and nature, as exemplified by the Emperor Ferdinand.[6]

Finally, according to Blessing, the characters in Döblin's earlier novels are searching for a meaning in life that they have lost. Life seems chaotic; it is a mere assumption to think that there may be order in the chaos. Particularly in *Wallenstein,* the author gives no indication that the characters may be anything but objects of random events in society and chaotic forces of nature.

In the early to mid 1980s, Axel Hecker published two articles and then a book on *Wallenstein.* In the first of the papers, "Die Realität der Geschichte und die 'überreale Sphäre' des Romans. Überlegungen und Thesen zum Problem der Fiktionalität in Döblins Romanprogramm und seinem 'Wallenstein,'"[7] Hecker analyzed the distinction Döblin makes between the historian and the author of historical novels in *Der historische Roman und wir,* making the epistemological point that the novel in Döblin's understanding was not designed to represent historical reality, but to reflect on our understanding of what we consider reality.

In a second paper of 1985, "Döblins *Wallenstein* und Flauberts *Salammbô.* Ein strukturaler Vergleich,"[8] Hecker demonstrates surprising parallels between the two novels and deals especially with the controversial aspect of cruelty and violence, asking if this aspect is gratuitous or can be justified for structural, that is, aesthetic, reasons. He sees a similarity in both works in terms of aestheticism, dehumanization in the description of human beings, excess, and the powerlessness of the individuals against mythical/historical forces. Hecker states a fundamental opposition between the historian's and the novelist's procedure in the dialectics of closeness and distance in the narrative perspective: "Der Historiker bemüht sich um einen *Ausgleich* zwischen der Annäherung des Vergangenen und seiner 'Entfremdung' zu einem möglichst objektiven, überschaubaren, von der realen Kontingenz gelösten Präparat" (213). Against this attempt to get close to the facts of history and then describe them from a distance that allows general developments to be seen, the two novelists in question undermine this synthesizing view: "Die beiden vorliegenden Romane dagegen *zerstören* gerade diesen Ausgleich und buchstabieren jenes merkwürdige Ineinander der Nähe und der Ferne durch alle denkbaren Extreme" (213). They don't do this for ideological reasons, according to Hecker, but "weil dies *gerade der Sinn der Literatur* ist: die uns bekannte Realität, zum Beispiel die historische, zu reflektieren, aber so, daß sich in dieser Spiegelung die Konstitution dieser Realität gleichsam *im Aufriß zeigt*" (213).

Hecker's 1986 book *Geschichte als Fiction* expands on this basic notion of history as fiction, of reality as something construed or created by the perceiving subject.[9] The historical novel, which Hecker says is between genres, a "Gattungszwitter" (11), is a most suitable subject of analysis through which to clarify the complex relationships between literature and reality, and *Wallenstein*, a most unusual example of the genre, offers deep insights. On the level of action, such analysis allows one to distinguish between purposeful actions of individuals (or attempts at them), and events, or "Abläufe," as Leo Kreutzer defined them, that happen as a consequence of several conflicting actions, or as natural phenomena. Hecker's real thrust is the deconstructionist analysis of fictionality, of the transformation of the story and history into a game, of reality into aesthetic structures. The fascinating point about Döblin's novel is that it works in both directions, reality into fiction, and fiction into reality, as can be seen in its imagery, where it is not always possible to determine whether a description is meant to portray reality or allegory or both, or whether a metaphor is "real" or just an image.

According to Hecker, Wallenstein personifies the irrationality of the supposedly rational action involved in war, which is perhaps more accurately termed calculating action. The novel is a demonstration of war and what it does to the human race. Wallenstein's and Slawata's actions are games that proceed from an attitude of a gambler who risks everything for victory, and who has no time or thought for humanitarian considerations. The book's aesthetization of risk-taking and war comes close to Walter Benjamin's definition of fascism, and aims at a perfect system and

the (impossible) end of all wars through war. In *Wallenstein* the historical sequence of structure-change-new structure is totally changed: any
emerging structures are transformed into movements. Döblin decon-
structs the idea of closure in his stories, and of "results" in history. In
fact, says Hecker, Döblin's radical destruction or deconstruction of the
tenets of the historical novel includes causality as such, and the potential
for human individuals to act and change the course of history. History
as humans understand it is seen to be an illusion when one considers the
laws and dynamics of nature. Thus Döblin's destruction of the historical
novel includes an "Irrealisierung" (327), and it is wrong to believe that
Döblin intends to describe and explain a historical epoch. It becomes
more and more evident that Hecker's critique goes far beyond *Wallen-*
stein, and as his subtitle indicates, it aims at a fundamental critique of
realism and the legitimacy of realistic literature. *Wallenstein* is a suitable
example insofar as it contains an immense amount of factual material,
and yet the author's approach transforms the facts into a world of the
work's own, which is the opposite of the conventional historical novel,
which aims at a mimesis of historical reality. Döblin, according to
Hecker, problematizes reality itself, together with its depictions by historians and novelists alike. For example, the Emperor Ferdinand becomes
a "real" person in aesthetic terms only when he ceases to be the historical
emperor; he has to exit from history to reach reality. This is how Döblin
generates an intricate game of contrasts between his material and his
aesthetic reality, or fiction.

Hecker finds out that for every strategy, point of view, structure, stylistic device, message, there is an equally valid opposite; for instance, Wallenstein against Slawata, Wallenstein against the emperor, the emperor
against Maximilian of Bavaria; the generals, the masses, the Jews of Prague,
they all find their opposites, as do natural objects and events. *Wallenstein*
presents its universe of chaos and conflict as a total of fictional structures
and linguistic combinations where nature acts through human beings
(using mostly their animal instincts) to create its own dynamics of life and
death. Hecker's analysis makes one understand why most of Döblin's
critics view this epic work with unease, although they feel respect for its
author's achievement. At the same time, it heightens our curiosity why it
is exactly this work that Günter Grass admires so much.

Waltraud Maierhofer approaches a mostly neglected subject in her
study "Zur Repräsentation der Frau und des Weiblichen in Döblins
Wallenstein."[10] Against the traditional reading of the text (supported by
Döblin himself) that women are of no importance, Maierhofer, through
a careful analysis, is able to relativize this general statement by defining

several distinctive functions of individual women or of "the feminine" in the framework of the epic and in its style. She finds few traces of misogyny, but a rather unconventional nonjudgmental view of women in a text that is devoted to war and the fate of men. Her study has significance beyond *Wallenstein*; for the earlier part of Döblin's oeuvre, her last sentence needs to be remembered: "Ein sorgfältiges Wiederlesen ist aber angebracht" (114).

Adalbert Wichert, in his 1978 book *Alfred Döblins historisches Denken*,[11] considers all of Döblin's historical novels as an expression of one philosophy of history, in spite of evident changes in his approach. According to Wichert, all Döblin's historical novels are guided by the conviction that "Unordnung ist ein besseres Wissen als die Ordnung" (22). The order that the human mind imposes on nature and history is totally misleading. Consequently, says Wichert, "das Motiv des Sich-nicht-zurechtfindens," the motif of disorientation, remains a dominant feature in Döblin (23). Wichert sees Döblin as presenting a "Hin und Her als Gegenmodell geschichtlichen Verlaufs" (34); he also calls this chaotic to-and-fro a "Sisyphos-Modell" (34). One of Wichert's most significant observations is that in Döblin's attempts at orientation amidst this chaos, which are similar to scientific experiments, there is a continual process of self-correction and revision by way of appendices or corrections (51). And this in turn explains the novels' lack of conclusive endings (52). Döblin's "endless" epics, which later grew into trilogies, are antihistorical, and the author's position of partiality ("Parteilichkeit") precludes a historian's view of the past. Wichert sees not harmony but struggle between the world of nature and of history (77). Döblin wants to provide "Wissen," "Erkenntnis," but due to his conviction that human beings, especially in crowds, are irrational by nature, he believes that efforts at enlightenment must use non-rational, non-intellectual means. Wichert sees Döblin, along with Brecht, as having attempted this (139). Döblin's ideas determine the form and content of his novels, and the priority of cognition is decisive for their form: they offer not actions, but the recognition of connections, *Zusammenhänge* (185). These connections are not causal connections, however: Wichert insists on mutual effects instead of causality (166). In Döblin's historical novels, *Erkenntnis* comes through comparisons and contrasts of different ages, of the present and the past (94, 209). All of this denies the one-directional flow of time and urges a reflection on the "Abläufe," the events. In other words: Döblin's books arrive at a point where it seems necessary to look back, take stock, and read them backwards: "Döblins Bücher wollen rückwärts gelesen werden" (97). Wichert draws a line between Döblin and Marxist historiography. With reference to Döblin's attitude toward power and the state, he considers Döblin closer to Burckhardt than to Engels (147). He also sees close parallels with the views of Kurt Breysig (73, 130), although Breysig's notion of "Entwicklung" would seem to make such comparison unlikely. Wichert cannot fail to notice Döblin's proximity to anarchistic philosophies of solidarity and mutual help.

Wichert's generalizations may read more system into Döblin's ideas than there is, especially considering his aversion to abstractions and abstract reasoning, but they indicate the philosophical underpinnings of Döblin's open forms as well as his nature images and his fundamental distrust of progress. All of this can be applied, as Wichert shows, to a fundamental revision of the image of Wallenstein (60–70). But we may conclude that much more is at stake: a revision of the concept of human history and the power (or lack thereof) of the individual to determine and influence the outcome of historical events. Döblin's pessimistic position, possibly influenced by Schopenhauer, was very much in opposition to Marxist optimism, even as early as the period around 1920.

Bernd Hüppauf examines the "history of mentalities" in his 1991 article "The Historical Novel and a History of Mentalities. Alfred Döblin's *Wallenstein* as an Historical Novel."[12] Hüppauf approaches *Wallenstein* as an "attempted fusion of the experimental novel with an historical subject" (71). In *Wallenstein*, Hüppauf notes the "lack of cohesion of the fable, the discontinuity in time and disparity in place and action and the general impression of chaos" (75), all of which convey the idea of being trapped in a labyrinth. At such a catastrophic point in history, there is no chance for a narrator to find a safe distance or for contemplation: narrator and reader are drawn into a vortex. Thus the narrative structure can be seen as "a negation of a hermeneutical approach to history" (79). Döblin's narrative, according to Hüppauf, does not lead to a clarification of historical facts and developments, but to "a construction of a poetic reality with specific philosophical qualities" (81). The novel presents the results of the experience of the First World War, "the common discovery of irrationality and destruction as integral elements of the modern world" (82). *Wallenstein* could be read, if history is seen according to the concepts of Schiller and Lukács, "as a historical novel of *posthistoire*" (83), expressing the "disintegration of teleological views" (85). Hüppauf links *Wallenstein* with the new developments in historiography, specifically the history of mentalities. "Destructiveness as a constitutional element of modern society" — not just in war, which is but an allegory (89) for the true nature of modern society — leads to this new form of narrative work that looks into the depths of history.

Döblin's *Wallenstein* provides the opportunity to reflect on the lost meaning and teleology of history and the heroic attempts to regain a sense of it later in the face of the Nazi barbarism, for instance in Heinrich Mann's *Henri IV*. This perspective places Döblin's later confrontations with history in *Amazonas* and *November 1918* in the wider context of the history of the catastrophic twentieth century.

Notes

[1] Wolfdietrich Rasch, "Döblins *Wallenstein* und die Geschichte," *Alfred Döblin zum 70. Geburtstag*, ed. Paul E. H. Lüth (Wiesbaden: Limes, 1948), 36–47; quoted from Rasch, *Zur deutschen Literatur seit der Jahrhundertwende: Gesammelte Aufsätze* (Stuttgart: J. B. Metzler, 1976), 228–42.

[2] *Akzente* 14, 4 (August 1967): 290–309; quoted from Günter Grass, *Über meinen Lehrer Döblin und andere Vorträge*, LCB Editionen, vol. 1 (Berlin: Literarisches Colloquium, 1968), 7–26.

[3] Dieter Mayer, *Alfred Döblins Wallenstein: Zur Geschichtsauffassung und zur Struktur* (Munich: Wilhelm Fink, 1972); the dissertation had been completed in 1970.

[4] Klaus Müller-Salget, *Alfred Döblin: Werk und Entwicklung* (Bonn: Bouvier, 1973; 2nd rev. ed. 1988).

[5] Karl Herbert Blessing, *Die Problematik des "modernen Epos" im Frühwerk Alfred Döblins*, Deutsche Studien, vol. 19 (Meisenheim am Glan: Verlag Anton Hain, 1972).

[6] Blessing's major thesis goes beyond an analysis of *Wallenstein*. On the basis of *Wang-lun, Wallenstein, Berge Meere und Giganten*, and *Manas*, Blessing wants to arrive at a definition of Döblin's narrative works. They are not "novels" in a traditional sense, as Döblin himself emphatically declared. So what are they? Can they serve as examples for a reborn genre of the "epic"? Eventually, Blessing comes to the conclusion that while combining archaic and progressive-avantgarde elements that exceed the boundaries of the "traditional" novel, Döblin's works did not and could not restore the epic genre of Homer, but remained as gadflies within the realm of novelistic writing, always testing the limits of the genre.

[7] Axel Hecker, "Die Realität der Geschichte und die 'überreale Sphäre' des Romans. Überlegungen und Thesen zum Problem der Fiktionalität in Döblins Romanprogramm und seinem 'Wallenstein,'" *Internationale Alfred-Döblin-Kolloquien 1980–1983*, ed. Werner Stauffacher (Bern: Peter Lang, 1986), 280–92.

[8] Axel Hecker, "Döblins *Wallenstein* und Flauberts *Salammbô*. Ein strukturaler Vergleich," *Internationale Alfred-Döblin-Kolloquien 1984–1985*, ed. Werner Stauffacher (Bern: Peter Lang, 1988), 196–214.

[9] Axel Hecker, *Geschichte als Fiktion: Alfred Döblins "Wallenstein" — Eine exemplarische Kritik des Realismus*, Epistemata: Würzburger Wissenschaftliche Schriften, Reihe Literaturwissenschaqft, vol. 21 (Würzburg: Königshausen & Neumann, 1986).

[10] Waltraud Maierhofer, "Zur Repräsentation der Frau und des Weiblichen in Döblins *Wallenstein*," *Internationales Alfred-Döblin-Kolloquium Leiden 1995*, ed. Gabriele Sander (Bern: Peter Lang, 1997), 95–114.

[11] Adalbert Wichert, *Alfred Döblins historisches Denken: Zur Poetik des modernen Geschichtsromans* (Stuttgart: J. B. Metzler, 1978).

[12] Bernd Hüppauf, "The Historical Novel and a History of Mentalities. Alfred Döblin's *Wallenstein* as an Historical Novel," in *The Modern German Historical Novel: Paradigms, Problems and Perspectives*, eds. David Roberts and Philip Thomson (New York/Oxford: Berg, 1991), 71–96.

7: *Berge Meere und Giganten*

B ERGE MEERE UND GIGANTEN, Döblin's immense vision of future
history, impressed his contemporaries when it appeared in 1924,
but seems to have embarrassed rather than fascinated academic scholars,
who found ways to avoid it. Klaus Müller-Salget has noted that it is
almost de rigueur to speak in negative terms about this work; and he
mentions Muschg, Martini, and Leo Kreutzer as examples of this.[1] Erwin
Kobel, in a book dealing with Döblin's early short stories and all major
novels, even *Manas*, avoids *Berge Meere und Giganten* as well as
Wadzek.[2] Ingrid Schuster's collection of essays of 1980, *Zu Alfred Döblin*, also omits it. Sebald dismisses the book simply as science fiction —
meaning that he judges it worthless. But others who have confronted the
monstrous text have felt compelled to dive into the intricacies of
Döblin's philosophy of nature. Roland Links pursues Döblin's own
(later) question as fundamental for the text: "Was wird aus dem Menschen, wenn er so weiterlebt?" (83). There is a close correlation between
critics' avoidance of the issues of Döblin's philosophy of nature and their
avoidance of *Berge Meere und Giganten*. Therefore, the amount of scholarly literature on this text is relatively small; yet as interest began to grow
in *Das Ich über der Natur* and *Unser Dasein*, *Berge Meere und Giganten*
seemed to deserve a second and third look. Since most scholars agree on
a shift in Döblin's theory of epic narration and in his views on nature and
the human race in general in the mid-twenties, before the writing of
Manas, *Berge Meere und Giganten* and Döblin's travelogue *Reise in
Polen*, both written just prior to *Manas*, take on new significance as
documents of transition. Thus recent studies of *Berge Meere und Giganten* show evidence of more attentive reading and a real attempt at understanding and evaluation of a text that defies generic definitions.

The 1948 Festschrift *Alfred Döblin zum 70. Geburtstag* contained
only two studies on Döblin's works, one being Rasch's article on *Wallenstein* and the second a study on *Berge Meere und Giganten* by Max
Herchenröder.[3] Herchenröder uses an essayistic style, but has a concise
thesis. He underscores the relevance of the book after twenty-four years;
he even mentions a number of scientific predictions that had come true
in the interval. But predominantly he dwells on what he sees as the

novel's main point: the hubris of human technology that will destroy the human race after robbing it of its humanity — and for Herchenröder the best possible outcome is a return to "primitive" life in the country, as Döblin depicts it at the novel's end. Herchenröder's own thesis about the driving force behind this mad rush to self-destructive technology and away from nature is "the will to power" (54), in two forms: the brutal sadistic will to subjugate and its correlate, the masochistic willingness to be dominated (54). There is no "materialism" in Döblin's book, Herchenröder asserts; instead, the worldview expressed is a remarkable, purely western version of Taoism (56). The moral consequence of this worldview is the modesty and humility of the human being (56). *Berge Meere und Giganten* remains "ein Hymnus auf das Leben," "ein furchtbarer Psalm auf die protoplasmatischen Schicksale," a warning about the heroic but impossible struggle of the mind against the fundamental conditions of existence (57). Herchenröder's strictures against rationalism and technology, reinforced by the shock of the atomic bombs, echo the postwar mood of humility and religiosity. And this humility and religiosity fits in with the predominantly Catholic view of Döblin's work in the Festschrift, where the pagan exuberance in Döblin's earlier texts appears only, as it were, against the express will of the authors.

Ardon Denlinger's University of Massachusetts dissertation, *Alfred Döblins Berge Meere und Giganten: Epos und Ideologie,* published as a book in 1977,[4] starts out with the thesis that Döblin's concept of the epic is designed to restore on a modern basis the unity of the world as it had existed at the time of the gods (4). Denlinger refers to Georg Lukács's classic *Theorie des Romans,* and says that Döblin wants to return the divine to the novel, the absolute in the form of an all-encompassing concept of nature (3). Denlinger seems to mean by this a pantheistic view and foundation for the structure and content of the epic; for him *Berge Meere und Giganten* narrates the attempt of humanity to transcend nature by means of technology (4). Denlinger continues and modifies previous analyses by Müller-Salget, Kreutzer, Blessing, and Kort by paying special attention to the interconnections between the main plot and the digressions, and also to the second version, *Giganten,* of 1932, and its major differences from the book of 1924. (*Giganten* is commonly mentioned in passing, but hardly ever examined in detail by critics.)

In the technological revolution, according to Denlinger, the real driving force is the human psyche (11). Thus all human emotions, love above all, are entering into the relationship with the newly invented machines and procedures. The machines, however, become independent of their inventors — a common theme in science fiction. Whereas in the text of 1924, technology overpowers the inventors to the point of eventual self-destruction, the *Giganten* text is much more benign: it assigns total responsibility for the destruction to the human race, but posits the chance for a balanced and beneficial use of technology, even for solving the social conflict between rich and poor, by elevating the masses out of their misery into a decent life. Equally, the ending of *Berge Meere und Giganten* can be easily construed as anti-city and in favor of the "healthy" life on the farm; but in *Giganten*, Döblin tried to minimize that effect. The text is much more positive and less critical of Western civilization. Whereas in *Berge Meere und Giganten* it is the West, against the resistance of the Asians, that pushes technology forward and generates war, *Giganten* largely eliminates this difference. The fact remains that the development of technology, which feeds on itself, is not caused by economic or social necessity, but by psychological drives for power.

One of the progressive symptoms of the disintegration of Western civilization through the lust for technological power is the disappearance of the differences between the sexes; women in particular become more masculine, which Denlinger finds exemplified in the figure of Melise and her rule in the name of Persephone, the queen of the underworld. According to Denlinger, the women in *Berge Meere und Giganten* still represent the anti-technological side: *Lebensphilosophie*, or vitalism. But at this point, this vitalism turns into a longing for death: *Todessehnsucht*.

Berge Meere und Giganten describes the evolution of humanity to a menacing impasse, and the attempts to rescue the human race. The text is, however, less than clear on whether certain movements, and the leaders who represent them, are benign or destructive. A case in point is Marduk, who takes things to the brink of an annihilation of free humanity that is only prevented by love, by erotic relationships. The action then proceeds to the figure of Kylin, who unites within himself all the contradictions of the human condition and resumes within himself all the previous conflicts (76). His search for a solution leads to "the new man" ("den neuen Menschen") rather than to a new form of society ("neue Gesellschaftsform")(80). It is within the human being that the transformation has to occur. And it is Kylin who personifies this process, as he changes through his encounters with different women. Here it seems that the action turns into a quest for salvation.

Denlinger illustrates Döblin's efforts to bring about a new epic narrative that would go beyond the conventional psychological novel of his day — efforts which are much more clearly expressed in Döblin's essays than in his novels — through a comparison of the essays with Georg Lukács's *Theorie des Romans*. For Denlinger, Döblin's primary purpose is to present (and restore) the totality of the world (109). In *Berge Meere und Giganten,* this leads him beyond human proportions and human history. Specifically, Döblin has to exclude the entire economic-social dimension (116). The search for "den neuen Menschen," typical for Expressionism, is compatible with Döblin's negative attitude toward political parties, the socialist parties in particular, and his refusal to accept Marxist historical materialism. For Denlinger, Döblin's theory and practice of the novel is consistent with his natural philosophy and his anti-Marxist political attitude. However, Denlinger finds in all of Döblin's philosophies, theories, and practices a fundamental ambivalence and inability to take sides, which was evident in Döblin's political position in the years leading up to 1933. *Berge Meere und Giganten,* in other words, is remarkable on the one hand in its attempt to grasp the totality of human existence in nature and its conflicts, and on the other hand in its failure to stake out a concrete moral and political position. This is in spite of the fact that the novel has a clear didactic trend, a message that is considerably heightened and simplified in the *Giganten* version of 1932.

The most detailed study of Berge Meere und Giganten is Gabriele Sander's book of 1988, *"An der Grenze des Wirklichen und Möglichen . . .": Studien zu Alfred Döblins Roman "Berge Meere und Giganten."*[6] Sander's review of the previous reception leads her to conclude that the early reviews are mostly helpless attempts to get a handle on the problems raised by the book (7). This is due to what she calls "irritating experiences" in reading the work (9), and not least to the difficulty of determining its genre (15). This uncertain attitude did not change substantially in later evaluations (23). There are vast differences in the determination and evaluation of Döblin's "Schreibart" (33), meaning style and approach to problems, and the ending has remained particularly controversial. Another point of divergence has been Döblin's representation of the human race in this novel, of individuals, if they can be called individuals, and especially the masses. There is a consensus that this book marks the end of the "collectivist phase" of Döblin's writing (20). One might say that he reached an extreme, a non plus ultra. Sander points out that structural and stylistic analyses of Döblin's work must be much more refined if they are to give an adequate account of its formal and substantial complexities (63). Her own long and detailed study provides an example of a more sophisticated analysis that does better justice to Döblin's intentions and achievement.

Döblin, in his customary manner, read a considerable number of books, especially on geography, for this project, but Sander shows that he used surprisingly little material in a direct way (96). Rather, he transformed such realia in a way that suited his more important poetic intentions (97). The novel's complex interplay of imagery and multi-perspectival narration, says Sander, conforms to its fundamental "Doppelgesicht" (183): "Mythisierung" on the one hand versus the natural sciences and technology on the other. Never again did Döblin make such an effort to grasp such a totality of life in all its multitudinous variety (253). Sander also points out that although the text can be called "historical" (in a futuristic way), it is striking that the temporal dimensions are de-emphasized while the spatial dimensions in their "Maß- und Grenzenlosigkeit" remain in the forefront (147).

For Sander, the gigantic projects depicted in the novel, which aim at domination of nature and demand total sacrifice of freedom and individuality on the part of the human masses (such as the de-icing of Greenland), result in the system of government taking on a totalitarian character (259). This leads to man-made catastrophes from which only small farming communities emerge, localized in the idyllic setting of Southern France. Their non-technological way of life means also a liberation from a political system of enslavement. While the narrator had previously preferred the impersonal forms of "man" and "niemand" to refer to human beings, the ending brings the return to "real" people with personal names (146).

Klaus Müller-Salget's chapter on *Berge Meere und Giganten* emphasizes the novel's transitional character in Döblin's development and the opposing forces portrayed in it:[6] the book is not only the final climax of Döblin's fatalistic period, but shows his new emphasis on the dignity of the individual (202). Müller-Salget finds nearly all Döblin's strengths and weaknesses expressed in this text: his imagination had run away from him, and the conception changed drastically during the process of writing. The dominant theme of the book, as Müller-Salget sees it, is man's struggle to rise above the "allbeseelte Natur" that he is a part of and to achieve mastery of the world through technology (209). This is hubris, "Größenwahn," and Döblin has taken the concept literally, and transformed it into the book's reality. But Müller-Salget's main point goes beyond this view, which is shared by most critics. He emphasizes the opposing trend, Döblin's representations of individuals and of individual relationships, love in particular. For him as for others, the novel has a "Doppelgesicht," but one of both collective and of individual forces (214). His interpretation focuses on the individuals, Marduk and Kylin. He points out that in spite of the dominant impression of anonymity and purely natural forces at work, a personal narrator emerges repeatedly.

Wolfgang Reif focuses in the concluding chapter of his 1975 book *Zivilisationsflucht und literarische Wunschräume* on the combination of nature mysticism and fascination with technology in *Berge Meere und Giganten*.[7] He considers that Döblin turns the topic of the problems of technology into a hymn to nature, the novelistic project into a prose epic (158). Döblin's mystical philosophy considers all nature — even inorganic nature — to be "beseelt," possessed of a soul. Nature tries to remain in balance and does not tolerate the preponderance of one element or quality, such as technology. There is no "evolution" in nature as portrayed by Döblin, but constant flux. According to Reif, *Berge Meere und Giganten* is characterized by an aggressive technological "progress" followed by regressive reactions, a back-and-forth movement without a dialectical synthesis. In the end the catastrophe can no longer be prevented: technology self-destructs and the natural world is brought back into its balance with even more force than before (164). Reif notes that Döblin's novel includes all the trappings of science fiction in a regressive sense: the fear of "inner Africa," Frankenstein monsters, creatures from prehistoric ages (but no dinosaurs!), artificial food, and technological miracles, like the de-icing of Greenland. In the end, Europe regresses to a peaceful farmland, a new Arcadia. This, says Reif, is an impossible dream of escapism and a monster of a novel; in spite of moments of great writing the whole thing remains an unrestrained dream of destruction (168). For Reif, what is unique about *Berge Meere und Giganten* is that it claims to be high literature, whereas other similar works are relegated to the realm of trivial literature.

Wolfgang Kort, in his monograph of 1974,[8] considers *Berge Meere und Giganten* a turn to mysticism, one that is typical for Döblin's works whenever perception, knowledge, and technology have reached their limits (80–81). On the positive side, he notes with some surprise that female characters appear here as independent figures for the first time in Döblin (86). This is obviously a sign of a "return" to the real world. Leo Kreutzer, in his 1970 monograph on Döblin's work up until 1933, sees Döblin's "Zug ins Gigantische" (93) as a symptom of aiming for extremes; he finds the book's continual eccentricities tiring (95).[9] He also notes, in keeping with his overall approach, a background political problematic with contradictions of the same kind as Döblin's other texts from the period (95).

Torsten Hahn, in his article "'Vernichtender Fortschritt.' Zur experimentellen Konfiguration von Arbeit und Trägheit in *Berge Meere und Giganten*,"[10] analyzes the novel as a grand panorama of "Posthistoire," of the time after the end of history. On one hand, it is the description of an experiment that eventually fails; it can also be seen as an example of Döblin's idea of the eternal sequence of decadence and renewal; but the novel demonstrates even more the self-destructive features of Western civilization, which were analyzed by Ernst Jünger, first in *Der Kampf als inneres Erlebnis* (1922), later in *Der Arbeiter* (1930), and by Gottfried Benn. The rebarbarization leads to the point where war is considered a kind of sport that is undertaken to achieve new records, but not for any other goal: war for war's sake. Torsten Hahn analyzes in particular the phenomenon of the masses in *Berge Meere und Giganten,* who are characterized by their "Trägheit," meaning their passivity, laziness, and lack of initiative. This laziness leads, paradoxically, to occasional explosions into riots that resemble revolutions but are without purpose and lead only to destruction. They are only a useless discharge of accumulated energy. An essential part of this picture of "post-history" is that the awareness of the past has disappeared except for meaningless fragments.

Nevzat Kaya considers the struggle between patriarchal and matriarchal forces in "'Tellurische' Rationalitätskritik: Zur Weiblichkeitskonzeption in Alfred Döblins *Berge Meere und Giganten.*"[11] The basic thesis is that the novel is a "Literarisierung von Friedrich Nietzsches *Die Geburt der Tragödie aus dem Geiste der Musik*" (133), except that in Döblin's novel the development is backward, from the "olympischen Zauberberg zu seinen Wurzeln, den titanischen Mächten der Natur" (133), in the words of Nietzsche. This polarity of the Apollonian and Dionysian principles is equated with the patriarchal and matriarchal poles, following Johann Jakob Bachofen's controversial 1861 work *Das Mutterrecht.* The images of the "Great Mother" and the struggle between the Apollonian rationality and Dionysian irrationality are described, especially in connection with the crucial episode in the novel depicting the de-icing of Greenland. In the end, according to Kaya, there is indeed a renewal of humanity through the matriarchal forces, and thus a positive outlook into the future.

Kaya compares this with texts that are similar in theme and of the same time period as *Berge Meere und Giganten:* Alfred Kubin's 1909 novel *Die andere Seite,* Hugo von Hofmannsthal's *Märchen der 672. Nacht,* and most of all, Thomas Mann's *Der Zauberberg,* which appeared in the same year as Döblin's novel, 1924. All of them are much more pessimistic about humanity's future than Döblin's work is.

Notes

[1] Klaus Müller-Salget, *Alfred Döblin: Werk und Entwicklung* (Bonn: Bouvier, 1973; 2nd rev. ed, 1988), 201.

[2] Erwin Kobel, *Alfred Döblin: Erzählkunst im Umbruch* (Berlin/New York: Walter de Gruyter, 1985).

[3] Max Herchenröder, "Berge, Meere und Giganten," in *Alfred Döblin zum 70. Geburtstag*, edited by Paul E. H. Luth (Wiesbaden: Limes Verlag, 1948), 48–57. Döblin wrote the title *Berge Meere und Giganten* without a comma, with the clear purpose of totality in mind, but many critics disregard that signal and "conventionalize" the phrase.

[4] Ardon Denlinger, *Alfred Döblins Berge Meere und Giganten: Epos und Ideologie* (Amsterdam: B. R. Grüner, 1977).

[5] Gabriele Sander, *"An der Grenze des Wirklichen und Möglichen . . .": Studien zu Alfred Döblins Roman "Berge Meere und Giganten"* (Frankfurt: Peter Lang, 1988). The book has 634 pages.

[6] Klaus Müller-Salget, *Alfred Döblin: Werk und Entwicklung* (Bonn: Bouvier, 1973; 2nd rev. ed. 1988), 201–25.

[7] Wolfgang Reif, *Zivilisationsflucht und literarische Wunschträume: Deutsche exotische Romane im ersten Viertel des 20. Jahrhunderts* (Stuttgart: J. B. Metzler, 1975), 158–68. Reif's analysis of *Berge Meere und Giganten* gains added significance in his book as the concluding segment and the negative conclusion of his entire investigation.

[8] Wolfgang Kort, *Alfred Döblin*, Twayne World Authors Series 290 (New York: Twayne Publishers, 1974).

[9] Leo Kreutzer, *Alfred Döblin: Sein Werk bis 1933* (Stuttgart: W. Kohlhammer, 1970).

[10] Torsten Hahn, "'Vernichtender Fortschritt.' Zur experimentellen Konfiguration von Arbeit und Trägheit in *Berge Meere und Giganten*. *Internationales Alfred-Döblin-Kolloquium Bergamo 1999*, ed. Torsten Hahn (Bern: Peter Lang, 2002), 107–29.

[11] Nevzat Kaya, "'Tellurische' Rationalitätskritik: Zur Weiblichkeitskonzeption in Alfred Döblins *Berge Meere und Giganten*," *Internationales Alfred-Döblin-Kolloquium Bergamo 1999*, ed. Torsten Hahn (Bern: Peter Lang, 2002), 131–40.

8: *Manas*

ONE OF THE LARGELY UNEXPLAINED RIDDLES of Döblin's oeuvre is his attempt to write a verse epic on a topic from ancient Indian mythology at a time when he was closely involved in the political struggles of the Weimar Republic and in the happenings of the literary scene of Berlin. Döblin did not help matters by declaring *Manas* a mere prelude to *Berlin Alexanderplatz*. In spite of Robert Musil's enthusiastic review at the time of its publication, *Manas* never found an audience, and is rarely seen by critics as a work in itself, but instead only as a transition to the real event, which is *Berlin Alexanderplatz*.

Despite the passage of time, Heinz Graber's 1967 study of *Manas*[1] still stands out as a careful analysis of the text, based on the thesis of a circular movement of the text that progresses in order to reach the past. Reminding the reader of Expressionist works dealing with "der neue Mensch," Döblin's character Manas needs to die to be reborn to a new existence as a demigod. This transformation and rebirth is the work of his beloved wife Sawitri, the incarnation of a new type of woman in Döblin's oeuvre beginning with Venaska in *Berge Meere und Giganten*, the woman who stands for redemption, for transformation, for the guide to a higher existence — variations of whom reappear in all subsequent texts, although their functions vary considerably. Manas, Graber reminds us, is the "Heimkehrer," the heroic military leader who, returning home, carries the trauma and the guilt of the slaughter with him despite his victories; hence Manas's subsequent death, or voyage to the "Totenfeld" of pain and suffering from which he is rescued by his wife. Döblin uses Indian mythology to describe the need for and pain of the necessary cleansing to make the memory of the war bearable — which is impossible without the active participation and love of Sawitri.

Graber underscores the change of Döblin's views during the years preceding *Manas* and the new significance of the individual in his cosmos. But even after this change, the individual never appears alone, but always within a system of "Beziehungen," of relationships, both to other individuals and the mass of anonymous people. This network of relationships involves the answering of calls for action and engagement, responses whose manner defines the character of each individual. In this way, Graber sees Döblin taking gradual steps from his idea of "resonance" in nature and history, expounded in *Unser Dasein*, to the answering of the call of a God beyond nature. Sawitri's self-sacrifice for Manas brings them both eternal life.

In his 1985 book on Döblin's novels, Erwin Kobel devotes a fairly substantial chapter to *Manas*.[2] He sees the epic in the tradition of German longing for India and refers specifically to Hölderlin, Schelling, and early Indologists, like Max Müller. Kobel states that *Manas* belongs to those works by Döblin that were created as a counterpoint ("im Gegenzug") to previous works (228). The preceding text against which *Manas* was conceived, according to Kobel, is *Berge Meere und Giganten*, a book in which Kobel finds no redeeming value: for Kobel it is rather a work of "Phantastik" than of "Phantasie" (229–30), meaning a work resulting from calculating play with non-reality rather than from poetic inspiration. In contrast to such a work of rational calculation, whose message can be easily summarized in one single sentence, *Manas* is an example of the opposite danger: the author getting lost in the complexities of Indian mythology. Yet Döblin could have confidence in the affinities between Germany and India that were discovered by Schelling and the Romantics.

For Kobel, the central event of the epic is what he calls the "Hadesfahrt" (231), the voyage to the underworld. Kobel recognizes the dreamlike quality of the events and their circular structure, and he associates this with the psychological processes after the experience of trauma: the trauma of soldiers who return from war, but keep repeating the battle scenes in their dreams. While Kobel emphasizes that the action of *Manas* cannot be explained entirely as "innerlich," that is, psychological, as dreams and visions of a person afflicted with the repetition of unbearable events, he downplays the reality of the myth and wants to bring the story close to the present.

Kobel, like Graber before him, wonders why Musil's emphatic prophecy that *Manas* will be an enduring work with universal response did not come to pass. He mentions as the first obvious reason Döblin's style and form, his epic verse, which, technically speaking, may not be verse at all, but is still much harder to read than prose, and precludes a simple, fast reading. Kobel stresses the musical qualities of this verse, and it may indeed be worth a test to see if an oral recitation would do more justice to this text than silent reading does.

Scholars have routinely associated the thematics of *Manas* with those of Döblin's subsequent and most successful novel, *Berlin Alexanderplatz*, to the point that Kobel calls Biberkopf "Manas auf berlinerisch" (251). Therefore, in analyzing *Manas* they often concentrate primarily on similarities with *Alexanderplatz*. Thus a focus on *Manas*'s themes — those of the aftermath of war and of guilt and redemption — has been preempted by comparison to *Alexanderplatz* and the later works. Moreover, studies on the modern verse epic have been rare. In any event, *Manas* remained a special experiment among Döblin's many and varied explorations into the field of epic narrative.

Notes

[1] Heinz Graber, *Alfred Döblins Epos "Manas,"* Basler Studien zur deutschen Sprache und Literatur, vol. 34 (Bern: Francke, 1967).

[2] Erwin Kobel, *Alfred Döblin: Erzählkunst im Umbruch* (Berlin/New York: Walter de Gruyter, 1985), 223–50.

9: *Berlin Alexanderplatz*

The Resounding Success

THE YEAR BEFORE DÖBLIN PUBLISHED *Berlin Alexanderplatz* in 1929, he had been honored widely for his fiftieth birthday, and he was a dominant figure in the Berlin cultural scene, but his publications remained texts for other writers, critics, and the happy few. The public at large knew the man but not his work. Furthermore, his stormy relations with his publisher Samuel Fischer had reached the point of crisis. It was only after much hesitation that Fischer consented to publish one more book by the quarrelsome author who brought in little or no money. Fischer disliked the title *Berlin Alexanderplatz* and insisted on adding the subtitle *Die Geschichte vom Franz Biberkopf.* But then the unforeseen happened: the book sold more copies in the first weeks than all Döblin's previous books combined. *Berlin Alexanderplatz* became one of the bestsellers of the last years of the Weimar Republic, together with other assorted novels, including Erich Maria Remarque's *Im Westen nichts Neues,* Hans Fallada's *Kleiner Mann, was nun?,* Hans Grimm's *Volk ohne Raum,* Edwin Erich Dwinger's *Die Armee hinter Stacheldraht,* most of them war and anti-war novels. The success of Döblin's novel is all the more surprising because of his modernist style, and can only be explained by the attraction of the topic, the Berlin underworld, which found its classic depiction in Fritz Lang's film *M. Berlin Alexanderplatz* has been designated as a big-city novel, and as the German equivalent of John Dos Passos's *Manhattan Transfer* and James Joyce's *Ulysses.* The big city and crime aspects of the novel, along with Döblin's montage technique, have ensured the enduring interest of the media, culminating in Fassbinder's 1979 television series (later released as a film), as well as the interest of literary scholars beyond the field of German studies. As the following discussion shows, emphasis has been on the narrative techniques, on the big city milieu and the related theme of the masses versus the individual, on Franz Biberkopf's development as a character, and on the inconclusive ending with its political and religious implications. Also, the psychological or even pathological aspects of the figures, Biberkopf in particular, have often been scrutinized.

Living in the Metropolis

Fritz Lang's film *Metropolis* (1926) and Walter Ruttmann's *Berlin. Die Symphonie einer Großstadt* (1927), the later documentary by the young filmmakers Robert Siodmak, Fred Zinnemann, Billy Wilder, and Edgar Ulmer, *Menschen am Sonntag* (1928), and still later Brecht's *Kuhle Wampe* are all witness to the unending fascination with the big city Berlin, which had already been depicted by the Dadaists and George Grosz, and would later be in Erich Kästner's *Fabian*, Hermann Kesten's *Glückliche Menschen,* Mascha Kaleko's poems in *Das lyrische Stenogrammheft,* Kurt Tucholsky's short pieces, and all that was printed in the papers and magazines. Berlin was the first really modern city in Germany, and the fastest growing metropolis, with all the accompanying ills and excitements. Berlin was the epitome of proletarian housing, the *Mietskasernen* and *Hinterhöfe,* and of all their misery and idyllic poetry, as portrayed by Heinrich Zille. All of this Döblin knew only too well, and he made use of it in his novel.

Günter Anders wrote an essay on *Berlin Alexanderplatz* at the time it appeared, but did not then publish it; he communicated it only to Döblin personally, and they had intense debates on the issues it raised. Anders published the piece in 1965, as "Der verwüstete Mensch," in a Festschrift for Georg Lukács, and again in his book *Mensch ohne Welt.*[1] In Anders's view, *Berlin Alexanderplatz* is a demonstration of "Weltlosigkeit." He defines "Menschen ohne Welt" as those who are forced to live within a world that is not theirs (*Mensch ohne Welt,* xi). This is surprising, as Anders characterizes Biberkopf and Döblin as true Berliners. While Anders admitted in retrospect in 1965 that only this great novel has truly preserved this monster of a city that has been destroyed (3), he defines *Berlin Alexanderplatz* as a "negative" novel: "Biberkopfs Leben und die Romanform sind aufeinander nicht zugeschnitten. Sie dementieren sich gegenseitig und zwar dauernd" (4). Biberkopf does not live, rather "er wird gelebt"; the novel is negative-bourgeois (9) describing a "subjektloses Leben" (12). The "non-subject" does not speak — "Niemand spricht, niemand formuliert" — it is the "Sprache der Sprache" (14). The novel thus advances to the limits of nothingness, but "Im Augenblick, da das Nichts beginnt, springt die Sprache zurück ans Ufer des Seienden" (16). This novel tries to embrace the entire world, not just a segment of it; it is plagued by the angst that (according to Spinoza) determinatio equals negatio: whatever is defined will disappear in nothingness (20). The novel is an exploration, especially through its montage technique, which as Anders says, does not invent but discovers: "die

Montage *erfindet* nicht, sondern *entdeckt*" (27). In sum, the novel's dialectic reveals not the totality of the system, but the totality of chaos (28). The city which is not the "world" speaks for itself, engulfing people like Biberkopf, who become passive objects of passing time.

Theodore Ziolkowski, in his early study "Berlin Alexanderplatz,"[2] characterizes the image of the city as chaos, as it appears to Biberkopf's eyes and mind when he steps out of prison and is unable to make sense of his life and his environment. His search is a search for order, *Ordnung,* which eludes him. Biberkopf considers the catastrophes that befall him to be *Schicksal,* fate, and in this sense, subjectively, the story has the form of a Greek tragedy, with the hero blind against almighty fate. Biberkopf's blind conviction that everything is just fate is a fatal flaw: he has to learn to accept responsibility for his actions, which he will do at the end. The city, although presented by a narrator, is really seen through Biberkopf's eyes and responds to his attitude and actions. Ziolkowski points out that Biberkopf's physical appearance and his psyche are in very close agreement with the theories of Ernst Kretschmer's enormously influential book of 1921 *Körperbau und Charakter* (Ziolkowski, 135–37), which is also true for Biberkopf's friend and enemy Reinhold, the opposite type. According to Kretschmer, a person of Biberkopf's physique would tend to manic-depressive states of mind, which is indeed the case. Reinhold on the other hand would be characterized by alternate states of coldness and sentimentality. Reinhold, Ziolkowski reminds us, has striking resemblances with Adolf Hitler, both physically and psychologically.

This is how Ziolkowski defines the different aspects of the story: From an aesthetic point of view it is a modern tragedy, following closely the laws and the rhythm of the classical Greek tragedy. Psychologically, Döblin demonstrates the crisis and cure of a case of manic-depressive illness that defines the personality of Biberkopf. From a sociological point of view, it is the rehabilitation of a criminal who ends up in spring 1929 as the assistant gatekeeper of a factory; here is evidence of Döblin's social conscience. Finally, from a political point of view, this "Deutscher Michel" is eventually disenchanted with a dictatorial leader (Reinhold) who seemed to satisfy for a while his masochistic urge for order and obedience (147). In this way, Ziolkowski considers the book a prophecy of Hitler's dictatorship, which was to begin four years later. All of this takes place and can only take place in the big city. The chaotic city needs an ordering framework; and this framework is the structure of Greek tragedy, which allows the elements of reality to float free.

Albrecht Schöne's often cited article of 1963 on *Berlin Alexanderplatz*[3] is divided into two parts: one on Biberkopf and one on the city. In

Schöne's view Döblin does not tell the criminal Biberkopf's story for Biberkopf's sake but for the example that it provides (296). But this is in no way a variant of the educational or developmental novel ("des Erziehungs- und Entwicklungsromans") (298), since the main characteristic of Biberkopf is precisely that he won't allow himself to be educated: he requires a total collapse to come to his senses; he refuses to listen to the voice that speaks to him (298). Döblin tells "the old parable of Everyman" (300). This Everyman is blind and denies all guilt and responsibility until the end — an end that Schöne characterizes as contradictory.

However, the novel holds more than just the stations of Franz Biberkopf's life. Schöne characterizes the novel's "Nebenerzählungen" as "Entsprechungen und Spiegelungen" (304) and detects many warnings and omens. He points to the universal principle of "Resonanz," as Döblin expounded it in *Unser Dasein*, as the indication of the interconnections among individuals and between humans and their environment, in this case the city. "Handeln," action, arises from such mutuality. The city and Biberkopf's environment provide a system of coordinates and of universal communication, of which he is a part — which is one aspect of the message of *Berlin Alexanderplatz*. Döblin does not "describe" this city life, he makes the reader a part of it. If one talks about collage, montage, inserting quotations, it is important to remember that all these inserted elements become part of the process, they are transformed into moving particles — just as in futuristic paintings. Döblin's narrative technique, however, does not destruct the elements into a dissociated chaos; on the contrary, he uses them to build up correspondences and resonances. Quotations and the use of "prefabricated" elements of language, such as idioms and conventional phrases, are a special case: they reflect the speakers, Biberkopf in particular, who have no control over language; language runs through them as an indication how little they control their own behaviors and fates. But beyond such citations, other texts seem to be voiced, if not by the narrator, then by some collectivity, by the city itself. In large parts of the novel, it seems that the city is the narrator who narrates itself, its own story. However, the voice of a personal narrator is there and persists; and the narrator integrates all elements so that montage, inner monologue, and the like are not just formal experiments, but part of a meaningful story with a powerful message.

Volker Klotz, in the Döblin chapter of his book *Die erzählte Stadt*,[4] posits the city as one "sujet" that stands against the other, Biberkopf. They are equally significant. But whereas Biberkopf cannot live without the city, the city can very well live without him. Klotz demonstrates how the seemingly random facts and documents that the author inserts into the narrative are well designed to give an understanding of the many ways in which the city operates, and how its lines of communication flow through its entire body. The narrator can penetrate from the front of a building to its apartments and their inhabitants, to the back of the building and adjacent houses to show how a mini-community functions. This also means that the novel as such is unending; all of these details can be amplified and continued. For Klotz, the Berlin dialect of the speakers is the language of the city itself; the narrator does not impose a style and language on the city, but instead he reproduces the city's language that he has soaked in, language including the noise of the construction sites, the shouts of the street vendors, the screeching of the streetcars. The facade of a department store that is to be torn down leads the narrator to associations about past splendors of cities now totally vanished, such as Babylon, Nineveh, and ancient Rome.

Klotz calls the frequent use of quotations "Koalition durch Kollision" (393). Quotes from the Bible, classical German literature, folksongs, and current popsongs are amalgamated into the Berlin vernacular. While the narrator and the characters leave at first an impression of purely associative speaking, there is a distinct structure and meaning, and frequently a distinct irony, in this flow of heterogeneous language elements.

For Biberkopf, Klotz says, Berlin is life (397). And it has the flavor of George Grosz and the Dadaists, of Georg Heym and Expressionism, and taken all together the story and the tone of the narrator resemble a *Moritat*, just as Brecht presented it in his *Dreigroschenoper*. Whereas other scholars prefer to speak of modern media, meaning film, Klotz reminds us of the "Bildtafeln" of the *Moritat*, the pictures of the crucial scenes to which the singer/narrator points with his stick while he tells them.

Klotz also confronts the question of the contradictory ending. First it seems clear: Biberkopf understands that solidarity is needed, but one has to choose one's comrades with care and reason, and one has to know where one belongs. But then comes the last paragraph, the trumpets and drums of the marchers. For Klotz, they are clearly a signal for what the narrator rejects, what Biberkopf does not want anymore: no more blind marching into war, slaughter, or ideological battles, "Kriegskameraderie als falsche Solidarität" (407). The leitmotif of war that runs through the novel indicates the path to disaster.

Berlin Alexanderplatz modifies two literary models, according to Klotz: Everyman and Goethe's Faust figure. Biberkopf, the test figure, the unwilling Faust, is saved and reborn in the end, reborn for an earthly existence of considerable uncertainty. Berlin, the space of Biberkopf's life, is a "kämpferische Herausforderung" (411). It is "Kampfplatz und

Kampf," "Agon" (411). Berlin, the city, is the real presence in the novel, not the figure of Death, not Job and the Babylonian Whore. It is a living space, once one has learned to recognize "die gewichtigen Gesellschafts-antagonismen" (417). Which means to be above the *Kampf*, the struggle. Helmut Schwimmer, in his 1973 book, analyzes *Berlin Alexander-platz* primarily as a "Großstadtroman."[5] Schwimmer offers a short de-scription of all the elements customarily associated with the text, but focuses particularly on "das Bild der Wirklichkeit" and "das Menschen-bild" in the novel. He diagnoses "Großstadtbegeisterung" and "Natur-feindlichkeit" (50) in the narrator of the text, but not without contradicting himself — the author Döblin feels attracted to "nature," but in a different sense. The reality of the metropolis is not only dynam-ized, but anthropomorphized. This shows itself in the behavior of its inhabitants, as the big city and its people reflect on each other. One aspect is collectivism and its anonymity. The image of this living chaos is rendered sharply and precisely through Döblin's medical or scientific lens, his specific kind of observation and description.

In spite of the seeming chaos and the spontaneous manner of narra-tion, Schwimmer finds the structure of *Berlin Alexanderplatz* to be carefully planned and symmetric (69–71). The narrator guides the reader throughout the book. Schwimmer agrees, however, with the chorus of critics who declare themselves unconvinced by the open ending of the action and Biberkopf's sudden transformation (74–79). Schwimmer enumerates in detail the types of inner monologue, of montage, the uses of advertising slogans, literary quotes, and popular songs, and focuses especially on the use of religious figures and texts (115–27). The lan-guage is characterized by the Berlin dialect, street jargon, Jewish idio-lects, by metaphors and other figures of speech such as similes, by repetitions and rhymes, alliterations and assonances, by onomatopoetic effects, resulting in some reminiscences of Expressionist poetry, but largely a parodistic pathos. All of this reinforces the language of the metropolis speaking for itself in its own inimitable language.

David B. Dollenmayer in his chapter on *Berlin Alexanderplatz*[6] con-siders Biberkopf, the "Everyman," a new type of hero for Döblin (63). Whereas his previous protagonists were "leaders" as revolutionaries, emperors, generals, supermen, here he turns to an ordinary man from Berlin. Dollenmayer sees the novel in connection with Döblin's new theories presented in *Der Bau des epischen Werkes* of 1927, specifically in the presence of the authorial voice and in new types of exemplary figures and actions. The plot of *Berlin Alexanderplatz* is straightforward and undistinguished; it is not this but the way the story is told that lends it its fascination and greatness (65). In this novel, place, specifically the area around the Alexanderplatz, is as important as character (66). Dollenmayer analyzes the significance of montage, first noted by Walter Benjamin in 1930, for the authenticity of the depiction of the city and the presentation of the protagonist, finding that it is well suited aesthetically to the big city theme. The similarities to techniques of montage as used in film are obvious. The narrator digresses into a glimpse of a multitude of individual lives, creating a "telescopic perspective" of the metropolis (79). Dollenmayer tackles the question whether Döblin's image of the city is one of chaos, of an unfathomable demonic power that engulfs the struggling individuals, or of a "complexly ordered fabric with both positive and negative aspects" (81), opting for the second choice, which has fundamental consequences, for instance for understanding the ending of the novel. Dollenmayer does not fail to see the similarities of Biberkopf with the Spanish picaro and its many descendants (84). He goes on to discuss two larger issues that will be taken up later: the controversial ending of the novel and the role of women.

An unexpected perspective on the city and the novel is offered by Roger Hilman in his article "Döblin's 'Symphony of the Big City': *Berlin Alexanderplatz* and the Historical Novel,"[7] in which he considers the big city story as history in the making. The book offers a general critique of Georg Lukács's and Hans V. Geppert's definitions of the historical novel; the two world wars have radically changed the concept of history and blurred the boundaries between history and the historical novel, as well as that between the historical novel and the *Zeitroman*. For Hilman, *Berlin Alexanderplatz* "stands at the crossroads of all these transformations" and "combines the Zeitroman, the Bildungsroman, and the historical novel as commonly understood" (103), since it is characterized by an "overlaying of time levels" (103) and the continual reference to the past and the future. The novel responds to the needs of its epoch, as it is "an amalgam of sub-genres and of documentary historiography, but also of other art forms" (105). Hilman sees a number of common features with Walter Ruttmann's documentary film of 1927, *Die Sinfonie der Großstadt*. In this manner, *Berlin Alexanderplatz* offers both a panorama of the city as space and the city (with Biberkopf in it) as history, past, present, and future.

James Joyce and John Dos Passos

It was evident for a good number of the early reviewers that *Berlin Alexanderplatz* could and should be compared with James Joyce's *Ulysses*, whose German translation had appeared while Döblin was working on his novel and was reviewed by Döblin himself, among others. Dos Passos's *Manhattan Transfer* was mentioned less frequently, but still seemed to be close enough to define a new type of big city novel and a new narrative technique characterized by inner monologues, montage, fleeting, movie-like images, and the individual wandering in the streets crowded by faceless masses. In Matthias Prangel's 1975 volume *Materialien zu Alfred Döblins "Berlin Alexanderplatz,"*[8] Joris Duytschaever summarizes and evaluates the previous scholarship on this point. The two opposing viewpoints, one that the reading of *Ulysses* confirmed and reinforced previously existing trends in Döblin, the other, that after reading *Ulysses*, Döblin rewrote and radically changed his novel, are complicated by the fact that the impact of Dos Passos cannot be excluded, and that Dos Passos, in turn, was also deeply impressed by *Ulysses*. When *Berlin Alexanderplatz* appeared, the critics jumped on this question, affirming either a direct influence, or just analogies, or the influence of other sources on both writers (138–39). The attribution implied value judgments on the originality and substance of Döblin's text. Döblin himself tried to clarify the issue on several occasions, but when critics and scholars persisted in seeing direct imitations, he got angry and finally denied any similarities.

The translation of *Manhattan Transfer* was published by S. Fischer in October 1927, and with Döblin's close connections with the publishing house, it is very likely that he read the prepublication excerpts and heard about the character of the novel. However, he never mentioned the book directly, although he later read Dos Passos's *USA* trilogy. Apparently *Manhattan Transfer* did not affect him in the same way as *Ulysses* did.

After a review of pertinent scholarship, Duytschaever comes to the conclusion that the impact of Joyce and Dos Passos on Döblin cannot be compared to that on Hermann Broch and Hans Henny Jahnn: it served mainly to clarify and crystallize what Döblin had already been trying to achieve (148). Furthermore, if the question of influence is raised, other sources may be relevant as well, for instance Joseph Conrad's novels, which Döblin read about the same time (148). Still, a more thoroughgoing study of the manuscript or typescript of *Berlin Alexanderplatz* might yield different results.

The Döblin chapter of Breon Mitchell's 1976 book, *James Joyce and the German Novel 1922–1933*[9] tries to demonstrate the overwhelming impact of Döblin's reading of *Ulysses* with evidence from the *Berlin Alexanderplatz* manuscript. Mitchell insists especially on the inner monologues, the montage elements, and the use of "realia" such as advertising as elements taken from *Ulysses*. Werner Stauffacher, in the afterword to his 1996 edition of the novel, summarizes the evidence and the valid objections against Mitchell's readings and his view of Döblin's dependence on Joyce (840–42). There is a consensus, however, on the surprising number of similarities, in spite of fundamental differences, between *Ulysses, Manhattan Transfer,* and *Berlin Alexanderplatz*. Indeed, it was the similarity of Döblin's novel to the great book by his friend Joyce that motivated Eugene Jolas to translate *Berlin Alexanderplatz* into English.

That this problem should be seen in a wider context and taken beyond questions of direct intertextual evidence is demonstrated by Eva Banchelli in her "'Berlin Alexanderplatz' und der Großstadtroman der amerikanischen Moderne: Reflex, Anregungen, Polemiken,"[10] published in 1993, in which she points to surprising textual similarities between the novel and Theodore Dreiser's *Sister Carrie* (a German translation of which appeared in 1929), Dos Passos's *Manhattan Transfer,* and Upton Sinclair's *The Jungle,* which had an enormous impact on German writers, particularly for its slaughterhouse scenes. But much more important, according to Banchelli, is that the American literature of the big city and "amerikanische Großstadtmetaphern" (212) influenced Döblin's writing in a general way. Artists and writers of the twenties in Berlin were part of an intense Americanism, according to Banchelli, and Berlin was the American "capital" in Europe, sharing major aspects with New York, such as its modern architecture — especially around the Alexanderplatz — the chaotic impression of city life, the cosmopolitan, multilingual population, even the vision of an apocalyptic Babylon. Thus, while it may be futile to pursue specific influences and imitations, Döblin was well aware of the image of the American big city and shared in the common image of the metropolis, as it was expressed in literature, film, and visual arts in all Western countries during that period.

Albrecht Schöne is typical for scholars of *Berlin Alexanderplatz* in that he mentions the similarities with Joyce and Dos Passos (292, 315, 318), but totally disregards the question of influence or imitation. So does Erwin Kobel (351–53). David Dollenmayer relegates it to a footnote (192).

In his book *Alfred Döblin: Werk und Entwicklung,* Klaus Müller-Salget reviews the different stages of the composition of *Berlin Alexanderplatz,* using Döblin's manuscript and serial publications in newspapers that preceded the publication of the complete novel, and finds a consistent evolution rather than a radical change caused by influence from an outside source.[11] In his later, much more detailed study of the matter, "Zur Entstehung von Döblins *Berlin Alexanderplatz,*"[12] Müller-Salget leaves the door open for more substantial revision of the manuscript after Döblin's reading of *Ulysses* (127). However, he still insists that the work evolved in a consistent way.

In sum, scholarship has considered the topic of influence, which caused heated debates among the first reviewers, to be largely irrelevant, particularly since many of the narrative techniques can be found in Döblin's earlier works; and even if Döblin shared in some of the aspects of the German "Americanism" of the twenties.

The Controversial Ending

No part of the novel has generated so many contradictory opinions as its ending. In fact, there are two endings (or none at all, depending on one's view): one is the redemption, healing, or revival of Franz Biberkopf as a "new man"; the second is the very last scene, in which Biberkopf has taken his position as *Hilfsportier* in a factory, and from his post watches the masses marching by amid fanfare and drum rolls, keeping himself at a wise distance. Who are these marchers? Don't they rather look like Nazi troops, although they are not defined as such? Dollenmayer recognizes that troubling possibility (86–88), and Winfried Sebald has denounced Döblin's choice of images. Klaus Schröter considers Döblin (and Biberkopf) entangled in contradictions without a way out.[13] Even if one discounts the direct political attacks that were directed at it from the BPRS journal, *Linkskurve,* and continued by later Marxists, the ending leaves much to be desired in clarity, and Döblin's hint that he considered it the beginning of a second volume does not solve the problem either. Ulrike Scholvin, in her 1985 book *Döblins Metropolen,* calls it simply "mißlungen," a failure.[14] Otto F. Best, in an article published in 1979, tries to solve the problem by going back to the fundamental difference between the Oriental and Occidental views of the individual: "Aufgehen im Allgemeinen oder Erstarken im Besonderen."[15] According to Best, Döblin's affinities with the Orient have their philosophical underpinnings in the teachings of Spinoza: his "Urgrund," his intuitive knowledge, his insistence on the unity of thought and action (99) and his definition of freedom as mastery of the emotions (100). Biberkopf emerges from his self-destructiveness through submission, which, paradoxically, means self-preservation (100). Thus the example of Spinoza can be amalgamated with the Wu-wei of Taoism, and Biberkopf's acceptance of his fate at the end equals "Nichtwiderstreben," non-resistance.

Roland Links, in his 1976 book *Alfred Döblin: Leben und Werk,* considers the ending logical, but says that it gives the impression of being a foreign body and is difficult to understand, and he puts this down to the aesthetic weaknesses of the book, Döblin's mode of representation, and his political position, or rather his lack of one.[16] Links says that Döblin is content with vague, general declarations, visions rather than realities, both because he has no concrete idea of the revolution and because the mere readiness of the individual to act, to achieve consciousness and achieve change, seems to him to be more important than a clear political program. Links echoes the attacks on *Berlin Alexanderplatz* by the *Linkskurve* critics: Döblin, he says, was unable to overcome the contradictions inherent in the bourgeois mentality and ideology.

Hans-Peter Bayerdörfer's 1970 article, "Der Wissende und die Gewalt. Alfred Döblins Theorie des epischen Werkes und der Schluß von *Berlin Alexanderplatz*," remains the most thoroughgoing investigation of the question of the novel's ending.[17] Bayerdörfer begins with Döblin's own thesis of the "Unabschließbarkeit des epischen Werks" (150): while closure is a generic problem of the modern novel, it is of particular urgency for Döblin, and especially in the case of *Berlin Alexanderplatz*. The examination of preliminary versions shows that Döblin hesitated in choosing his ending and may not have selected the best alternative (153). Bayerdörfer analyzes the path taken by Biberkopf, who begins his new life after prison with an unattainable goal and thus must flounder. The narrator, according to Bayerdörfer, construes the story as if from its end; he tells the story "indem . . . er diesen Ablauf schon vom Ende her entwirft" (155). How does the narrator form the end of his "Moritat"? (156). The entire plot has an "Enthüllungscharakter" (156), it is relevatory, an unveiling, like a detective story, so that when the reader sees the resurrected Biberkopf, the "new man," he can grasp the truth. Biberkopf's past becomes transparent to him: he understands where self-assertion ("Selbstbehauptung") and violence left him, and that knowledge and insight ("Wissen") represent his first step into a new life (157). The marching columns at the end are not new or unexpected, but a hidden leitmotif of the entire text (158–59). In the end, Biberkopf escapes them and becomes aware that he must avoid whomever they are marching for. He has arrived at the insight that worldly power is perishable and must be judged (160). Biberkopf's breakdown is a judgment on the social order that is ruled by violence, *Gewalt*. Therefore, the line between criminality and lawfulness is of little importance (162). The narrator's last word, like that of a *Moritat*, is equivocal: he ends with an aporia. For Bayerdörfer, what makes this ending open to doubt is the question whether the new knowledge and insight of Biberkopf can be put into action in the society he finds himself in, and if so, how.

For Bayerdörfer, unlike Links and others, the text is eminently political, albeit non-partisan and without a recipe for a specific course of action. The existing collective bodies, political parties for instance, are only there to prevent the individual from becoming a true person — which would only be possible in a give-and-take between man and nature and man and community, as exemplified in *Wissen und Verändern!* and *Unser Dasein*. These works are closely connected with *Berlin Alexanderplatz*, where the political and anthropological views of the narrator are evident throughout the text.

Döblin's views on socialism, socialist parties, and the crisis of 1930 are anything but original. He remains a fundamental critic of capitalist society and its principle of "Machtzuwachs," ever-increasing power (170). But he saw the socialist parties, especially the communist party of the Soviet Union, as having abandoned their utopian goals and settled down to pursuing permanent class struggle and the dictatorship of the proletariat instead of a classless society. Instead, the liberation and development of the natural human being, including liberation of his economic means, should replace the rigid hierarchies generated by the socialist class struggle. The long-term goal would be the abolition of all power structures — state governments, party organizations — which are the centers of coercive power and violence in order to pave the way for the utopian age of spontaneous and cooperative forms of community. But of course there was no formula for immediate political action and for an organizational structure to oppose the violence-bearing collectives. *Berlin Alexanderplatz*, *Wissen und Verändern!*, and *Unser Dasein* all end on a tentative note, maintaining the clarity of reflection above the onslaught of the masses, but without a plan for their reorientation.

For Bayerdörfer, Biberkopf is not an exemplary figure, not a Wilhelm Meister; he is exemplary only in that he is the vehicle for the unmasking of his environment (180). In this sense, he is what Döblin later called "eine Sonde" (a probe): he reveals the structures and problems of society. Therefore, his environment, his milieu, is as significant for the novel as is Biberkopf himself. Döblin uses the technique of montage for this purpose. The narrator plays the role of the scientist, who brings Biberkopf into the proletarian milieu of Berlin for the purpose of an experiment whose outcome he predicts at the outset of the story. The figure of the narrator provides Döblin with the space for the message, which, as tentative as it may be, he insists on repeating at the end: only *Wissen*, knowledge and insight, can overcome the pervasive system of violence that rules and ruins our present world.

Bayerdörfer aims to prove, by integrating the various texts and theories, that the seemingly abrupt ending of *Berlin Alexanderplatz* is the only possible one under the circumstances, and a logical consequence of the structure and dynamics of the text. But it is not surprising that such a provocative and enigmatic text has since brought about many more exegeses, although most of them reference Bayerdörfer's article.

Matthias Prangel represents a different view in his short article published in 1995, "Franz Biberkopf und das Wissen des Wissens. Zum Schluß von *Berlin Alexanderplatz* unter der Perspektive einer Theorie der Beobachtung der Beobachtung."[18] Prangel divides the previous explanations into three groups: the first, exemplified by Leo Kreutzer, considers the ending as a *salto mortale* out of the social and political realm. It is worse than superfluous, an unnecessary appendix, typifying the disorientation of the left-liberal writer at the end of the Weimar Republic. The second group accepts a real transformation in Biberkopf and interprets it from a Christian perspective or as an individual struggling to remain true to himself against the collectivities. This was advocated by Walter Muschg, and for different reasons by Albrecht Schöne and James Reid. The third group sees the conjunction of the opposites as the real result of the process: the individualistic and collectivistic attitudes come together in a symbiosis of opposites. Klaus Müller-Salget, Erwin Kobel, and Otto Keller hold varying forms of this view, which seems to have the strongest support among Döblin scholars.

On the basis of such divergent opinions, Prangel analyzes the tripartite structure of Döblin's thinking. He says that Döblin sees the processes of nature and history as running in concurrent antithetical dynamics, which arrive finally at a crisis and conflict point that generates a new "Absprung und Umschlag in die neue Qualität" (172), a third stage, not a utopian ideal or a Platonic idea, but something real that can happen here and now. Prangel cautions that similarities between this theory and Hegelian or Marxian dialectics are more apparent than real. This understanding of Döblin's thinking leads to an interpretation of the ending of *Berlin Alexanderplatz* that Prangel formulates as follows:

> Döblins *Berlin Alexanderplatz* beschreibt den im Mehrwissen und Vorauswissen des Erzählers immer schon vorgegebenen Übergang schließlich auch des Romanhelden selber von einer zweiwertigen zu einer dreiwertigen Logik, von einer Beobachtung erster zu einer Beobachtung zweiter Ordnung als avancierte Erkenntnissituation des modernen Menschen. Unter solchem Gesichtspunkt ist der paradoxale Schluß des Romans weder angehängte unverbindliche Zugabe, noch Spiel im Himmel, das Biberkopfs irdisches Scheitern idealistisch verklärt. Es ist

jener Schluß hingegen der nicht nur erzählerisch konsequent verfolgte, sondern auch erkenntnistheoretisch konsequent gesetzte Zielpunkt eines instabilen, prozessierenden modernen Kontingenz- und Selbstbezüglichkeitsdenkens, mit dem die Aporien der dualistischen Metaphysik aufgebrochen werden und neue Anschlußmöglichkeiten für das Fortbestehen lebender Systeme wie Individuen und Gesellschaft eröffnet werden können. (173)

Such a *Zweiwertigkeit* is the opposition of subject and object, of individual and collectivity, in actual practice: the choice between the self-assertion of the individual against society and the total acceptance of society's dictates. It is not enough to observe the world around us; we must observe the observer. Or, as Prangel understands Döblin's phrase: "Wir wissen, was wir wissen" — the point of departure for Bayerdörfer — we know our own knowledge, we are able to reflect on ourselves. And we understand the "polykontexturale und subjektdependente Konstruiertheit von Wirklichkeit" (178), which is in simpler terms the independence from fate (*Schicksal*), and from the simple alternatives between subject and object. For Prangel, this also implies the seemingly contradictory cohabitation of activity and passivity, of subject-centrism and object-centrism: action and insight have become one and the same (79). This new epistemological level of insight, which can be defined as reason or wisdom, does not, however, solve the quandary of how to respond to a society and world gone wild.

For Klaus Müller-Salget, the political dimension in the novel, and especially its ending, is essential but not dominant, as he argues against Roland Links and James Reid, who had termed *Berlin Alexanderplatz* a "political novel" and subordinated all other dimensions to this aspect.[19] It has to be understood as a part of the overall theme of the self-limitation ("Ichverkrampfung") of the individual and his blindness to reality (348). The ending has to achieve two goals: first, to break Biberkopf's pride and arrogance ("Hochmut"), his stubborn belief that he alone is right (349), and second, to destroy the misguided belief in an almighty fate (349). Only through a middle point between these extremes can he survive. Thus, for Müller-Salget, the ending of *Berlin Alexanderplatz* is in full agreement with Döblin's position in *Wissen und Verändern!*, and *Wissen*, knowledge, is indeed the prerequisite for all actions, for joining any group or cause. The egotism inherent in modern Western civilization has to be dismantled to create the conditions for a community of mutual solidarity in harmony with the cycles of life and death.

David Dollenmayer, whose views on the ending are close to Bayerdörfer's, but who sees Biberkopf in a transitory no-man's land in which he is coming to the point of espousing a real cause for a community not of "Ochsen" but of reasoning people, points forward to *Pardon wird nicht gegeben,* in which Karl finds himself in a similar position between the two fronts and pays with his life for his eventual choice. For Dollenmayer the ending of *Berlin Alexanderplatz* does not mean disengagement or an "idealistic" escapism into a Christian model of guilt and redemption, but remains fundamentally ambiguous.

Wolfgang Düsing considers the novel's ending in the framework of his 1982 book *Erinnerung und Identität,*[20] focusing on an unending search for the self, or "Ich-suche." He bases his analysis of Biberkopf on *Das Ich über der Natur* and *Unser Dasein* and posits the striving for a balance between the active and the passive-receptive ego, between "Handeln" and "Nichthandeln" as a quest for the complete personality, which is impossible to achieve. He defines *Berlin Alexanderplatz* as an "Enthüllungsroman," revealing the past and one's own ego to oneself, in this case to an unwilling and stubborn Biberkopf. The "new" or newborn Biberkopf of the ending, ambiguous and perhaps vague in his contours, is characterized by the independence of the individualization that he has achieved, but also by the awareness of the need for participating in the community, in the entirety of his environment. For Düsing, the personal process of cognition, transformation, and awareness is dominant above the societal and political issues, which is the point that had drawn the ire of the *Linkskurve* reviewers and critics: Biberkopf is not a class-conscious proletarian. For Düsing there is, for a moment, an uncertain balance between knowledge and action, individualism and collectivism, megalomania and self-negation (141), but it is evident that the balance cannot last.

Helmut Koopmann, in his article "Der Schluß des Romans *Berlin Alexanderplatz* — eine Antwort auf Thomas Manns *Zauberberg?*"[21] surveys the previous scholarship and comes to this conclusion: "Die Ursituation des Erkennenden als solche — sie sollte wohl dargestellt werden" (188). He then proceeds to a comparison of the endings of the *Zauberberg* and *Berlin Alexanderplatz* and finds surprising parallels and similarities, with the decisive difference that Hans Castorp stumbles into the First World War without thinking and without taking stock of his Davos experience, while Biberkopf has finally come to his senses and understands what happened to him and why.

Peter Bekes surveys the different views on the ending of *Berlin Alexanderplatz* in a 1995 book designed to assist teachers in German Gymnasien,[22] which thus serves to replace the earlier book by Helmut Schwimmer mentioned above. Bekes rejects both the religious and political interpretations and sees the ending as open, in that it shows Biberkopf with a new awareness of himself and of society, but still wary about whether he should engage himself in the struggle of his time, and if so, how. But he realizes that no man can isolate himself, and that he must live in solidarity with his fellow men under the principle of mutual help (101–10). Bekes's basic thesis on *Berlin Alexanderplatz* is that of a fundamental antinomy expressed in the polarity Biberkopf vs. Alexanderplatz/the city. The open ending does not overcome this antinomy, but shifts it to a new plane. Without mentioning the book, Bekes sees the ending as an exemplification of *Wissen und Verändern!*

Mythology

Döblin's montage inserts not only realia from newspapers and similar documents, but also a complex mythological dimension — predominantly biblical, with figures like Job, Isaac, and the Babylonian Whore from Revelation — retold by the narrator seemingly with no connection to the plot. Inevitably, these pieces, juxtaposed to Berlin dialect and newspaper reporting, called for an explanation as to their meaning and integration into the entire text. Some scholars, like Leo Kreutzer and Erwin Kobel, however, ignore the mythical figures and allusions completely. This is not easy to do; attention to the figure of Death would seem essential for any analysis, and the same is true for Job and the Babylonian Whore. However, scholarship seems to be much less concerned with problems of meaning and integration than one should expect, and studies of the mythological aspect are almost non-existent. In 1966, Dieter Baacke, in the *text & kritik* volume devoted to Döblin, pointed out many uses of figures from classical mythology in Döblin's novels from *Berlin Alexanderplatz* to *Hamlet*.[23] He pointed out that all of these figures are integrated into the texts with a clear didactic intention; they are never there for their own sake, but to serve as parallels to the action, and lead to a deeper understanding.

For Müller-Salget, the Isaac and Job figures, who are parallels with Biberkopf, are not meant as sacrificial victims; but Döblin's treatment of these figures stresses their stubborn refusal to acknowledge their weakness, their need for help and for redemption. They want to go it alone, and until they acknowledge their need for help, there is no way to help them (322–24). The Babylonian Whore appears in connection with Biberkopf's decision to join the Pums gang with the other criminals; the figure points to the criminal underground of the big city, but it also reminds us of the image of Babylon, the city of the Jewish exile where the Jews lived comfortably ignoring the exhortations and warnings of the prophet Jeremiah (331–33). In other words, the biblical leitmotifs function similarly to others that permeate the text. Their specific "biblical" character seems irrelevant.

Two studies by Georg Fromm, a student of Otto Keller, emphasize fundamental differences between the text of the Bible and Döblin's paraphrases of Job and the Isaac sacrifice.[24] Fromm finds that Döblin used the Bible for explicating the necessity of Biberkopf's admission of weakness and need for help, whereas the motif of sacrifice is deemphasized, especially since Döblin does not want to speak of God.

Otto Keller, in his 1980 book *Döblins Montageroman als Epos der Moderne*,[25] emphasizes the structural integration of the seeming digressions on Job, Isaac's sacrifice, and the Whore of Babylon. In each case, it is important to notice how Döblin uses and modifies Luther's Bible text to suit his purposes, and where exactly the digression is inserted. Each has a specific function for Biberkopf's story and development, and each is designed to give the reader insight into what happens with and in Biberkopf. In this manner, the mythical parallels provide a "Tiefendimension" for the story that goes beyond the allusions to German classical literature, for instance *Faust*.

Kathleen Komar, in her 1981 article "Technique and Structure in Döblin's *Berlin Alexanderplatz*,"[26] analyzes the functions of the biblical allusions and digressions in the novel. Following Theodore Ziolkowski's presentation of the novel's structure, she finds in this "postfigurative" novel "a triad of temptations and trials" (319) symbolized by Adam and Eve, Job, and Abraham and Isaac. Parallel to this, Komar detects three "groups of references": from Jeremiah, Ecclesiastes, and Revelations (321). Whereas these biblical references "buttress an irresistible central pattern" of the book (323), the often "mock-heroic" citations and allusions from classical literature, such as Kleist's *Prinz von Homburg* and the *Oresteia* seem rather at counter purpose to the theme of redemption. She goes on to analyze the leitmotif "Es ist ein Schnitter, der heißt Tod" and its place in the later part of the novel (325–26).

The Women of Berlin

Robert Minder's characterization of Döblin's earlier novels as novels without women is not valid for *Manas* and *Berlin Alexanderplatz*, and it needs to be modified for the previous works as well, as was indicated above. However, homoerotic conflicts, between Reinhold and Biberkopf for example, undeniably occupy a major role in these stories, and a typical battle of the sexes erupts not between man and woman, but rather between mother and son, as in *Pardon wird nicht gegeben* and *Hamlet*.

Döblin is no Strindberg or Wedekind in this respect; the first depiction of a devastating marriage occurs in *Hamlet*.

The unforgettable woman figure in *Berlin Alexanderplatz*, Mieze, is a prototypical victim of male brutality. But there is more to the women figures, even if they tend to a type somewhere between the mother figure and the prostitute. In her study "Döblin und die Berlinerin," Ute Karlavaris-Bremer surveys the women figures in *Wadzek*, *Berlin Alexanderplatz*, and *Pardon wird nicht gegeben*.[27] Although they are generally seen in connection with male figures and not as independent agents, they are by no means mere passive creatures, and are crucial to the plots of the novels; indeed, they are at times superior to the men. Since *Kampf* — combat, struggle, conflict — is the basic ingredient of these stories, the women cannot help but be involved in conflicts. Gaby in *Wadzek* and Eva in *Berlin Alexanderplatz* are in their own way emancipated women who fight their way through the big city jungle. Although they make their living through sexual favors, they are helpful to other women and try to rise above their condition. The other women tend to be in one of two categories: the "edle Dirne" or the mother figure. Remarkably, solidarity with other women turns out to be a common character trait. From a sociological point of view, it is significant that not all of these women are born and raised in Berlin: many come from the provinces and have to survive in a hostile, alien environment.

For David Dollenmayer, who analyzes Mieze's relationship with Biberkopf mostly from Biberkopf's own perspective, and who notices that she receives her own biography, a *vita sancta*, only after her death (94–95), the "missing" mother figure in *Berlin Alexanderplatz* is present in the Babylonian Whore, representing the monstrous, fearful aspect of the mother (96–97). Whether one sees it in terms of sadism and masochism or not, it is clear that the double image of the woman is pervasive in Döblin's work and reoccurs in a great number of variations until and including *Hamlet*.

A dissident feminist voice is raised by Maria Tatar in her 1992 article "'Wie süß ist es, sich zu opfern.' Gender, Violence, and Agency in Döblin's *Berlin Alexanderplatz*."[28] Whereas previous critics have focused on Biberkopf as victim or perpetrator, little attention has been paid to the victimization of the women — all the women in the text, not just Mieze. From this perspective the book offers a picture of "female suffering and male aggression" (518). Tatar argues both against attempts to harmonize the chaotic text and the notion of "developmental paradigms" (495), that is, the idea of *Berlin Alexanderplatz* as a Bildungsroman of sorts. It is a continual scene of conflict and power struggle over women

— who are seen as objects (502). This becomes clear only when the "non-dominant" discourse of the women and about the women is unearthed beneath the dominant male discourse. This offers a conflictual and disturbing picture of the sexes and the place of the women in German society in the late twenties.

The Modern Media

All critics mention film techniques in *Berlin Alexanderplatz*. One should equally think of radio techniques. Döblin wrote a radio play version of *Berlin Alexanderplatz*, which was supposed to be broadcast from Berlin on 30 September 1930, with Heinrich George as the voice of Biberkopf. This version was preserved on a record and finally broadcasted in 1959 and published in 1962.[29] Heinrich George played Biberkopf in the film version of 1931, which was generally considered too conventional and too centered around the protagonist, with an optimistic ending showing Biberkopf the *Stehaufmännchen*, as a street vendor on the Alexanderplatz.[30] Hans-Peter Bayerdörfer, in his more recent interpretation of the novel,[31] begins and ends with film, referring to Rainer Werner Fassbinder's gigantic production, which places the story in the shadowy interiors of proletarian Berlin and focuses almost entirely on the human relationships, on the contacts between people — friendly, hostile, erotic, businesslike — but puts the Biberkopf-Reinhold story clearly in the center.

Several studies have tried to go beyond the general notion of film technique to analyze more specific elements. Ekkehart Kaemmerling[32] enumerates a number of techniques: the manipulation of time and of perspective, the use of closeups, and especially the different kinds of montage, including contrasting, parallel, synchronizing, and symbolizing montage. Even in the dialogues and the narrator's commentaries, similarities with film scripts can be detected. However, not all of these devices were necessarily borrowed from films. On the contrary, early cinema also borrowed heavily from modern literature, so that the relationship should be seen as a give and take, contrary to the usual point of view.

Three contributions to the Döblin colloquium of 1991, by Helmuth Kiesel, Achim Haag, and Andreas Rost, are devoted to Fassbinder's film, and to Döblin's affinities to the film technique.[33] Helmuth Kiesel traces Döblin's view of cinema, which was by no means as unreservedly enthusiastic as is often believed. It was, however, sophisticated and free from the usual arrogant rejection of the educated classes. Kiesel defends the 1931 film against its early negative reviewers, and argues that the montage technique was adopted by filmmakers from literary models and not vice versa. Finally, he points out the fundamental problems of the version of Fassbinder, who limited himself largely to a focus on Biberkopf (even more than the 1931 film had) and the erotic and homoerotic, and especially sadomasochistic aspects of it.

Achim Haag and Andreas Rost offer the perspective of the film scholar, as opposed to the scholar of literature. Haag discusses common prejudices of literary scholars, whose interest is limited primarily to how the words are transposed into images, and not to the many aspects of film as such: image, music, dialogue, contrasting montage, etc. It would be erroneous and misleading, says Haag, to develop a strict philological concept of faithfulness to the original work (301). Fassbinder's films adapted from works of literature are characterized by a critical assessment of the literary work, an assessment that is then integrated into the film; this has clear indications for the viewer. In the case of *Berlin Alexanderplatz*, it needs to be remembered that collage, montage, and similar devices have different functions and character in the different media. They cannot be simply transferred from novel into film, although they may be "filmic" devices in the text. Haag goes on to invalidate Heinz Brüggemann's arguments against Fassbinder[34] with the basic point that no comparison of the two versions based simply on similarities and analogies is valid; rather, what is needed, according to Haag, is an analysis of the aesthetics of the film that considers it as a work of art in its own right (310). Brüggemann's basic points had been that Fassbinder disregarded the interpenetration of Biberkopf and the big city, so that the boundaries of the outer and inner worlds in Döblin's text are destroyed (57), and, more important, that Fassbinder's film is a negation of the book's modernity. It is a "Widerruf der Modernität durch Re-Psychologisierung" (59) and a "Melodramatisierung" (60) because of Fassbinder's idiosyncratic reading of the text, following the maxim, "das erinnert mich an mich" (62). Brüggemann does not argue that the film should reproduce the book, as it were, following the plot and settings religiously, and he does not hold the fact that Fassbinder does not follow the text this way against him, but he does argue against a misreading of the text that cheapens, distorts, and destroys the fundamental point of the story.

Andreas Rost points out that the idea of a "vorbildliche Literaturverfilmung" is absurd (318): when literary scholars look at movies made from literary works, they always look for a "Reliterarisierung" of the work in filmic form, in which deep narrative structures can be inferred (319). According to Rost, three points are essential when judging a film adapted from a literary work: first, the text needs to be preserved with regard to the logic of its plot and action and its essence, which is constituted by its literary form; second, the filmmaker has the right to his own personal reading ("Lesart"); and third, the "filmische Gegebenheiten," the specific conditions of film, have to be observed. In the case of Döblin, literary scholars have been seduced by his term "Kinostil" to think that his texts are ready-made movies. But Rost points out that Döblin's ideas of filmlike narrative were quite distinct from real film-making, and, moreover, that the film techniques of 1930 cannot be a guide for filmmaking in 1980. Rost compares the films of Döblin's time with those of Fassbinder to point out the essential differences, for instance in the montage. He goes on to analyze Fassbinder's television series/film from the point of view of entertainment and film genres, especially the often-used term "melodrama." It is evident to Rost that Fassbinder took up once more the tradition of the German film of the twenties brought to Hollywood by the German exiles and continued by Douglas Sirk. It needs to be kept in mind in these discussions that *Berlin Alexanderplatz* was planned as a television series and broadcast in 1979, but had a very mixed reception among the general audience and was much better received when it was released as a film, albeit one of monstrous length. Therefore it is difficult to define precisely the genre of Fassbinder's work.

A different view of Döblin and film, along with a consideration of Döblin and radio, is provided by the dissertation of Andrea Melcher, *Vom Schriftsteller zum Sprachsteller?*[35] Melcher analyzes first Döblin's remarks on cinema, its theory, and its effects on audiences, as well as his reviews of individual films. Döblin viewed film in the context of "das Theater der kleinen Leute," as popular entertainment, and as an instrument to reach and influence the masses. He was, therefore, less interested in avant-garde experiments and in Expressionist German film, which, from our perspective, would be seen in close proximity to Döblin's own avant-garde style and form. While Döblin shared the stereotypical contempt for American movies, he, like Brecht, was fascinated by Charlie Chaplin, and he saw considerable merit in the new Soviet cinema, although he remained averse to the combination of art and ideology, and the use of films as political propaganda. It is surprising that he did not respond publicly to Eisenstein's *The Battleship Potemkin*, which was shown in Berlin in 1926, and its famous use of montage (68–72).

Of special interest is Melcher's analysis of Döblin's use of film techniques, exemplified, however, mainly by *Berge Meere und Giganten* rather than *Berlin Alexanderplatz*. What did Döblin actually mean by his term "Kinostil"? Melcher lists the following as belonging to a "filmische Erzählung": cutting and montage, which is basic for any film work; camera angle and distance, from close-up to panorama; camera movement, a decisive innovation in film; standpoint and perspective, which can vary from the normal human perspective to a viewpoint above, below, close or distant; the blending back and forth and between images; and fast and slow motion effects (88–92). Montage as a literary device, however, is quite different from its use in film (92–94). Döblin's use of these devices in *Berge Meere und Giganten* is designed to achieve his goal of a discontinuous, polylinear, paratactic narration. *Berge Meere und Giganten* can be regarded, at least in some parts, as a film script, which aims at achieving the impression of "moving images" (111–20).

The second half of Melcher's study deals with radio. In the present context it is pertinent to mention her section on Döblin's radio play adaptation, *Die Geschichte vom Franz Biberkopf*, in which he concentrated on Biberkopf's story (189–97). She details the circumstances of the production and why it was never broadcast. Even more interesting is Melcher's discussion of the extent to which the play incorporated elements that can be called radio-specific. She finds that Döblin's experiment indeed contained a nucleus for a possible further development of the radio play genre.[36]

Montage, Interpolation, and a New Form of Epic Narration

Hardly any feature of *Berlin Alexanderplatz* has raised more questions than the striking element of montage, especially since it comes in combination with all the other elements typical for modernist prose of the early twentieth century: the inner monologue or *erlebte Rede;* the willful mix of stylistic levels in which language of all stylistic registers and cultural provenances is used, including dialect, jargon, quotes from "high" literature, pop songs, and advertising slogans; and the abrupt changes of perspective. Hardly any study of the text fails to analyze or at least mention some or most of these features. It was Otto Keller who defined *Berlin Alexanderplatz* as a *Montageroman* and as paradigmatic for the age of Modernism. His book of 1980[37] traces the central element of montage back to Döblin's earliest published novel, *Der schwarze Vorhang*, and places it in the framework of the fundamental transformation of the genre of the novel. As a corollary, Keller sets out to prove the surpassing greatness of the "Epiker" Döblin among the prose writers of the century, and hopes his book will help Döblin's reputation, making him, up until now a loser, into a winner (12). Keller's conviction is strengthened by comparisons with Brecht, Kafka, Musil, and Grass.

Keller's analysis of *Der schwarze Vorhang* and Döblin's other contemporary essays and short stories leads him to conclude that the central theme of Döblin's first decade of writing is the dissociation of the Ich ("der Ich-Zerfall"), and that this new theme makes the old structures obsolete and requires new ones (48). The abandonment of what Döblin called "Seelenentwicklung" led to the dissolution of the personal unity of the narrated figure and the auctorial narrator, who loses control over the destiny of his characters, a destiny which reverts back to the forces of nature and society. In terms of narrative technique, this can be seen in the abandonment of an identifiable, firm perspective. Along with the identity of the person, the meaning of words becomes questionable, as does the motivation of actions and the idea of a unified plot. It is in this context that montage enters into the structure of narration. Keller's conclusion is that Döblin conceives of the idea of montage largely in a formal way, rather than in a formal-thematic, or unified way (49). Keller agrees with other critics that the origins of Döblin's montage technique, first evident in *Der schwarze Vorhang*, are not to be seen in his understanding of film, but in his "Sprach- und Ideologiekritik" (49).

One of the earliest types of montage used by Döblin were "Mythenmontagen" (51), which were later so prominent in *Berlin Alexanderplatz*. Such montages of myths and mythical figures are not only alienating elements within the narration, but also tend to bring the myths into new, foreign contexts, as Döblin does in *Der schwarze Vorhang* with the figure of Lilith. Such analogies and comparisons are frequently a tool for critical reflection. The insertion of a myth into a foreign context can startle the reader into critical reflection and can assign new meanings to the myth; it can also result in a parody of the myth and offer an ironic commentary on the characters and the action.

Keller pursues his basic points, the fragmentation of the narrated character and the narrator, in his examination of *Wang-lun*. "Döblins Wang-lun fehlt das Moment der Kontinuität, das allmähliche Wachsen und Reifen. Auch von stufenweiser Entwicklung kann man kaum reden" (116). Döblin has replaced gradual development with the "leap." "Döblin weist durch das Bild des Sprungs auf das Neuartige bei der Gestaltung seiner Titelfigur hin" (117). If the firm contours disappear, it becomes difficult to recognize him as the same person: "Wang-lun erhält so etwas Vielschichtig-Unberechenbares und Zwiespältiges" (117). The consensus of critics about the "collective hero" is seen here in a new light: "Wang wird motivlich mit verschiedensten Kräften verbunden, von ihnen aus gespiegelt. Es sind kollektive Kräfte, gesellschaftliche und triebhaft-archaische. Ihre Struktur ist antinomisch, zu ihr gehört eine unlösbare Polarität und eine radikale Dynamik" (121). Keller emphasizes the priority of "Gestus" over "Charakter." Such a gestus are the leaps: "Im Titel des Romans werden vor dem Helden seine drei Sprünge genannt. Der Blick wird schon hier zuerst auf eine bestimmte Gebärde, auf ein mit ihr zusammenhängendes Grundverhalten, einen Gestus, gelenkt"(126). The term "Gestus" refers to Bert Brecht. Keller considers Brecht's dialogue with Döblin decisive for both authors. The new definition of "character" in the narrative implies a new role for the narrator. He does not control events or lead them to a given goal; he is rather like a surveyor of an unknown land whose *Gestus* is that of pointing out the features without value judgment and without guiding the reader to a specific endpoint. Döblin gains a "Tiefendimension" through the montage of parables and legends whose connection with the action becomes gradually apparent during its course. In this manner, the unilinear action is replaced by a multifaceted panorama with multiple temporal dimensions.

While Keller detects constitutive elements of montage in the earlier novels, he devotes his most detailed examination, nearly ninety pages worth, to *Berlin Alexanderplatz* (140–227). He finds a network of military metaphors, beginning with Biberkopf's intent to "conquer" Berlin. It is the *Gestus* of conquering, repeated three times (like the three leaps of Wang-lun), that invites the three blows and Biberkopf's final crisis and the transformation that results in his accepting the message of Death. This idea of a conquest reveals itself as the arrogance of a Job-figure, in that Biberkopf believes that he can do it by himself alone, until he is humiliated and understands his limitations. He has to understand, and the reader has to understand, with the help of the inserted myths, parables, and realia, that life is ruled by hellish forces. But, says Keller, neither Biberkopf nor humans in general are simply delivered to these hellish forces (168). What Biberkopf wants to conquer in reality is not the city but his own fear of death. But as a conqueror, he carries the destructive forces within himself, and he is attracted to Reinhold, the ultimate conqueror. The narrator builds up another *Gestus* in opposition to this hubris of conquest: that of the helper, of the one who, like Isaac, is ready to sacrifice him/herself and be sacrificed, a *Gestus* embodied in Mieze.

For Keller, the perspective on the characters in *Berlin Alexanderplatz* is largely determined by their inner monologues, which present the "aufgelöste Einheit des Ich" (201). At the same time, this perspective undercuts the military images and the heroic gestures of conquest associated with Biberkopf and his companions. The novel, according to Keller, broadens itself into a comprehensive confrontation with the basic position of Western humanity, heroism (205). And it turns into a "satirical-humoristic" novel, reflecting and exposing the emptiness of this heroism after the First World War. Franz Biberkopf and his fate become a parable of the antinomian forces of the living, of existence (212). Keller discusses the new functions of the narrator in *Berlin Alexanderplatz*, maintaining that Döblin's narrative voice in this text is not a return to a "personal narrator," but it is an expansion of the function of the narrator. Much of the narration is in the mode of a commentary, and reinforces the satiric and parodistic tone. This helps to break up the *Bericht*, the mere report, as the events and the characters are viewed from several perspectives at once, and the temporal dimensions are intertwined. The fixed central character and the personal narrator are replaced by what Keller calls a "force-field that resides in history, in time" (220). This leaves the reader in a most insecure position, as the narrative position mirrors no unity for him, gives him no solid, static ground from which he can judge and come to terms with the conditions of the world (227).

Keller believes that in the center of Döblin's novelistic achievement are "die neuen Motivnetze, die montierten, gestisch angelegten, absoluten Bilderreihen" (239), and that these pictures have the character of parable (241). Döblin does not want to present things, objects, facts, but "das Lebendige": life in its fluctuating totality.

Keller considers the *Amazonas* and *November 1918* epics continuations of *Berlin Alexanderplatz*: they are "large-scale, satiric-parodistic epics, new-style montage novels" (261). Here he underscores the continuity of Döblin's work, as he emphasizes the significance of Döblin's early philosophical readings of Nietzsche and Fritz Mauthner, but also of Spinoza, Hume, Kant, and Schopenhauer.

Irony, Humor, and the Grotesque

Irony, satire, and humor are routinely mentioned as characteristic for the narrator and as results of the contrasts that emerge from the montage technique. There is humor involved in the use of the dialect and of classical quotes in everyday language or in advertising. One of the few studies on this subject is Henrietta S. Schoonover's *The Humorous and Grotesque Elements in Alfred Döblin's "Berlin Alexanderplatz."*[38] The larger part of her book is devoted to humor and satire. After an extensive review of the then-existing literature, Schoonover concludes that many critics neglect to mention the presence of humor and satire; Günter Grass's comparison of Döblin with Jean Paul being the exception rather than the rule. Schoonover points out that although Döblin's humor is apparent and has been acknowledged, it has not been analyzed across his entire oeuvre (11), and this is still largely valid today, even if humorous elements in works like *Wadzek* and *Babylonische Wandrung* have been analyzed.

According to Schoonover, treatment of the grotesque in Döblin's works has been even more rare. A very important ingredient of humor is the ability to laugh at oneself, and Döblin possessed it to a high degree, together with his Berliner *Schnauze* (12–20). Schoonover analyzes the different language-related devices that Döblin uses to produce laughter or amusement: word play, repetitions and variations, sound imitations, puns and pseudo-etymologies. She goes from there to define the range of registers Döblin employs: colloquial speech, children's language, bureaucratic and scientific language, biblical language, and literary language; the last, usually taken from Schiller and Goethe, is generally purposefully misapplied in a way that counts on the reader's common Gymnasium experiences to elicit parodistic or satirical effect. As Schoonover puts it, "the incongruity that jolts the reader into laughter is intended to present Döblin's particular view of the world" (95).

And that particular view of the world is often satirical, which is evident from the narrator's comments and intrusions. His willful ironies and warnings take the form of a *Moritat*, and make him into the "Bänkelsänger" (105) who retells in a parodistic manner the story of an unusual event, usually a crime. One major feature is absurd logic, or the lack of any logic, usually ending with the commentary: such is life. Döblin likes to satirize pretense and high-class demeanor, but also the behavior of the lower classes trying to imitate the behavior of higher-ups. Beyond the social satire, however, Döblin aims at the frailties of human nature as such in a satire that is mostly of a more gentle or humorous kind. The specific political satire is based on commonsense skepticism that understands that the revolution was no revolution, that the authoritarian structures are intact, and that the little man can claim little or no freedom or rights as long as the police are in control.

Schoonover echoes previous statements that *Berlin Alexanderplatz* stands in the tradition of the picaresque novel (157–77). However, she draws important distinctions: "Franz is no picaro, either traditional or modern. Until his crisis, Franz is of the world, but not in it. Unlike a traditional picaresque figure like Simplicissimus, Franz does not reject the world at the end of the novel. Unlike a modern picaro like Günter Grass's Oskar Matzerath, whose final refuge is a mental hospital, Franz stays in the world, but he is not of it" (176–77).

Schoonover's chapter on the grotesque elements (178–229) looks at specific aspects that both repel and fascinate the reader (179). She finds this quality in the "Dunkel-motif" (179), the threatening, dark world evident in many of Döblin's texts. Remarkably, the use of colors, for instance yellow, seems to enhance the grotesque (188–96). The widespread use of distortions would be readily expected as a grotesque element. Another source of the grotesque, however, is most unexpected: the view of order, *Ordnung*, that runs through the novel and is typical of Biberkopf's own views. Due to its incongruity with the chaotic, outsider milieu in which Biberkopf finds himself, this stereotypically "German" order takes on a grotesque quality.

As Schoonover summarizes, humor and the grotesque lace and color Döblin's texts; there are many reasons for this attitude, from his allergy against aestheticism and false idealism to his outright aversion to ideology and his view of the world as an irrational web of conflicting energies without superior order or purpose. A text like *Berlin Alexanderplatz* offers a rich web of conflicting strands of humor and irony that baffle and amuse the reader.

Berlin Alexanderplatz in English

Eugene Jolas's 1931 translation of *Berlin Alexanderplatz* was the first English translation of a Döblin text, and would be followed by only one more in his lifetime, *Men with Mercy*, a translation of *Pardon wird nicht gegeben*, which appeared in 1936. But Jolas's translation, although widely reviewed, was not a commercial success. The initial reviews had some comments on the language of the text, and differed in their evaluations of the quality of the translation. In his study, "Wessen Amerikanisch?" of 1989, David B. Dollenmayer began to examine the question of the quality of the language.[39] Eugene Jolas, who was born in Alsace and was trilingual, had a considerable reputation as a journalist and especially as the editor of the literary magazine *transition* that published American, English, French, and German avant-garde texts (Kafka, Trakl, Carl Einstein, Lasker-Schüler, etc.); he translated the German texts himself, but *Berlin Alexanderplatz* was his only venture as translator of an entire novel. Jolas's effort was certainly prompted by the novel's similarities with James Joyce's *Ulysses*, as Jolas was a close friend of Joyce.

Dollenmayer describes the very diverse responses of the American reviewers to Jolas's translation and Döblin's text. Many of them were baffled by the book's complexities and uncertain ending. However, the majority of the critics agreed that Jolas had done the impossible and hailed the translation as a masterwork. One question was immediately raised, however: what kind of slang was it that Jolas substituted for the Berlin dialect of Biberkopf? Was it really "American"? Or did Jolas possibly invent his own language?

Dollenmayer shares with the early reviewers an overall respect for Jolas's achievement, both in terms of the speed with which he worked and his faithfulness to the original. The rendering of lyrical passages is especially remarkable and proves Jolas's considerable talent as a poet. On the other hand, there are a considerable number of mistranslations and misunderstandings of idioms and proverbs. It is unavoidable, of course, that word plays, an essential part of Döblin's language, can rarely be rendered adequately. Dollenmayer offers examples that show how important a correct translation would be and how difficult it is to achieve.

As far as the slang is concerned, Jolas faced another insolvable problem. Since New Yorkers don't use a separate *dialect*, as Berliners do, but rather a specific vocabulary, that is, slang, he could not render a crucial dimension of the characters' language. Moreover, slang changes quickly, so that Jolas's terms are not only antiquated from our point of view, but they were already out of use at the time of the translation. Jolas had grown up in New York, but English was not his native language, and he had been out of the country for four years by the time he was working on the translation. Dollenmayer concludes his study with a list of representative examples of this outdated speech (202–4).

The recent dissertation of Anke Detken, *Döblins "Berlin Alexanderplatz" übersetzt*[40] compares the English, the French, and two Spanish translations, on the basis of recent translation theory (17–23). (The novel has been translated into twelve languages.) Detken offers a detailed comparison of the different solutions for the translation of names (of streets, persons, and places), quotes from pop songs, advertising, literary texts, the Bible, onomatopoetic passages, especially the sounds of road construction, for rendering Döblin's transforming objects into living beings, and then turns to the spoken idioms of the Berliners (68–83). In comparing the English and French translations, she observes that the English translation tries to imitate the oral language and understands that the use of the Berlin dialect is not restricted to speakers of the lower classes, whereas the French translation treats this as a low-class slang. The parodistic insertions of quotes from literary classics like Goethe and Schiller, but also from the Bible, present a special problem for any translator, and Detken observes again that Jolas, as opposed to the French translator, made valiant efforts to render some of the flavor of the original, although he could not expect the readers to recognize the citations.

Detken sees the considerable number of changes and cuts in the French translation in the context of the period around 1930 and specifically the French reception or non-reception of Expressionism. In the English-speaking countries Expressionism was much better known, so that Jolas could expect his readers to have fewer problems of comprehension. Also, because the city of Berlin looked so much more similar to

New York than it did to Paris, the French translator felt compelled to reduce the description of "Berlin" and put more emphasis on Biberkopf's story, whereas Jolas had fewer problems conveying the image of the city. Moreover, Döblin's narrative techniques were already known to many English-speaking readers through James Joyce and John Dos Passos. Summarizing her observations, Detken states that Jolas's translation follows principles that would be commonplace fifty years later, keeping much closer to the text and the flavor of the original. Detken asks why *Berlin Alexanderplatz* has not achieved more significance in the critical discussion on the modern novel in the Anglo-Saxon countries, and comes to the tentative conclusion that it may be because its place was already occupied by texts like *Manhattan Transfer* and *Ulysses*; thus Jolas's work could be called "eine Art Rückübersetzung ins eigene Genre, das des modernen Montageromans" (251), that is, a German work in a genre already established by Joyce and Dos Passos, and now brought back "second hand."

Notes

[1] Günther Anders, "Der verwüstete Mensch. Über Welt- und Sprachlosigkeit in Döblins *Berlin Alexanderplatz*," *Festschrift zum achtzigsten Geburtstag von Georg Lukács*, ed. Frank Benseler (Neuwied/Berlin: Luchterhand, 1965), 420–22; also in Anders, *Mensch ohne Welt* (Munich: C. H. Beck, 1984), 3–30; here it is followed by Anders's 1935 essay on *Babylonische Wandrung*.

[2] Theodore Ziolkowski, *Dimensions of the Modern Novel: German Texts and European Contexts* (Princeton, NJ: Princeton UP, 1969), 99–137; translated as *Strukturen des modernen Romans* (Munich: List, 1972), 94–126; reprinted in Ingrid Schuster, ed., *Zu Alfred Döblin* (Stuttgart: Ernst Klett, 1980), 128–48.

[3] Albrecht Schöne, "Döblin — Berlin Alexanderplatz," in Benno von Wiese, ed., *Der deutsche Roman vom Barock bis zur Gegenwart: Struktur und Geschichte*, vol. 2 (Düsseldorf: August Bagel, 1963), 291–325.

[4] Volker Klotz, *Die erzählte Stadt: Ein Sujet als Herausforderung des Romans von Lesage bis Döblin* (Munich: Carl Hanser, 1969), 372–418.

[5] Helmut Schwimmer, *Alfred Döblin: Berlin Alexanderplatz, Interpretationen für Schule und Studium* (Munich: Oldenbourg, 1973).

[6] David B. Dollenmayer, *The Berlin Novels of Alfred Döblin* (Berkeley/Los Angeles/London: U of California P, 1988), 54–97

[7] Roger Hilman, "Döblin's 'Symphony of the Big City': *Berlin Alexanderplatz* and the Historical Novel," in *The Modern German Historical Novel: Paradigms, Problems and Perspectives*, eds. David Roberts and Philip Thomson (New York/Oxford: Berg, 1991), 97–108.

[8] Matthias Prangel, ed., *Materialien zu Alfred Döblins "Berlin Alexanderplatz,"* Suhrkamp Taschenbuch 268 (Frankfurt: Suhrkamp, 1975), contains documents on the genesis of the novel, Döblin's own assessments, a choice of early reviews, four scholarly articles, the *Hörspiel,* and a few pages on the first film. Joris Duytschaever's article, "Joyce — Dos Passos — Döblin: Einfluß oder Analogie?" 136–49.

[9] Breon Mitchell, *James Joyce and the German Novel 1922–1993* (Athens, OH: Ohio UP, 1976); the book deals primarily with Hans Henny Jahnn's *Perrudja,* Döblin, and Hermann Broch. The Döblin chapter is found on pages 131–50.

[10] Eva Banchelli, "'Berlin Alexanderplatz' und der Großstadtroman der amerikanischen Moderne: Reflexe, Anregungen, Polemiken," *Internationale Alfred-Döblin-Kolloquien Münster 1989–Marbach a. N. 1991,* ed. Werner Stauffacher (Bern: Peter Lang, 1993), 206–16.

[11] Klaus Müller-Salget, *Alfred Döblin: Werk und Entwicklung* (Bonn: Bouvier, 1973; 2nd rev. ed. 1988), 280–93.

[12] Klaus Müller-Salget, "Zur Entstehung von Döblins *Berlin Alexanderplatz,"* *Materialien zu Alfred Döblins "Berlin Alexanderplatz,"* ed. Matthias Prangel, Suhrkamp Taschenbuch 268 (Frankfurt: Suhrkamp, 1975), 117–35.

[13] Klaus Schröter, *Alfred Döblin in Selbstzeugnissen und Bilddokumenten,* Rowohlts Monografien (Reinbek: Rowohlt, 1978), 102–14.

[14] Ulrike Scholvin, *Döblins Metropolen: Über reale und imaginäre Städte und die Travestie der Wünsche,* Ergebnisse der Frauenforschung vol. 2 (Weinheim/Basel: Beltz Verlag, 1985).

[15] Otto F. Best, "Zwischen Orient und Okzident. Döblin und Spinoza. Einige Anmerkungen zur Problematik des offenen Schlusses von *Berlin Alexanderplatz,"* *Colloquia Germanica* 12 (1979): 94–105.

[16] Roland Links, *Alfred Döblin: Leben und Werk* (Berlin: Volk und Wissen, 1976), 118–19.

[17] Hans-Peter Bayerdörfer, "Der Wissende und die Gewalt. Alfred Döblins Theorie des epischen Werkes und der Schluß von *Berlin Alexanderplatz,"* *Deutsche Vierteljahrsschrift für Literaturwissenschaft und Geistesgeschichte* 44 (1970): 318–53: reprinted in Prangel, ed., *Materialien,* 150–85.

[18] Matthias Prangel, "Franz Biberkopf und das Wissen des Wissens. Zum Schluß von *Berlin Alexanderplatz* unter der Perspektive einer Theorie der Beobachtung der Beobachtung," in *Internationales Alfred-Döblin-Kolloquium Leiden 1995,* ed. Gabriele Sander (Bern: Peter Lang, 1997), 169–80.

[19] James H. Reid, *"Berlin Alexanderplatz* — A Political Novel," *German Life & Letters* 21 (1967/68): 214–23.

[20] Wolfgang Düsing, *Erinnerung und Identität: Untersuchungen zu einem Erzählproblem bei Musil, Döblin und Doderer* (Munich: Wilhelm Fink, 1982).

[21] Helmut Koopmann, "Der Schluß des Romans *Berlin Alexanderplatz* — eine Antwort auf Thomas Manns Zauberberg?" *Internationale Alfred-Döblin-Kolloquien Münster 1989–Marbach a. N. 1991,* ed. Werner Stauffacher (Bern: Peter Lang, 1993), 179–91.

[22] Peter Bekes, *Berlin Alexanderplatz: Interpretationen,* Oldenbourg Interpretationen mit Unterrichtshilfen vol. 74 (Munich: Oldenbourg, 1995).

[23] Dieter Baacke, "Erzähltes Engagement. Antike Mythologie in Döblins Romanen," *text & kritik* 13/14 (1966): 22–31.

[24] Georg Fromm, "Hiobs Wachhund. Die erste Hiob-Paraphrase in Alfred Döblins *Berlin Alexanderplatz,*" *Internationales Alfred-Döblin-Kolloquium Paris 1993,* ed. Michael Grunewald (Bern: Peter Lang, 1995), 213–26, and "Die Isaak-Paraphrase in Alfred Döblins *Berlin Alexanderplatz,*" *Internationales Alfred-Döblin-Kolloquium Leiden 1995,* ed. Gabriele Sander (Bern: Peter Lang, 1997), 159–68.

[25] Otto Keller, *Döblins Montageroman als Epos der Moderne: Die Struktur der Romane Der schwarze Vorhang, Die drei Sprünge des Wang-lun und Berlin Alexanderplatz* (Munich: Wilhelm Fink, 1980).

[26] Kathleen Komar, "Technique and Structure in Döblin's *Berlin Alexanderplatz,*" *German Quarterly* 54 (1981): 318–34.

[27] Ute Karlavaris-Bremer, "Döblin und die Berlinerin. Frauengestalten in Alfred Döblins Berliner Romanen," *Internationale Alfred-Döblin-Kolloquien 1984–1985,* ed. Werner Stauffacher (Bern: Peter Lang, 176–84).

[28] Maria Tatar, "'Wie süß ist es sich zu opfern.' Gender Violence and Agency in Döblin's *Berlin Alexanderplatz,*" *Deutsche Vierteljahrsschrift für Literaturwissenschaft und Geistesgeschichte* 66 (1992): 491–518.

[29] In Heinz Schwitzke, ed., *Sprich, damit ich dich sehe: Frühe Hörspiele* (Munich, 1962); for the text, cf. *Materialien zu Alfred Döblin "Berlin Alexanderplatz,"* ed. Matthias Prangel, 199–236.

[30] Short excerpts from the script and some reviews in *Materialien zu Alfred Döblin "Berlin Alexanderplatz,"* ed. Matthias Prangel, 237–44.

[31] Hans-Peter Bayerdörfer, "Alfred Döblin: *Berlin Alexanderplatz,*" in *Interpretationen: Romane des 20. Jahrhunderts,* vol. 1, Stuttgart: Reclam, 1993, 158–94.

[32] Ekkehart Kaemmerling, "Die filmische Schreibweise," in *Materialien zu Alfred Döblin "Berlin Alexanderplatz,"* ed. Matthias Prangel, 185–98.

[33] Werner Stauffacher, ed., *Internationale Alfred-Döblin-Kolloquien Münster 1989– Marbach a. N. 1991* (Bern: Peter Lang, 1993). The three articles are: Helmuth Kiesel, "Döblin und das Kino. Überlegungen zur *Alexanderplatz*-Verfilmung," 284– 97; Achim Haag, "Fassbinder ver-filmt *Berlin Alexanderplatz.* Bilder und Töne jenseits ihrer Vorlage: Wider eine Dogmatik der Literaturverfilmung," 298–316; Andreas Rost, "Fassbinder ver-filmt *Berlin Alexanderplatz.* Bilder und Töne jenseits ihrer Vorlage: Von 'Sachzwängen' und 'Zwangsjacken' einer filmischen Ästhetik," 317–30.

[34] Heinz Brüggemann, "*Berlin Alexanderplatz* oder 'Franz, Mieze, Reinhold, Tod & Teufel'? R. W. Fassbinders filmische Lektüre des Romans von Döblin. Polemik gegen einen melodramatischen Widerruf der ästhetischen Moderne," in Heinz Ludwig Arnold, ed., *Rainer Werner Fassbinder, text & kritik* vol. 103 (Munich: Edition text & kritik, 1989), 51–65.

[35] Andrea Melcher, *Vom Schriftsteller zum Sprachsteller? Alfred Döblins Auseinandersetzung mit Film und Rundfunk (1909–1932)* (Frankfurt: Peter Lang, 1996).

[36] The play has been published in a version edited by Heinz Schwitzke in *Frühe Hörspiele*, vol. 2 of *Sprich damit ich dich sehe*, and in the volume *Drama, Hörspiel, Film* of Döblin's *Ausgewählte Werke*, edited by Erich Kleinschmidt, 273–317. Cf. especially Kleinschmidt's commentary and afterword.

[37] Otto Keller, *Döblins Montageroman als Epos der Moderne: Die Struktur der Romane Der schwarze Vorhang, Die drei Sprünge des Wang-lun und Berlin Alexanderplatz* (Munich: Wilhelm Fink Verlag, 1980).

[38] Henrietta S. Schoonover, *The Humorous and Grotesque Elements in Alfred Döblin's "Berlin Alexanderplatz"* (Bern: Peter Lang, 1977), which was originally a Canadian dissertation under the guidance of Ingrid Schuster.

[39] David B. Dollenmayer, "'Wessen Amerikanisch?' — Zu Eugene Jolas' Übersetzung von *Berlin Alexanderplatz*," *Internationale Alfred-Döblin-Kolloquien Münster 1989–Marbach a. N. 1991*, edited by Werner Stauffacher (Bern: Peter Lang, 1993), 192–205.

[40] Anke Detken, *Döblins "Berlin Alexanderplatz" übersetzt: Ein multilingualer kontrastiver Vergleich*, Palaestra vol. 299 (Göttingen: Vandenhoeck & Ruprecht, 1997).

10: *Babylonische Wandrung*

IN 1932, AMIDST THE TURMOIL of the disintegrating Weimar Republic, Döblin had started a novel that would take him far afield, the story
of a Babylonian god who finds out that he has been deposed, that no
one prays to him anymore, and that Babylon has disappeared. The work
might have been a tragedy, but it turned out to be a tragicomedy, with
many grotesque scenes and characters. The god Marduk, later called
Konrad, goes on an unending trip; thus the title *Babylonische Wandrung*.
The larger part of the book was written in exile in 1933 in Zurich and
Paris, and it was published in 1934, evoking little response even from the
exile community. Döblin scholars tend to avoid this very long text,
which does not lend itself to easy definitions and defies both political and
religious interpretations.

The most thorough examination of the entire novel was done by
Patrick O'Neill in *Alfred Döblin's "Babylonische Wandrung": A Study,*[1]
published in 1974. O'Neill begins with an introduction to Döblin's life
and work, the history of the writing of *Babylonische Wandrung* in
1932/33 at the very beginning of Döblin's exile, and the novel's publishing history, including Walter Muschg's meritorious but problematic
new edition of 1962. After an overview of the stations of the journey, he
zeroes in on crucial points. First, the complex of "Babylon," already
familiar to Döblin readers from previous works, especially *Berlin Alexanderplatz*. Beyond the image of Babylon as the exemplary big city of
arrogant sinners doomed to fall (the model of Byzantium, Rome, Paris,
and Berlin), and of Babylon as the place of Jewish exile and the object of
wrath of the prophet Jeremiah, the image of the deposed Babylonian god
sets off a series of mythological episodes and allusions, usually in a lighter
mode. These episodes and allusions often appear with elements of the
grotesque or with a Heinean break in mood, which have the effect of de-
mythologizing them (47–48). Together with all the other sources from
which Döblin draws, these mythological elements make up the complex,
chaotic voices of the world that he holds up to scrutiny (48). O'Neill
goes on to say that "*Babylonische Wandrung*, in its selection of examples
from our political and cultural history as well as in the sequence of cities,
the expression of this history, retraces the course of western civiliza-

tion"(48). In other words, Döblin offers a somewhat facetious history of civilizations from Babylon to twentieth-century Europe.

O'Neill follows this up with an analysis of the novel's three "Babylonians," Georg, Waldemar, and Konrad. The short section on Georg is especially illuminating, as it highlights the irony in the name "Georg" the dragon-slayer, since the evil god of the Babylonians, the power of chaos and darkness, is represented as the dragon to be slain by Marduk (49–52). Most of Döblin's text reverses this outcome with subsequent defeats of Konrad until his rather surprising victory, assisted by the crucified Christ, over Georg in the Cathedral Notre Dame de Paris. O'Neill confirms the need for the third Babylonian, Waldemar, although there is little to say about him, except that he personifies the lust for drinking. Konrad, the protagonist and a very complex figure, is given the most detailed attention by O'Neill (56–73). O'Neill pursues Konrad's "Wanderung" from station to station, as he tries to shed and reject his Babylonian heritage and become a real human being. Particular attention has to be paid to Konrad's dreams, which reveal his subconscious wisdom and knowledge, as well as his ongoing dialogue with the universe, the stars and the moon. Unlike previous critics, O'Neill sees the conclusion of the novel as being consistent with the rest. Konrad's way, he says, "proceeds quite consistently through the stages of realization of man's relationship to his world. Responsibility is the key concept of the novel" (72). For Döblin, this was connected with the responsibility of the German people, the exiles (and himself) included, for allowing Hitler to seize power. But, continues O'Neill, "the rise of Nazi Germany is merely a symbol of the march of Babylon through history" (77), Babylon standing for the idea of the evil and destructive power of states and ideologies, and thus Babylon becomes a symbol for the march of the Nazis to dominate and destroy the world.

Konrad can be seen as an exile, and the text is filled with other exiles: Waldemar, the gypsies, the Jews, Kamilla the camel, and the narrator himself all suffer the fate of exile, which means the fall. Exile, according to O'Neill, becomes the "penitential journey in search of the happiness which might have been ours" (79). As far as autobiographical links are concerned, O'Neill points to a striking similarity between Konrad and Döblin's father Max — whom he resembles much more than he does Döblin himself — Döblin's father who abandoned his responsibilities for the elusive enjoyments of life, and whose artistic talents and flights of fancy Döblin himself inherited (81–83). O'Neill also points to the women in *Babylonische Wandrung* as a reflection of Döblin's ambivalence toward women, which was characterized by his double image of women as enemies and as saviors of man, as personified in his wife Erna and his "muse" Yolla Niclas (84–88).

With these considerations in mind, O'Neill analyzes the form and style of *Babylonische Wandrung*. He claims that the form is "only apparently chaotic" (91) — previous critics having jumped to the conclusion of this chaos of form. As far as the structure is concerned, O'Neill adopts Döblin's description of his own autobiographical volume *Schicksalsreise*: "eine Reise zwischen Himmel und Erde" (92). The stations of the journey also conform to the stages in Konrad's life from youth to maturity and finally old age, but then the metaphysical nature of the journey is emphasized by the parodic allusion to Goethe's *Faust* and to the Book of Job (92). *Babylonische Wandrung* shares with its predecessor *Berlin Alexanderplatz* the central role of the narrator, from chapter headings to commentaries. This auctorial framework is again, according to O'Neill, "didactic, sometimes slightly patronising, usually faintly humorous" (96). A typical element of *Babylonische Wandrung* is what O'Neill calls "interpolations" (99). Whereas in *Berlin Alexanderplatz* they are treated as part of the technique of montage, in this text they seem more foreign and arbitrary. They are of two kinds: historical and mythological or literary. O'Neill notes that Döblin's style is highly associative (102). But even with all the seemingly heterogeneous material and Döblin's inability to restrain himself, the fundamental character remains: "*Babylonische Wandrung* . . . is the voice of a latter day Jeremiah warning a degenerate world of its downfall. The theme finds its fitting expression in the style, based, as Döblin himself had demanded, on the fantastic and the surrealistic" (106–7).

The humor in *Babylonische Wandrung* has seemed rather incongruous to most critics, pervasive as it is, and this gives O'Neill some pause for reflection as well, until he arrives at the conclusion that "*Babylonische Wandrung* is the laughter of a civilization on the brink of an abyss," maintaining that the book is not only a novel of exile but a religious novel (123). But it is written from the conviction later voiced by Friedrich Dürrenmatt, that the Jeremiad of the twentieth century must be voiced in the form of a comedy. Döblin used the term "Heiterkeit" to describe its mood, but one can call it a rather "trostlose Heiterkeit," as Heinz D. Osterle did with regard to *November 1918* (122).[2]

A short summary of O'Neill's findings is offered in his article "*Babylonische Wandrung*" of 1980.[3] Here O'Neill emphasizes the double process and perspective: it is that of Konrad's journey through the human world, in contrast with his alter ego, the evil Georg, leading from lack of responsibility to responsibility in a way similar to *Berlin Alexanderplatz*. O'Neill sees the two novels in close proximity with one another, especially because in the later novel there is a need for a "Babylonische Wandlung," a transformation out of Babylon, the place of evil. Paris and Berlin are echoes of the Biblical Babylon, and despite its many digressions, the general theme of the novel is the depravity of the human race and its need for a rebirth, a radical change. While O'Neill defends the ending as consistent with the drift of the novel, he nevertheless admits that it does not really matter — Konrad cannot really "arrive" at a specific goal. O'Neill agrees with other scholars that Döblin's own later disparaging remarks on the novel come from the perspective of the converted Christian, and that it is misleading to see *Babylonische Wandrung* solely from this point of view. Although Christianity enters into the plot, with Notre Dame de Paris, the last section and Konrad's death resemble much more the ending of *Berge Meere und Giganten* than an experience of Jesus Christ.

Since O'Neill's study, several aspects of *Babylonische Wandrung* have been examined by other scholars, particularly the theme of exile. Helmut F. Pfanner pursues the traces of exile in his article "Die Widerspiegelung der Exilerfahrung in Alfred Döblins *Babylonischer Wandrung*"[4] in close correspondence between Döblin's biography and the text. While Döblin had not yet experienced the most degrading aspects of exile, he knew already that he had lost his roots and was going to wander in foreign lands. The text is full of allusions to current events, but pogroms are mentioned only in historical digressions. Pfanner's main point is that Döblin's subtitle "Hochmut kommt vor dem Fall," a leitmotif of this novel, reflects his conviction that life before 1933 was *Hochmut*, hubris, and that the god Konrad, like other exiles, deserves his fall from his elevated station. Konrad, in his exile, begins to identify with the Jews, and specifically with the mythical figure Ahasverus the Wandering Jew, who is mentioned throughout the text (72). In this respect, *Babylonische Wandrung* echoes Döblin's 1933 *Unser Dasein*, and his 1926 *Reise in Polen*. Konrad begins also to see positive aspects of his exile, including the experience of a new world, just as Döblin initially tried to see his own exile. However, the text points to major stumbling blocks for a new life: the foreign languages and cultures, and the unending *Heimatlosigkeit*. Finally, for Pfanner, the text opens up the perspective of a metaphysical worldview that bestows meaning on the seemingly digressive and chaotic events in this life. For him, Döblin's multidimensional depiction of the exile condition offers a particularly substantial picture of the situation of 1933 and a key to understanding the shock and meaning of exile.

Wulf Koepke, in his article "Der Beginn von Döblins Babylonischer Wanderung,"[5] also places the novel in the context of Döblin's beginning exile. He sees two contradictory emotions emerge vividly from the text that are typical for this time: the optimism and *Leichtsinn* of a new departure, of a liberation from unsolvable difficulties in Berlin, and then the disorientation of rootlessness, of finding oneself in an empty space, nowhere. Both of these emotions combine to produce the parodistic tone, the playfulness, and the impression that life is a journey with no beginning and no end, and that everything in between is an episode without consequences. It is obvious that the major plot device of a god fallen into the human condition seems to contradict this view, but then contradictions characterize the text. While other of Döblin's narrators, in *Wallenstein*, for instance, devour the pieces of outside reality to create his world, this narrator and his protagonists, Konrad in particular, try to avoid coming into close contact with "reality"; they want to stay above the weighty topics and emotions like guilt, sorrow, and homesickness. Hermann Kesten's 1934 review of *Babylonische Wandrung* had focused on the word "half." Konrad is a half-hearted, passive dilettante; he is also the halfhearted Western Jew who considers his property more important than his Jewishness. Konrad is potentially an object of satire, as it seems at the beginning; but this changes in the course of the story, and this is possibly because he became the personification of Döblin's self-criticism. The goal of Konrad's life journey becomes Paris, and both Paris and Berlin are compared and contrasted with Babylon, the place of exile, but an exile of rich Jews who forget Jerusalem. The text of *Babylonische Wandrung* is filled with forebodings of a sad exile; but the narrator keeps up the tone of lightness between the Berlin past and the unknown future. Whereas the writers who remained in Germany could afford to write travelogues, the exiles understood that this was not a pleasure trip anymore, and that there would be no return.

Barbara Baumann-Eisenack, in her article "Zu Gebrauch und Funktion des Mythos in Alfred Döblins Roman 'Babylonische Wandrung oder Hochmut kommt vor dem Fall' (1934),"[6] refers also to the unsettled situation of the new exile Döblin in 1933, with specific focus on the use of mythological figures and tales. She mentions Döblin's visit to Thomas Mann in 1932, a time when Mann had embarked on his epic tale about Joseph and his brothers, and Döblin had started work on his Marduk-Konrad story (using some of the same sources), speculating that their conversation must have turned to the use of mythology in novels. Mythology and reason, mythology and deeper truth, a hot topic during the later twenties, emerges in *Babylonische Wandrung*, but only to be parodied. Although the novel begins on a mythological level, it is soon clear that — in contrast to *Berlin Alexanderplatz* — the use of mythology in this book is characterized by total arbitrariness, *Beliebigkeit*, and that there is no discernable connection between Konrad's fate and the inserted mythological tales. The montage pieces are non-functional. Döblin demonstrates rather "das Scheitern einer Denkgewohnheit Mythos" (238), together with the failure of the deposed god Konrad. The heightening of mythology into the realm of the grotesque makes it possible for the reader to distance himself from it (239–40). The text can be seen as offering a liberation from myth by making it look ridiculous. While the following narrative works *Amazonas* and *November 1918* would integrate mythological elements in a serious way, *Babylonische Wandrung* seems bent on debunking the entire debate on mythology, certainly not without reference to the political misuses of mythological images and figures by the National Socialists.

Helmuth Kiesel, in the chapter on *Babylonische Wandrung* in his 1986 book *Literarische Trauerarbeit*,[7] attaches special significance to this work, which he believes can be designated as Döblins true novel of exile ("eigentlicher Emigrationsroman") (96). This evaluation is contrary to that of most critics. Manfred Auer, in his 1977 book *Das Exil vor der Vertreibung*,[8] justifies his omission of *Babylonische Wandrung* with the argument that in this book Döblin "unternimmt . . . den forciert wirkenden Versuch, seiner Realität schreibend zu entgehen" (31). It is, according to Auer, Döblin's sole attempt at escapism (31); Döblin would face the new reality in his next novel *Pardon wird nicht gegeben*. But Kiesel argues from an opposite point of view. Marduk-Konrad, the deposed Babylonian god, is condemned to lead a human life, and indeed, to become human. His human life is to be an atonement for the guilt he has amassed as a cruel god of slaughter and devastation. Kiesel examines the meaning of the subtitle, "Hochmut kommt vor dem Fall": How does this square with the humoristic tone of the book, the numerous grotesque scenes, and the fact that Konrad, after many trials and also many moments of pleasure, never really feels the pain of *Buße*, and dies peacefully and in harmony with the environment? Döblin's own later answer that his story "derailed" while he was writing it, is at best misleading. Kiesel examines the nature of the novel's humor, its psychological aspects — predominantly with reference to Freud — and the view of history that informs this seeming kaleidoscope. It is the banishment of a god into permanent exile that provides the plot: the assimilated Jews, especially the intellectuals among them, thought they were gods, and now, after their banishment, their exile has begun — an analogy that inevitably comes to mind, but, in Kiesel's view, has only limited validity. Also, Konrad's encounters with Jesus Christ do not yet have consequences. Döblin does not yet accept the validity of the Christian view of evil and its causes. Only later, after the reading of Kierkegaard and Catholic theology, St. Augustine in particular, did he change his mind. In *Babylonische Wandrung*, Konrad remains unconvinced after his conversations on religion in Zurich. Döblin's text reveals in many instances his opposition to senseless violence and persecution; it maintains his stances on revolution and historical change as expressed in *Wissen und Verändern!* and *Unser Dasein*. Döblin was opposed to the Marxist idea of class struggle and violent revolution, and hoped for a transformation of the minds and a spontaneous formation of new and peaceful forms of community. It was here that he saw the task and responsibility of the writer: raising timely questions and preparing the awareness of the need for change. Therefore the message of this work is less in its end result than in the ongoing debate and the many facets of reality that Döblin brings to light. But the humoristic, even serene tone of the book does not hide the element of melancholy, or mourning, *Trauer*, over the loss of the previous glory of the "gods" in Berlin and their seeming security. In its multifaceted tone and structure, the text provides a fundamental outlook on the coming exile and its literary expressions, *Amazonas, November 1918*, and *Hamlet*.

Notes

[1] Patrick O'Neill, *Alfred Döblin's "Babylonische Wandrung": A Study* (Bern: Peter Lang, 1974).

[2] Patrick O'Neill also provides a careful listing of sources and citations from the Bible and literature (108–16). Appendix I offers examples of manuscript variants (135–40).

[3] Patrick O'Neill, *"Babylonische Wandrung,"* in Ingrid Schuster, ed., *Zu Alfred Döblin* (Stuttgart: Klett, 1980), 149–59.

[4] Helmut F. Pfanner, "Die Widerspiegelung der Exilerfahrung in Alfred Döblins *Babylonischer Wandrung*," *Internationales Alfred-Döblin-Kolloquium Lausanne 1987*, 68–82.

[5] Wulf Köpke, "Der Beginn von Döblins Babylonischer Wanderung," *Internationales Alfred-Döblin-Kolloquium Paris 1993*, ed. Michel Grünewald (Bern: Peter Lang, 1995), 67–84.

[6] Barbara Baumann-Eisenack, "Zu Gebrauch und Funktion des Mythos in Alfred Döblins 'Babylonische Wandrung oder Hochmut kommt vor dem Fall' (1934)," *Internationale Alfred-Döblin-Kolloquien Münster 1989–Marbach a. N. 1991*, ed. Werner Stauffacher (Bern: Peter Lang, 1993), 233–42.

[7] Helmuth Kiesel, *Literarische Trauerarbeit: Das Exil- und Spätwerk Alfred Döblins* (Tübingen: Max Niemeyer, 1986), 96–131.

[8] Manfred Auer, *Das Exil vor der Vertreibung: Motivkontinuität und Quellenproblematik im späten Werk Alfred Döblins* (Bonn: Bouvier Verlag H. Grundmann, 1977).

11: *Pardon wird nicht gegeben*

DÖBLIN'S FIRST NOVEL WRITTEN ENTIRELY IN EXILE — after the transitional work *Babylonische Wandrung*, which he began before leaving Germany in 1933 — was *Pardon wird nicht gegeben*, published in 1935. It is an anomaly in the author's oeuvre in that it is a well-built novel of modest length with a clear plot, fairly past-paced action, and an emphasis on psychological processes, albeit with a socio-political background. It also has easily discernable autobiographical elements. This has caused some scholars to surmise that this novel was written hurriedly between July and October 1934, under financial pressure, in order to reach the drastically shrunken audience, and was meant for swift and easy reading. But if it was an experiment in commercial writing, Döblin returned afterwards to the expansive epic forms of *Amazonas* and *November 1918*. *Pardon wird nicht gegeben* did indeed sell sufficiently well and had enough appeal for translations into English (*Men Without Mercy*), French, Italian, Russian, and Polish, all in 1937.[1] The postwar edition of 1960 went into a second edition in 1962, followed by a dtv paperback in 1964. Evidently Döblin had offered a readable story and achieved at least a moderate commercial success, whether this was his chief goal or not.

However, with a writer like Döblin, notorious for his disdain for "easy readers," such an explanation seems improbable, even under the pressures of exile. Robert Minder, whose review in the *Revue de l'enseignement des langues vivantes*[2] stood at the beginning of his friendship with Döblin, saw an influence of the French environment and French classical forms. Explanations that Döblin did not have access to a big library for extensive preliminary research, as he was used to doing, do not make sense in view of the conditions in Paris and the subsequent works. Indeed, the "conventional" or "traditional" structure and content of *Pardon wird nicht gegeben* beg for a better explanation. However, scholarly criticism has largely by-passed this novel as not worthy of consideration. Erwin Kobel is once more typical for this attitude: while he includes even the *Babylonische Wandrung* in his survey, he jumps from there to *Amazonas*, skipping *Pardon wird nicht gegeben* entirely.

Roland Links, in his book of 1976, *Alfred Döblin: Leben und Werk*,[3] contradicts Döblin's statements in *Epilog* that seemed to dismiss this "little novel" as merely private and transitional. Links emphasizes that the novel does something that was rare for bourgeois literature before the Second World War: it makes close connections between individual fates and societal and specifically economic relationships (155). The novel demonstrates the effects of the Great Depression on German society, and once more it exemplifies, much clearer than does *Berlin Alexanderplatz*, Döblin's idea of revolution. For Links, the novel is not an expression of Döblin's isolation, as *Babylonische Wandrung*, but a sign of Döblin's beginning involvement in the antifascist struggle.

The first major treatment of *Pardon wird nicht gegeben* was a chapter devoted to it in Manfred Auer's 1977 dissertation, *Das Exil vor der Vertreibung*.[4] Auer's starting point is that the alternative of either "Zeitroman" or "Autobiographie," as defined by earlier critics, is misleading and unproductive. He understands the reduction of the setting to an unnamed city at a period without dates (although easily recognizable), and of the cast of characters to a relative few, whose family names are not given, as a clear indication of the author's intent to transcend the level of documented facts: "Aufgrund dieser Reduzierung im strukturellen, erzähltechnischen, stilistischen und thematischen Bereich erscheint der dargestellte Kampf des Individuums um Selbstbehauptung als eine archetypische Konstellation des Lebens als ständigem Machtkampf und als Paradigma der menschlichen Existenz" (33). The theme of *Selbstbehauptung*, one of the constants in Döblin's oeuvre, is reduced in this text to the struggle between two persons, mother and son. This reduction or abstraction rules out identification of this novel as a *Zeitroman*. The mother-son conflict goes back to the father-mother relationship: the father, who is deceased, was a "Lichtgestalt" (34) who was attractive for the materialistic mother as an appearance of the "other," but who was living in a different sphere and was irresponsible in practical matters. Hence the mother's memory of him is still characterized by a mixture of love and hate, and the father's legacy of debt causes her bitter hatred against society. Karl, her oldest son, is destined to be the instrument to carry out her revenge. Karl's total dependence on his mother is reversed in his marriage to Julie: he is the master, until at the end, during the economic crisis, she liberates herself and leaves him. Karl's decision to follow the dictates of his mother and not his political mentor and friend Paul is not primarily motivated by political ideas. Political ideas and criticism of the capitalistic system are evident, especially on the level of the narrator, but they remain secondary for the plot.

Auer characterizes the narrative method in *Pardon wird nicht gegeben* as "Pragmatisierung des Erzählens" (38). The reflection on the past in autobiographical terms becomes a "Standortreflexion" in a more general sense, including the socio-political factors. There is the process of self-awareness of the author through narration, but also a distinct goal, a "Ziel des Erzählens" (38). Auer points out that in the section "Erster Rückblick" in Döblin's autobiographical 1928 book written with Oscar Loerke and published on the occasion of his fiftieth birthday, *Alfred Döblin: Im Buch — Zu Haus — Auf der Straße*, Döblin had written: "Meine Mutter, im Exil in Berlin" (40).[5] He was referring to the family's move to Berlin after their desertion by his father. In *Pardon wird nicht gegeben*, Döblin takes up where the 1928 book left off, focusing on his relationship with his (absent) father and his dominant mother, but he is also beginning to approach the roots of the problems of Germany, the dominant theme of *November 1918*. Involuntarily Döblin projected his "exile," his expulsion into a strange place, back into his childhood, thus making his "real" exile of 1933 into a second, a repeated trauma. Döblin would later treat the two realms of conflict — the family struggles and the revolutionary conflicts — shown in their interrelations in *Pardon wird nicht gegeben* separately and in all their complexities in *Hamlet* and in *November 1918*.

There is a substantial chapter on *Pardon wird nicht gegeben* in David Dollenmayer's 1988 book *The Berlin Novels of Alfred Döblin*.[6] For Dollenmayer, *Pardon* is the "diametrical opposite" of the preceding Berlin novel, *Berlin Alexanderplatz*, and it reminds him more of *Wadzek* than the last work. Also, although the name of the place is never mentioned in the text, it is obvious that Döblin means Berlin. Considering the autobiographical content, the links with the "Erster Rückblick" of 1928 become apparent as well. In Döblin's oeuvre, the novel is an exception, a *roman à thèse* with a clear didactic intent that limits its scope and form. All Döblin's other novels are more expansive: their message is ambiguous or at least complex, and their conclusions are tentative. Dollenmayer details the background of Döblin's family and Döblin's political involvement and positions before his escape in 1933. The sudden loneliness of the exile, he writes, "no doubt encouraged the inward turn of the novel toward self-reflection about his family and their fate" (110). Dollenmayer does not fail to mention the other striking aspect: that of the homoerotic overtones, which he finds to be at the center of the work (115). The political situation described, which is that of shortly before 1933 in Germany, echoes the dead-end view of Döblin's 1931 *Wissen und Verändern!:* "The only hope for change lies in the working class, but it has been led astray by its political leaders" (116). Karl, in contrast, is the prototype of the disoriented German middle class (119). He betrays himself and his society, with catastrophic results. As Dollenmayer writes, "On the level of both the family and society, *Men without Mercy* is a novel of betrayal and the possibility of redemption" (122). The ending, however, is "deeply pessimistic" (123), which could be a foreboding of Döblin's later conclusion that, since all political solutions fail, only religion can bring the human race out of the impasse.

Wolfgang Düsing, in his 1982 book *Erinnerung und Identität,*[7] focuses on Karl's primal traumatic experience, meaning being forced by his mother to stay at home and pursue a bourgeois career instead of leaving with his friend Paul. This leads to inner contradictions that are never to be resolved, and to Karl's uncertain position between social involvement and his role as an entrepreneur. According to Düsing, the book exhibits a "wechselseitige Abhängigkeit psychologischer und gesellschaftlicher Aspekte der Identitätsbildung" (145), and it is by no means a retreat into a mere psychological novel with a conventional structure and plot. Döblin tries hard to avoid an exclusively psychological or exclusively social determination of the characters and their actions. The ending shows the failure of Karl's compromises, but does not show a clear way out of the impasse.

Roland Dollinger, in his 1994 study *Totalität und Totalitarismus im Exilwerk Alfred Döblins,*[8] pays special attention to this neglected work, which he brings into the historical context of 1934/35. He sees a connection with *November 1918,* following Döblin's explanation that both works were written to elucidate "wodurch alles so gekommen war" (24). At the same time, he draws a line from *Berlin Alexanderplatz* to *Pardon,* which he sees as a substitute for the continuation of the first novel that was planned but never written (24–26). For Dollinger, the alternative interpretations of family story versus political/historical novel are misleading: *Pardon wird nicht gegeben* combines the two dimensions.

The conventional wisdom that Döblin was lonely and isolated in his Paris exile is seriously challenged by Dollinger's account of the events. Döblin was not only involved in the Jewish movement of Neo-Territorialism, but participated also in the anti-fascist activities of the cultural exiles in Paris, culminating in 1938 in the celebration of Döblin's sixtieth birthday. These activities were designed to combat Nazi Germany and to aid Republican Spain, and a major concern was the creation of a German popular front of solidarity among the exiles. For Dollinger, *Pardon wird nicht gegeben* is a document of politically active literature, both in its form and its content. For instance, the book sharply criticizes the "revisionism" of the Social Democrats that led to the avoidance of revolution in 1918, which was in Döblin's view the beginning of fascism, as a true democracy was never established. He later described the events in detail in *November 1918*.

In contrast to previous and subsequent texts by Döblin, Dollinger says that *Pardon wird nicht gegeben*'s presentation of history as the history of individuals has its corollary in the narrator's conception of man as a thoroughly social being (43). Dollinger agrees with Dollenmayer on the didactic intent of the text, which he considers to have been also directed at Döblin's colleagues in exile: "Er wollte seinen bürgerlichen Kollegen im Exil zeigen, was es heißt, weder der 'Parteipolitik' noch der weltabgewandten 'Mystik' zu verfallen" (45). Döblin comes close to Georg Lukács's concept of the historical novel (46–51).[9] In *Pardon wird nicht gegeben*, Döblin contributes one major point to the debate on the causes and precedents of National Socialism: the authoritarian family structure and society. This was analyzed at the same time by the Frankfurt Institute for Social Research, in particular by Erich Fromm, whose findings were published in Paris in 1936 (52–55).[10] *Pardon wird nicht gegeben* has an ambiguous ending, as Döblin seems to shy away from a partisan solution. He also fears, as would be evident in his subsequent texts, that the totalitarian regime of the Nazis might be replaced by other authoritarian or totalitarian systems and ideologies — a danger that drove him, together with Arthur Koestler and Manès Sperber, away from a communist-dominated popular front and once more into a position away from all party organizations.

Notes

[1] Müller-Salget, *Alfred Döblin: Werk und Entwicklung* (Bonn: Bouvier, 1973; 2nd rev. ed. 1988), 450–51; only *Berlin Alexanderplatz* had more foreign appeal, with its translations into twelve languages.

[2] Robert Minder, "Marxisme et psychoanalyse chez Alfred Döblin. A propos de son dernier roman *Pardon wird nicht gegeben*," *Revue de l'enseignement des langues vivantes* 54 (1937), 209–21. The article is now available in German, in R. M., *Die Entdeckung deutscher Mentalität*, ed. Manfred Beyer (Leipzig: Reclam, 1992), 267–82. Cf. Manfred Beyer, "Alfred Döblin und Robert Minder," *Internationales Alfred-Döblin-Kolloquium Paris 1993*, ed. Michel Grünewald (Bern: Peter Lang, 1995), 53–65.

[3] Roland Links, *Alfred Döblin: Leben und Werk* (Berlin: Volk und Wissen, 1976), 155–64.

[4] Manfred Auer, *Das Exil vor der Vertreibung: Motivkontinuität und Quellenproblematik im späten Werk Alfred Döblins* (Bonn: Bouvier Verlag Herbert Grundmann, 1977); on *Pardon wird nicht gegeben*, 31–41

[5] Döblin, with Oskar Loerke, *Alfred Döblin: Im Buch — Zu Haus — Auf der Straße* (Berlin: S. Fischer, 1928), 7–109

[6] David B. Dollenmayer, *The Berlin Novels of Alfred Döblin* (Berkeley/Los Angeles/London: U of California P, 1988), 98–123.

[7] Wolfgang Düsing, *Erinnerung und Identität: Untersuchungen zu einem Erzählproblem bei Musil, Döblin, und Doderer* (Munich: Wilhelm Fink, 1982), 103–72.

[8] Roland Dollinger, *Totalität und Totalitarismus im Exilwerk Alfred Döblins*, Epistemata. Würzburger wissenschaftliche Schriften, vol. 126 (Würzburg: Königshausen & Neumann, 1994), 21–67.

[9] Dollinger refers to Lukács's article of 1932 in *Die Linkskurve*, "Reportage oder Gestaltung?" as a programmatic text (47); Lukács's publications on the historical novel were not known to Döblin at the time. It makes sense that Marxist scholarship, e.g. Roland Links, has taken a generally favorable view of *Pardon wird nicht gegeben* as an analysis of the disoriented German bourgeoisie and the prehistory of National Socialism.

[10] Max Horkheimer, ed., *Studien über Autorität und Familie* (Paris, 1936). Erich Fromm was the main contributor to this work.

12: *Amazonas*

DÖBLIN HIMSELF DESCRIBED HOW he immersed himself in the maps of South America and was fascinated by the huge river system of the Amazon. In his trilogy *Amazonas*, also titled *Das Land ohne Tod*, Döblin used episodes from the history of the colonization of South America to voice his fundamental critique of modern Western civilization and his call for a return to a life more in keeping with the laws of nature. *Amazonas* was first published in two volumes in 1937 and 1938, titled *Die Fahrt ins Land ohne Tod* and *Der blaue Tiger*, but in his postwar edition of 1947/48 Döblin separated the last two parts of the second volume and presented it as a third volume, *Der neue Urwald*. This served as a pretext for Walter Muschg, who considered *Der neue Urwald* aesthetically inferior and without organic connection with the other parts, to eliminate the section altogether in his 1963 edition, an unpardonable act for an editor and one which was eventually rectified in 1988 with Werner Stauffacher's new edition for the *Ausgewählte Werke*.

Two early dissertations were devoted to *Amazonas*. Jacob Erhardt wrote his dissertation at Case Western Reserve University in 1968, and published a reworked version in 1974 as *Alfred Döblins Amazonas-Trilogie*.[1] After an introduction about the writing and publication of the trilogy, Erhardt demonstrates the close connection between *Amazonas*, especially the first volume, and Döblin's philosophy of nature. Erhardt describes in detail Döblin's use of the nature myths of the Indians (without comparing the sources), and analyzes the structure, language, and style of the work, noting that while the third part, *Der neue Urwald*, is an integral part of the entire work, it would be futile to seek too many parallels and connecting links with the previous volumes. Thus the integration remains predominantly on the thematic level. Erhardt offers examples of the superabundance of imagery and how metaphors are changed into personifications, illustrating Döblin's tendency to transform nature images into processes and actions. A striking structural feature in a work characterized by paratactic accumulation is the element of *Steigerung*, the mounting intensity of description (77–79). This conveys the constant change of life and death within the general framework of the eternal return of the same.

George Bernard Sperber published his *Wegweiser im "Amazonas"* in 1975.[2] The first section of the book deals with the reception of *Amazonas* during three periods: at the time of its first publication in 1937/38; in the early postwar period, that is, after the re-publication of 1947/48; and after Döblin's death. The responses to the 1947/48 edition were mindful of Döblin's conversion and his sometimes overzealous Catholic faith (24–32). They tended to ask the question whether this work, though written before his conversion, was already a product of his Christian faith. Hostile reviewers dismissed it not for its own faults, but as a text by the man Döblin, whom they disliked. A more nuanced evaluation was given by Fritz Knöller in *Welt und Wort* in 1948 (26–27), where he tried to do justice to the literary achievement and described Döblin's critique of occidental attitudes. On the other hand the articles published on the occasion of Döblin's seventieth birthday in 1948 did little to deepen the understanding of the South America trilogy. Later it became clear to the critics that *Amazonas* was the beginning of a new phase: "der dritten, gezwungenermaßen letzten Phase der geistigen Entwicklung Alfred Döblins" (33). Sperber's detailed discussion of the critical response to *Amazonas* between 1957 and the publication of his own book also includes a critique of Jacob Erhardt for his failure to provide a real structural analysis (32–64). A good deal of the energy of the critics of the 1960s was spent condemning Walter Muschg's editorial practices and justifying the significance of the third part of the trilogy, which Muschg had omitted. The critics also rediscovered Döblin's powerful language and his ability to come close to the magic words of the "primitive" Indios. The question remained, however, whether Döblin's scenes of brutality and slaughter were essential or gratuitous, and whether the alternative, the timeless idyll of the precolonial Indios, represented merely escapism or a genuine way out for the failed Western civilization. Sperber points out that in general critics move in their assessments between the poles of nature, history, mysticism or religion, and politics. The political aspects are emphasized in the books of Roland Links, Karl-Ludwig de Vries, Leo Kreutzer, and Louis Huguet.

Sperber devotes the rest of his book to an urgent desideratum of Döblin scholarship and of the *Amazonas* trilogy in particular: the establishment of a reliable text (65–208). This leads him from the consideration of the *Amazonas* manuscripts and variants to a discussion of what the concept "text" means in connection with Döblin's work. Sperber believes that the text of a work by Döblin includes the entire process from the first drafts to the definitive version (if there is one), and to the reception of the reader, who "completes" the text through reading.

Döblin conceived his texts, especially his novels, in a form that made the reader became part of the production process. The inserted texts in *Amazonas*, especially those from the books of Theodor Koch-Grünberg,[3] which Sperber calls "Prätexte," indicate clearly Döblin's intentions. These pre-texts from historical sources, says Sperber, are integrated into the narrative framework, but their claim to historicity is subordinated to the narrativity of the whole, and their chronology is relativized, as historical coherence gives way to textual coherence (197). This analysis would also be true for *Wallenstein*, and perhaps for *November 1918* as well, according to Sperber.

Another conclusion Sperber draws from his research on the variants bears out Döblin's own statement "Man schreibt sich an sein Thema heran" (200). The manuscripts show how the author (literally) approached his theme, getting closer to it in each subsequent version. Somewhat connected with this is Sperber's idea of a "werkimmanenter Erwartungshorizont" (201). Döblin builds up the reader's expectations only to throw the reader off at the first opportunity. Finally, the examination of the manuscripts proves Döblin's statements that, on the one hand, the epic work is limitless, but on the other hand, every individual narrative carries its own dynamics and proportions, and, therefore, its own closure.

Sperber justifies his "textsynoptische Methode," which shows the different stages of the text side by side, as a demonstration of the transformation from "Prätext" to a text that may in turn become a "pretext" for another text by the peculiar nature of Döblin's narratives (207). Döblin understood epic writing as that form of art that represents itself in its process of production. The published versions of Döblin's works are no privileged texts, but rather just stages of the entire process of production and interpretation, comparable to performances of musical compositions that are captured for sale on records or compact discs.

Roland Links's section on *Amazonas* is noteworthy for its polemics against Walter Muschg and its emphasis on the significance of the third part, *Der neue Urwald*, especially in political and philosophical terms.[4] Döblin identifies himself with the humanism of Las Casas, who rises to prominence in the first part of *Amazonas* when he raises his voice against the slaughter and exploitation of the Indians. This sixteenth-century humanism links the beginning and the ending of the trilogy when the Europeans entering the *Urwald* of South America begin to understand man's participation in and dependence on the entire system of nature, and acquire a new humanism, paradoxically in the process of disappearing in the jungle, just as Döblin's Las Casas had disappeared in the jungle (173). Still, for Links, Las Casas's Christian attitude and the attitude expressed in *Der neue Urwald* reaffirm Döblin's basic humanism, and Links sees the continuation of the same attitude after Döblin's Christian conversion, which was not a "capitulation," as it was considered by friends like Brecht. Muschg, says Links, distorts the meaning of the trilogy in a fundamental way by omitting *Der neue Urwald* — he changes it into a Christian epic.

Manfred Auer, in his 1977 book *Das Exil vor der Vertreibung*, concentrates his analysis on the "Zeitbezug" of *Amazonas*, its relation to time and history, since he considers the message of the trilogy as such to be unambiguous.[5] Thus he sees the book as a "historischer Schlüsselroman," a view that is reinforced by the inclusion of the third part, *Der neue Urwald* (42). *Amazonas* is both a historical novel and one that offers criticism of the present time, or in a term used by Döblin in a letter of 1936, it is "ein europäisches Schlußbuch" (43). Auer agrees with Walter Muschg that there exists a continuity from the Chinese Wu-wei in *Wang-lun* to the Jesuit republic in Paraguay in *Amazonas*, the latter of whose depiction also shows the traces of Döblin's preoccupation with the Jewish Neo-Territorial movement and his disillusionment about its goals and methods at the time of his writing.

Auer analyzes in considerable detail the contradictions within *Der neue Urwald* and the superficial or missing connections with the previous parts, which lead him to the conclusion that here the *Geschlechterkampf* becomes Döblin's fundamental theme, unduly replacing the historical perspective, the critique of European civilization since the Renaissance, and the specific critique of the European situation between the world wars. *Amazonas*, in its South American parts, shows Döblin's increasing interest in the Christian faith and his increasing focus on the problems of the Christian — specifically the Catholic — church, but it would be erroneous to detect early signs of Döblin's future conversion, or read the trilogy backward from the point of view of the converted Christian.

Auer detects an inhibition on Döblin's part against dealing directly and in a realistic manner with the events of 1933, their precedents and their consequences. In *Pardon wird nicht gegeben*, the conscious effort to eliminate specific references to historical events, although they remain clearly recognizable, points to an inner difficulty that is equally evident in *Der neue Urwald*, where the author still avoids the word "Nationalsozialismus." However, this text, with all its imperfections and inner contradictions, draws closer to the central problems that Döblin would finally confront in *November 1918*.

Helmuth Kiesel's chapter on *Amazonas* is titled "Generalabrechnung mit der europäischen Zivilisation" (A General Accounting with European Civilization). He uses Döblin's own characterization of the novel in his book of 1938 *Die deutsche Literatur (im Ausland seit 1933)* (48). This reckoning with Western civilization is, as Kiesel sees it, intertwined with another overriding concern, the search for a "Noah's Ark" (232) before the coming flood engulfs humanity and specifically the Jews. Döblin's description of the Jesuit republic in Paraguay includes the beauty, the limitations, and the necessary downfall of such a haven in the midst of war's violence, and it mirrors Döblin's skepticism with regard to the search for a safe Jewish homeland.

Kiesel observes that *Amazonas* in its three diverse parts is characterized by an almost total absence of a discernable narrator. This makes it more difficult to define the author's standpoint in regard to the basic dichotomy of Western civilization versus the "primitive" Indios. While Döblin's harsh criticism of the conquistadors and, by extension, of twentieth-century Europe is unmistakable, his attitude toward the pre-Columbian world of South America is less obvious. His depiction of the Indian mentality and way of life is sympathetic and largely positive, although he does not idealize it as a peaceful idyll; he makes clear that there had been bloody conflicts and enslavement before the arrival of the white conquerors. But Döblin finds that the history of the Indian civilizations indicates a way to escape from barbaric slaughter and sacrifices and reach a peaceful world. When the white soldiers appear, the Indians see them first as gods and then as evil demons, until they recognize them for what they are: desperados, "unglückliche und verzweifelte Menschen," ejected from the volcano Europe. The European murderers are accompanied by some saints. For Kiesel, Döblin's representation of this process of colonization, of conflict between rational and mythical attitudes, is something like a prelude to Horkheimer and Adorno's discussion of rationality and myth in *Die Dialektik der Aufklärung* (252).

Roland Dollinger, in his *Totalität und Totalitarismus im Exilwerk Döblins,* offers an analysis of the text as an allegory in the sense of Walter Benjamin, comparing Benjamin's interpretations of the Baroque *Trauerspiel* with Döblin's view of history and nature. Dollinger considers Döblin's views as expressed in *Der historische Roman und wir* and his use of allegory in the novel as closely connected with the debate on Realism, in which Döblin came down on the side of the avant-gardists like Brecht against Lukács's concept of realism and the symbolic form of literature, although Döblin differed sharply with Brecht on the application of Marxism.

Amazonas offers, as Dollinger demonstrates, a series of examples demonstrating the powerlessness of man in a struggle with nature and the futility of all attempts to achieve progress in the face of the eternal repetition of the same. The antithesis of the two views — eternal repetition and the Western idea of progress — is articulated in Döblin's essay "Prometheus und das Primitive," as well as in the "Zwischenspiel" that introduces *Der neue Urwald,* an episode that takes place in St. Mary's Church in Cracow, where Twardowski, a Faustian figure of Polish legends, confronts the founding fathers of modern Western thinking, Copernicus, Galilei, and Giordano Bruno, with the disastrous consequences of their worldview.

For Dollinger, the experiment of the Jesuit republic in Paraguay proves the impossibility of a truly Christian government and state, as both their pacifism and their total mind control are doomed to fail. The Jesuits cannot escape the wheels of history, and their experiment results in a retreat to the jungle. The colonization of world by the white peoples becomes total at the point when the other races internalize "white" thinking and aggression. In the end, says Dollinger, nature wins the struggle between nature and God for the men of history in the *Amazonas* trilogy (151). Döblin opposes the course of Western civilization since the Renaissance and sees hope only in small groups of heretics and mystics who seek a different path.

Erwin Kobel's short chapter on *Amazonas* dwells on the contradictions between the "Unbehausten," the Europeans who have no home and thus strive to conquer the world, and "das Häusliche," being rooted in one's own world, as the Jesuits try to create it for themselves and the Indios.[6] Both the Jesuits and the Indios are destroyed, and in a pessimistic view of history it is up to the reader to supply the hope for a third path between the extremes, for a center that no one reaches in this work. Neither the Promethean principle nor the primitive world can be models for a livable future.

In his article "Der entfesselte Prometheus oder die Eroberung Südamerikas aus der Sicht Alfred Döblins"[7] Helmut F. Pfanner emphasizes two points: first, the relevance of the third part of the work, "Der neue Urwald," and its close thematic connection with the other parts; and second, its relation to Döblin's essay of 1938, "Prometheus und das Primitive." For Pfanner it is the overall perspective on humanity and its history, and not the specific experience of the white colonization of South America, that determines the structure and the narrative manner of the trilogy. Pfanner poses the question whether the customary title *Amazonas* really corresponds to the intention of the author or whether it would be preferable to call the trilogy for instance *Das Land ohne Tod.*

Teresa Delgado, in her article "Poetische Anthropologie. Interkulturelles Schreiben in Döblins Amazonas-Trilogie und Hubert Fichtes *Explosion. Roman der Ethnologie,*"[8] considers *Amazonas* in the context of a critique of the anthropological perspective. Döblin makes the effort, especially in the first part, to view the world, and colonization in particular, from the point of view of the Indios, who were by no means "Naturvölker," but nations with a very different civilization. Döblin was not primarily interested in the facts, but tried to give a voice to the Indios, lending them a language that historical discourse had denied them. In this way, Döblin seems to be the first German author since Chamisso to explore "the other side"; he tries to establish in his novel the communication that the white conquerors have denied to the natives.

Notes

[1] Jacob Erhardt, *Alfred Döblins Amazonas-Trilogie,* Deutsches Exil 1933–45, vol. 3 (Worms: Georg Heintz Verlag, 1974).

[2] George Bernard Sperber, *Wegweiser im "Amazonas": Studien zur Rezeption, zu den Quellen und zur Textkritik der Südamerika-Trilogie Alfred Döblins,* tuduv studien, Reihe Sprach- und Literaturwissenschaften vol. 2 (Munich: tuduv-Verlagsgesellschaft, 1975).

[3] Theodor Koch-Grünberg, *Zwei Jahre unter den Indianern* (2 vols., Berlin, 1910); most importantly: *Indianermärchen aus Südamerika* (Jena: Eugen Diederichs, 1920), one of the volumes of the series *Märchen der Weltliteratur;* and *Zwei Jahre bei den Indianern Nordwest-Brasiliens* (Berlin 1921).

[4] Roland Links, *Alfred Döblin: Leben und Werk* (Berlin: Volk und Wissen, 1976), 164–80.

[5] Manfred Auer, *Das Exil vor der Vertreibung: Motivkontinuität und Quellenproblematik im späten Werk Alfred Döblins* (Bonn: Bouvier Verlag Herbert Grundmann, 1977), 41–56.

[6] Erwin Kobel, *Alfred Döblin: Erzählkunst im Umbruch* (Berlin/New York: Walter de Gruyter, 1985), 312–35.

[7] In two somewhat different versions in *Literatur und Geschichte: Festschrift für Wulf Koepke zum 70. Geburtstag,* ed. Karl Menges. Amsterdamer Publikationen zur Sprache und Literatur 133 (Amsterdam/Atlanta: Rodopi, 1998), 155–170, and *Internationales Alfred-Döblin-Kolloquium Leipzig 1997,* ed. Ira Lorf and Gabriele Sander (Bern: Peter Lang, 1999), 135–50.

[8] "Poetische Anthropologie. Interkulturelles Schreiben in Döblins *Amazonas*-Trilogie und Hubert Fichtes *Explosion. Roman der Ethnologie.*" *Internationales Alfred-Döblin-Kolloquium Leipzig 1997,* ed. Lorf and Sander, 151–66.

13: *November 1918*

DÖBLIN CALLED NOVEMBER 1918 an "Erzählwerk," not a novel, since it narrates the events of German history from November 1918 to January 1919 on the basis of documents, and mixes historical and fictional characters. It was to be a trilogy, but the second volume grew to be too long, and Döblin divided it into two parts, thus creating the tetralogy *November 1918: Eine deutsche Revolution.*[1] Döblin began writing the work at the end of 1937, and the first volume, *Bürger und Soldaten 1918,* was published in Holland in 1939. The manuscript of the second and third volumes, *Verratenes Volk* and *Heimkehr der Fronttruppen,* was virtually complete in 1940 when Döblin had to flee from Paris to escape the advancing German army, and was revised in Los Angeles. The last volume, *Karl und Rosa,* was written there in 1942 and 1943. Döblin was unable to publish any of the volumes either in German or in English during his exile in the United States, except for an episode entitled *Nocturno,* which was published by the Pazifische Presse of Los Angeles in 1944, and segments of the non-fictional part, titled *Sieger und Besiegte* and published by Aurora Verlag of New York in 1946. The second, third, and fourth volumes were first published by the Alber Verlag, Munich, between 1948 and 1950; the first volume had to be left out of this edition because of French censorship. In 1978, the Deutscher Taschenbuch Verlag re-published this edition along with the first volume of 1939; a fully satisfactory edition did not appear until the 1990 *Ausgewählte Werke* volume.

This tortured and delayed publication history helps explain the very belated and hesitant reception of the work, one of Döblin's major texts. It was the 1978 dtv paperback that finally made a noticeable impact and generated critical attention, which first became evident in the Basel and New York symposia of the nascent Alfred Döblin Society between 1980 and 1983.[2] The dtv edition included an afterword by Heinz D. Osterle, which had first been published in *Monatshefte* in 1970 and later reprinted in an abbreviated version in Ingrid Schuster's collection *Über Alfred Döblin.*[3] Osterle confronted the bias of previous critics who considered *November 1918* problematic for ideological reasons and inferior in aesthetic terms, and maintained that it is one of Döblin's major works, and worthy of attention on precisely the same counts on which it had been criticized: ideology and aesthetics (161). Osterle recognizes a basic contradiction in this long narrative work between utopian hope for a radical transformation of society and religious hope for a radical transcendence of all earthly things (163). For Osterle, the last volume, *Karl und Rosa*, is in every respect the climax of the work (164). The revolution appears as a sad comedy with all the comic devices, chief among them irony, satire, and grotesque (166). Döblin transcends all limits of conventional realistic narratives. Becker, the central figure for the religious dimension, is a Faustian being who is saved in spite of his bet with the devil, a parodistic descendent of Goethe's Faust and a strange predecessor of Thomas Mann's Doktor Faustus (167–70).

Osterle reminds us however that the central theme is the German revolution (170–76), as Döblin attempts to humanize its leaders Karl Liebknecht and Rosa Luxemburg — although in the case of Luxemburg it is undeniable that he invented or disproportionately exaggerated her pathological traits, presenting her as all too human. The true revolution embodied by them can be compared to what Ernst Bloch called "das Prinzip Hoffnung" (172). Luxemburg became in Döblin's eyes a mystic and a "Gottsucherin," as Robert Minder had already noted (176). The "epilogue," the last part of the last volume, while dominated by the eternal journey of Friedrich Becker, also demonstrates how the revolution (personified) had left the country and tried to find another home or at least a refuge.

One of the first positive reactions to the Deutscher Taschenbuch Verlag edition came from Hans Mayer, first in *Der Spiegel* in 1978, and later reprinted in a volume of his essays.[4] The original title of the review, "Eine deutsche Revolution. Also keine" indicates Mayer's primarily political reading, and he underscores its significance. He says of Döblin's account of the assassination of Liebknecht and Luxemburg: "Größeres hat Döblin nicht geschrieben" (69–70). Mayer goes on to say that despite the book's literary weaknesses, which in no way mitigate its great epic accomplishment, it is in its conception and narrative form Döblin's most important and consistent work (67–68). Mayer contrasts the novel's reception with that of Thomas Mann's *Doktor Faustus* and Hesse's *Das Glasperlenspiel,* two other novels of the same period that he believes it rivals in stature, contending that Döblin's epic should have been debated as vigorously as those books during the postwar years. Mayer sees clearly the dual combat depicted in *November 1918* "auf der Erde wie in den Lüften" (67). But he points the readers' attention to the earthly struggle and to Döblin's account of so many assassinations and irreplacable losses for German society in the twenties: *November 1918* is more than the account of a failed revolution, it is the narration of a fatal bleeding of the German people and its spirit. For Döblin, neither Lenin nor Liebknecht found the right way out of the impasse. Therefore a political solution had become impossible, and the religious or metaphysical turn was a logical consequence.

Two studies of 1979, by Wolfgang Düsing and Roland Links, can be seen as a response to the 1978 centennial of Döblin's birth and to the new edition of *November 1918*. Wolfgang Düsing's article "Das Epos der Weimarer Republik. Döblins Romanzyklus *November 1918*" appeared in a volume edited by Werner Link with the title *Schriftsteller und Politik in Deutschland*.[5] Düsing refers to the added attention given to Döblin's work since the centennial, and specifically to *November 1918*. He mentions the studies of Osterle and Auer, and summarizes the publication history. *November 1918* is, for Düsing, "eminent episch": it offers the depiction of a world in its totality (51). In accordance with the overall topic of writers and politics, Düsing concentrates on the failed revolution and Döblin's views on the political events. It is a fragmentary picture, seen from changing perspectives (53). The chaotic events, which lead to no real conclusion, are reflected in the narrative structure and perspective. In its fight against the danger of a communist revolution, the Weimar Republic disregarded the fascist threat that would later bring it down. Düsing disagrees with previous scholars who thought that Döblin identified himself with the point of view of the Spartacists, specifically Luxemburg. Rather, he finds that Döblin criticizes Liebknecht and Luxemburg from a political or strategic point of view, although he may agree with their ideals. There seem to be no solutions in the political realm, and this is where the fictional characters come in; they also have a connecting and integrating function (57). Düsing sees an integration of these figures, Friedrich Becker in particular, into the context of the political events, as the historical misery of the Weimar Republic is shown in the individual fates of the fictional characters (59). Becker is the only one who knows how to read the signs of the times (60). However, even he does not arrive at a total insight. *November 1918* is for Düsing a transitional work in its structure and outlook, leading to a next definitive step, Döblin's last novel, *Hamlet*. The open ending of *November 1918*, typical for most novels of Döblin, indicates that he is still on his way.

Roland Links's article "Mit Geschichte will man etwas. Alfred Döblin: *November 1918*" is part of the collection *Erfahrung Exil*, edited by Sigrid Bock and Manfred Hahn, and consisting of contributions from scholars from the GDR offering interpretations of fourteen novels by exile authors.[6] The overall thrust of the volume is antifascism, and Roland Links, who was later able to edit a four-volume edition of *November 1918* for publication in the GDR, felt obliged to justify Döblin's kind of antifascism and his "unorthodox" representation of the events of 1918/19. The first section of the article, under the subheading "Parteilichkeit des Tätigen," introduces the reader to the gestation period of the work and to Döblin's views on history and the historical novel, as expressed in *Der historische Roman und wir* of 1936 (328–37). Links stresses the crucial importance of the first volume of *November 1918, Bürger und Soldaten 1918,* which had been largely omitted in the three-volume edition of 1948–50 because of French censorship. This is the volume in which Döblin provides the description of the German masses, which makes the subsequent failure of the revolution comprehensible. Links also refers to Brecht's praise of this volume and his characterization of *November 1918* as a "Roman von Experimentalcharakter" (335), with the caveat that in 1940 Brecht had called Döblin's works "Dokumente der Ausweglosigkeit" (336). Still, Döblin had taken up a partisan position in the novels on the revolution, even if he left it up to the reader to draw the final conclusions (336).

Links emphasizes the sometimes neglected ironic distance of Döblin's narrator from the events and the characters. Even Friedrich Becker does not escape occasional ironic remarks by the narrator, although it is "beyond doubt that the author has taken the side of this character from the beginning. Inordinate demands are placed on the reader with this figure Becker" (340). The reader has to decide in each instance whether the narrator is identifying himself with Becker, using him as a "Sonde" or probe, or treating him with irony. This is complicated even more by the fact that it is possible to interpret Becker's crises as being due to mental illness — which according to Links they are not. Links reminds us of Döblin's original subtitle "Waffen und Gewissen," weapons and conscience, which are the two poles between which the characters are located. The writer Stauffer, a caricature of the author, represents the German intellectuals who did not take sides or whose ideas were so unrealistic as to deprive the revolution of a possibly crucial support (343).

For Links, the last volume, *Karl und Rosa,* does not continue the theme of revolution in the same manner, but begins again on a different basis. Whereas the previous volumes reflected Döblin's involvement in the antifascist struggle during the years of his exile in Paris, the last volume is an expression of his "Abgeschiedenheit," his total isolation in Los Angeles. Still, it is significant that Becker gets involved in the revolution, and that Döblin wrote an essay titled "Christentum und Revolution" as late as 1950. Links agrees with other critics and with Döblin's own statement from his *Epilog*: "Jedes Buch endet (für mich) mit einem Fragezeichen. Jedes Buch wirft am Ende einem neuen den Ball zu" (351). And referring to the entire text, Links notes that "Viel steht in diesem 'Erzählwerk' neben-, manches gegeneinander," for instance: "der Fatalismus Beckers neben seiner Aktivität" (350). But according to Links, Döblin's account opens up the realization that an individual endeavor to help or to change a situation "can culminate in a revolutionary action when it is demanded by a decision of conscience" (351). The revolutionary deed comes from the depth of the individual's conscience, the depth of the individual soul. We must presume that "revolution" still means socialist, that is, political revolution.

Manfred Auer devotes a long chapter in his 1977 book *Das Exil vor der Vertreibung* to this work, which at the time of his writing had been undervalued if not ignored.[7] His investigation includes work on the manuscripts and on the sources for Döblin's account of the events of 1918/19.[8] He was the first who was able to give a precise description of the extant manuscripts and typescripts of *November 1918*, of the subsequent changes and corrections, and of Döblin's extensive use of historical source material. Döblin often quoted verbatim, but more often he paraphrased and used only specific formulations. In this manner, he amalgamated the historical documents with his overall fictional framework.

Auer discusses in detail the then very relevant question of whether the work is a trilogy or a tetralogy. The evidence leads him to the conclusion that Döblin intended to write a trilogy; however, the second volume, *Verratenes Volk*, grew to be too long and had to be separated, "zerlegt," into two parts, the second receiving the title *Heimkehr der Fronttruppen*. Therefore, while it is necessary to print the entire work in four volumes, as was done by dtv in 1978, the inner structure remains that of a trilogy, and the second and third volumes should be called II,1 and II,2 — as was done in the edition of the *Ausgewählte Werke*. This problem is much more significant than it seems at first sight, and although Auer's very detailed discussion has resulted in a consensus of the scholars and thus seems irrelevant today, it still offers the first decisive insight into the structure of the work and the specific character of its three parts, which after all comprise a text of more than 2000 pages.

Auer offers several examples of how Döblin uses specific sources, newspapers and books, usually by shortening the original text and giving it a more explicit and provocative point (65–78). Döblin preferred books that offered a partisan view of the facts and thus provoke a partisan response; in other words, he is anything but neutral in his choice of texts, and consequently in his narrative stance. This is even more pronounced in the case of his portrayal of Rosa Luxemburg and Karl Liebknecht, whom he shows from a personal, intimate, rather than a public point of view. In general, Auer finds it remarkable how Döblin succeeds in integrating the most heterogeneous materials and details and never fails to follow his main direction. Inevitably, some of the innumerable facts are wrong or only partially correct, but the overall picture remains factual, although Döblin manages to stamp his own very personal interpretation on the events, sometimes by his choice of details, sometimes by direct or indirect value judgments, sometimes by irony and sarcasm.

In the "fictional" part of *November 1918*, the action dealing with figures like Friedrich Becker, Maus, and Hilde, among others, it is evident to Auer that, while the factual historical context is preserved, the characters experience fundamental problems known from Döblin's previous works: the disorientation of the soldier returning from the war, the quest for love as a way out of a senseless life, and the Ich-Suche (search for the self), especially in the case of Becker. Becker's Ich-Suche is connected with his guilt feelings stemming from the war and its atrocities. For him, the acknowledgment of this guilt and responsibility is the first step to a new life and the needed transformation of society. But his *Heimkehr*, his return home, proves to be a failure, like the German revolution, and like Döblin's own return to Germany in 1945.

Auer considers the parallel scenes of the last volume, *Karl und Rosa*, around Becker and Rosa Luxemburg respectively, as "Engführung," like a stretto in a musical fugue of the themes of Christianity and revolution (85–88). He does not deny the contradictions between these two ideals, which had already clashed in earlier texts by Döblin, but here he finds that what he calls a "christlich motivierten Humanitätsgedanken" brings them together (87). Auer is able to reach this conclusion because he downplays the religious component, finding that despite the book's religious tendencies, it is not on the whole edifying ("erbaulich") and that its telos is not comprised only of its religious component (87). There is a telos and a "Tendenz," and just as in *Wallenstein*, Döblin does not narrate the events for their own sake. Rather, he appropriates historical facts and figures for the purpose of the "Tendenz": this is a basic creative mode of Döblin's (89). The word "Inbesitznahme" is most significant; Döblin appropriates the facts for his own cause. This implies that Döblin's appropriation is not directed by aesthetic considerations, but that instead he forms the past "unter Gegenwartsaspekt," that is, according to the moral and political criteria of the present (90). The narrator of *November 1918* never predicts National Socialism, although indirectly it becomes clear why the Nazis were able to come to power, but it is evident from the text that preparations for the next war have already begun. Two main points have to be considered, according to Auer. First, for Döblin, 1918/19 was a historical threshold, a moment of openness with the potential for movement in opposite political directions, for the good or the bad (91). This must be seen in connection with the second point, which concerns Döblin's view of socialism and revolution. Döblin wanted to amalgamate his humanitarian socialism, opposed to class struggle, with his Christianity, claiming that Christianity and revolution are one and the same. They are transpolitical, above politics, above political parties and their ideologies and conflicts. This brings Döblin close to Ernst Toller, Gustav Landauer, and Kurt Eisner. For Döblin, this is the "Menschlichkeit" that Rosa Luxemburg was striving to achieve. But for Auer the humanitarian and socialist aspects and the Christian part represented by Friedrich Becker cannot be completely integrated, and this remains the unsolvable contradiction of the trilogy (96). This is also evident from the point of view of narrative techniques and structure.

Auer offers short comparisons with other fictional representations of the German revolution: Bernhard Kellermann's *Der 9. November,* Georg Hermann's *November achtzehn,* and Theodor Plievier's *Der Kaiser ging, die Generäle blieben.* Kellermann's emphasis is on the pre-history of the revolution, Hermann fictionalizes aspects of Kurt Eisner's role in it, and Plievier is primarily interested in the political events of the November days to understand how the foundations for the new Germany were laid. The comparison makes evident how ambitious Döblin's project was, and that he really wanted to achieve too much, resulting in an inevitable (at least partial) failure — a fact, according to Auer, which would be equally true for *Hamlet.*

Eight of the papers from the Döblin symposia of 1980 and 1981 and one from 1983 focused on specific parts and aspects of the *November* trilogy. Two of them deal with Antigone: Otto Keller's "Tristan und Antigone. Gestus, Verfremdung, und Montage als Medien der Figurgestaltung in Döblins 'November 1918'" and Heinz D. Osterle's "Auf den Spuren der Antigone: Sophokles, Döblin, Brecht."[9] Keller identifies the Antigone paradigm as that of helping others, overcoming death, and opposing the spirit of conquest and destruction, and he opposes this with the Tristan paradigm, meaning Isolde's "Liebestod" after Tristan's death, characterized by egocentric ecstasy and the longing for death. Keller recognizes the variations of the Antigone model in Becker's participation in the director's funeral, Heinz's refusal to turn against the director, and Minna Imker's fight in the Polizeipräsidium. These two models reappear, always in competition: most prominently in Rosa Luxemburg's struggles for the dead Hannes' love and against Satan. They demonstrate Döblin's new way of looking at character as something changing and unstable and his following the structural principles of *Gestus* and montage, as Keller had demonstrated them for *Berlin Alexanderplatz*. Döblin's use of these models turns his epics into parodies, as the journeys of both Becker and Rosa Luxemburg reveal themselves as parodies of Goethe's Faust and his striving. As Keller expresses it: "Liest man den November-Roman von dem Gestus aus, als eine in gigantisches Maß gesteigerte Partitur, so erhält man hier ein Epochengemälde von einer geistigen Dichte und Intensität, wie es sonst in der deutschen Literatur in der ersten Hälfte unseres Jahrhunderts nur ganz selten zu finden ist" (18).

Heinz D. Osterle goes back to Sophocles and to the reception of *Antigone* by the late Goethe and by Hegel and Hölderlin. There are three ways to look at the Antigone-Kreon conflict. Kreon can be seen as an unjustified tyrant (as by Goethe), Kreon and Antigone can be shown as representatives of two opposing, yet both partially justified principles in a dialectic process (Hegel), and finally, Kreon can be seen (by adherents of "law and order") as defending society and the state against Antigone's revolutionary chaos. Osterle analyzes Döblin's point of view and then proceeds to a comparison with Brecht, Hasenclever, and Anouilh.

Friedrich Becker appears before his Gymnasium students initially as a severely injured war hero, but they cannot comprehend his siding with Antigone and her right to fulfill her duty, ordained by the divine powers, to bury her fallen brother. For them, Kreon represents the authority of the state. Moreover, the "girl" Antigone has no right to interfere with the male order of the nation. For the students, the correct attitude is represented by Heinrich von Kleist's Prinz Friedrich von Homburg, who comes to recognize the supreme authority of the state. They reject completely Becker's talk of guilt, sin, and atonement. Becker and the students are primarily interested in the parallels between the Antigone-Kreon conflict and the German situation of 1918/19. Becker feels the need, like Antigone, to mourn the dead in the proper manner and to come to grips with the guilt of the living, who caused the slaughter. But the students deny that Germany bears any guilt in causing the war; to them, such guilt is only something the Allies want to impose on the German people from without. This would be repeated after 1945, when the Germans fiercely denied any "Kollektivschuld," collective guilt, in the Holocaust. Döblin, writing in 1942/43, remembered 1918 and feared a repetition of the same after the end of the Second World War. Döblin/Becker's interpretation of *Antigone* shows clear traces of both Hegel's and Kierkegaard's positions. The significance of these three "lessons" by Becker is underscored both by allusions to Antigone in Becker's future nomadic life and by a connection between Antigone and Rosa Luxemburg. Osterle refers to Hans Mayer's definition and description of the "Außenseiter," the outsiders, as a paradigm for their personal revolution and the fate of both Antigone and Luxemburg (100–101).

The importance of the Antigone paradigm and Döblin's debate on Sophocles' tragedy is much enhanced, according to Osterle, by a comparison with contemporary and subsequent plays and reinterpretations. He cites Walter Hasenclever, Bertolt Brecht, Jean Anouilh, Käte Hamburger's discussion of them, Walter Jens's *Sophokles und Brecht,* and finally, Heinrich Böll's script for Volker Schlöndorff's segment of *Deutschland im Herbst.* Although only an episode in Döblin's vast panorama of Germany and its history, the *Antigone* lessons touch on central issues of revolution and authority, of duty, guilt, and freedom.

Wolfgang Frühwald, in his contribution "Rosa und der Satan," views *November 1918* from the perspective of its last volume, *Karl und Rosa.*[10] The volume is a result of a conversion in a religious, political, and literary sense, says Frühwald:

> Der darwinistisch-naturwissenschaftliche Grundzug früherer Texte Döblins ist besonders im letzten Band von *November 1918* zurückgenommen und durch eine Position ersetzt, die das Christentum dem Heidentum, den Jenseitsglauben der Selektionstheorie (als einem Glaubenssatz), den Willen zur menschlichen Gemeinschaft dem Sozialdarwinismus jener Generation von 1890 bis etwa 1910 gegenüberstellte, aus deren Handlungs- und Tatorientierung sich der Nationalsozialismus ideologisch nährte. (242)

Frühwald refers specifically to the *Antigone* episode and Döblin's understanding of the figure of Antigone in Kierkegaard's terms. This "menschliche Gemeinschaft" can be identified as the community envisioned by the anarchist philosophers Peter Kropotkin and Gustav Landauer, the ideal of authors close to the USPD, such as Ernst Toller. For Frühwald, Döblin's depiction of the human being as a "Kampfplatz zwischen Gut und Böse" is a modern re-enactment of the mythical "Engelkampf," the struggle between the loyal and the fallen angels — that is, Satan — translated into the confrontation between the Darwinist theory of natural selection and Peter Kropotkin's emphasis on solidarity based on natural law (240).

For Frühwald, part of this struggle is for a new form of art. In *Karl und Rosa* Döblin turns sharply against art as aestheticism, the prime example of which is the work of Richard Wagner (246). But he does not aim to oppose only music, opera, and *Tristan und Isolde*, but also the "intellektual-essayistische Roman," which for Döblin has become the "literarisch-künstlerische Erscheinungsform des darwinistischen Monismus, der die Zerstörung der Person und die Etablierung des Nichts erstrebt" (247). For Friedrich Becker, Richard Wagner has poured poisonous drugs into the legend of Tristan and Isolde, and he has become particularly hostile to the idea of the "Liebestod," death as the highest fulfillment of love (and life), which is similar and related to the idea of heroic death in war (247).

Frühwald believes that Döblin wanted to undertake in this last volume of *November 1918* the great experiment of a renewal of the religious epic, which has no tradition in Germany except for Klopstock (248). But his model and "mythische Rahmen" is not, as the majority of the scholars seem to think, Goethe's *Faust*, but John Milton's *Paradise Lost*, if not Dante's *Divina commedia* (249). *Paradise Lost* is quoted by Karl Liebknecht to Rosa Luxemburg in the last hours before their arrest; but beyond this scene, there are many parallels between Milton's story of the Fall and *Karl und Rosa* (250). Frühwald also points to connections between this volume and *Berlin Alexanderplatz,* beginning with the paradigm of Everyman, by which he refers both to Biberkopf and to Becker. Thus, on the whole, he removes the volume from the realm of secular literature and views it as the revival of a religious epic.

Heidi Thomann Tewarson, in "Alfred Döblins Geschichtskonzeption in *November 1918,*"[11] examines Rosa Luxemburg's character in *Karl und Rosa* on the basis of the historical facts. Döblin wrote a historical novel, and his later review of Luxemburg's letters to friends indicates his familiarity with them and understanding of her life and personality. It is obvious, however, that Döblin is not concerned with Rosa Luxemburg the genius, the social scientist, the woman totally devoted to the cause, and her enormous self-discipline (67). Instead, he follows a few leads in her letters from prison indicating a tendency toward daydreaming and fantasizing, and builds her entire character on this basis. But contrary to Döblin's depiction, says Tewarson, Luxemburg stayed very much in contact with the "outer world," the real world, and her occasional hallucinations could be called normal under the circumstances. Döblin's characterization produces an image of a hallucinating woman with a masochistic relationship with her dead lover Hans Diefenbach, and largely eliminates the significance of her intellectual and political activities (68). This is glaringly true for the account of her activities after her release from prison: "Luxemburg ist im Roman die schwache, verzweifelte Frau, die nicht ein noch aus weiß" (69). In real life Luxemburg kept her belief in the necessity and the advent of the real revolution intact, but Döblin makes her the voice of his pessimism and ahistoricism (70). There is no evidence in historical documents for the Christian humility Döblin portrays Luxemburg showing at the end of her life. Finally, concerning masochism, with its aspect of subjugation, Tewarson points out that it is documented how Luxemburg fought for liberty and equality, especially of man and woman, not only in the public arena, but also in her relationship with Diefenbach. Thus, although Döblin wrote a historical novel, he did not really confront the crucial historical questions, among them the position of women, and could not, therefore, render a fair and adequate portrait of one of the eminent personalities of the age. Instead, he merely integrated her portrait into his previous views on women and of conflicts between the sexes.

Several contributions deal with Döblin's concept of history in *November 1918* in a more general way. David Dollenmayer offers an overview in "Der Wandel in Döblins Auffassung von der deutschen Revolution 1918–1919."[12] He traces the concept of revolution and revolutionaries from Döblin's first commentary on November 1918, "Revolutionstage im Elsaß," to *November 1918*, including pertinent passages from the Linke Poot columns, from 1928's *Erster Rückblick*, and from *Pardon wird nicht gegeben*. Döblin's preoccupation with a German revolution was a constant in his writings, but he came to believe early on that the idea of "revolutionary masses" was an oxymoron, that revolution came from rare individuals, and particularly in Germany, from outsiders. Consequently he portrayed Liebknecht, Luxemburg, Eisner, and eventually the fictional Friedrich Becker as exemplary outsiders. The idea of their preordained failure, which transformed them into *Opfer*, victims, could be made consistent with his growing Christian faith. Dollenmayer elaborates these ideas in the *November 1918* chapter of his 1988 book *The Berlin Novels of Alfred Döblin*.[13] Dollenmayer finds that Döblin had a clear social and political purpose, namely the examination of the origins of the German disaster, and what individuals could have done to prevent it (125). He states that the similarities with the previous Berlin novels are rather superficial, and that there are more genuine parallels with Hermann Broch's *Die Schlafwandler*, specifically its third part, and Anna Seghers's *Die Toten bleiben jung* (125–26). The cities around which the action revolves, Strasbourg and then Berlin, have ambiguous faces. Strasbourg is deceptively lovely, yet it engulfs the unsuspecting Germans, who are suddenly declared unwelcome strangers. Berlin emerges as dangerous and chaotic; its inhabitants have lost control of their lives (132). Here the montages of *Berlin Alexanderplatz* reappear in a new form: "Döblin still has the sudden shift of narrative tense and tone and the film-like cuts of *Berlin Alexanderplatz* at his command, but now the psychological truth they convey is simultaneously a political truth about the sources of both the revolution and of the counterrevolution which would crush it" (135). From the point of view of Friedrich Becker, the city appears at first sight as a "good city filled with helpers" (139), but this is deceptive; very soon it will unmask its murderous brutality. The narrator, according to Dollenmayer, while omniscient in comparison with the narrator of *Berlin Alexanderplatz*, is also "heterogeneous in his modes" (142). He declares his sympathies and antipathies openly, for instance in the case of Friedrich Ebert, who is mercilessly satirized (144–46). However, there is something more powerful involved: "Throughout the tetralogy the suggestion recurs that the revolution ultimately founders on the German character itself" (153). Thus there is no political solution. Instead, the narrator gives us "the story of Friedrich Becker as a counterpoise and commentary on the aborted revolution" (156). Tortured by guilt and self-doubt, Becker begins to change: "Personal change is . . . thrust on Becker by the catastrophe of war and is structured by narrative reference to three literary-mythical antecedents: Faust, Antigone, and Christ" (159). The Faust connection is the least explicit one, yet it is unmistakable (159–61). There is the repeated reference to Mephisto, the melancholy of the isolated man, and the parallels between the suicide attempt of Faust and that of Becker. The "postfiguration" of the life of Christ ends with the disappearance of Becker's body. As Dollenmayer says, "It is one of the most anticlimactic of Döblin's many anticlimactic endings" (168).

Dollenmayer discusses briefly Döblin's very ambiguous treatment of women, especially Hilde and Rosa Luxemburg, whose characterizations seem to be as uncertain and misplaced as that of the writer Stauffer. And while Becker's conversion is conceived as the spiritual center of the novel, for Dollenmayer it is its most problematic aspect (177). The total failure of the revolution and the death of idealists like Ede Imker seem to mirror the writer's "despair in his helpless exile in Los Angeles" rather than being a signal pointed to the future (178). As Dollenmayer puts it, "this is a highly problematic resolution of the dichotomy of rebellion and submission" (183).

Erich Kleinschmidt, in his article "Parteiliche Fiktionalität,"[14] deals with Döblin's "Schreibanliegen" in exile, his motivation to write, the concerns he wanted to address with his writing, and the forms that he chose to write in. Kleinschmidt finds that Döblin's motivation to write was, despite his rejection of plainly partisan writing, still defined by social and political concerns (117). Kleinschmidt senses in Döblin's exile texts a sometimes more, sometimes less veiled "Trauerarbeit an Deutschland" which he believes held a true existential necessity for him at the time (120). (This formulation by Kleinschmidt predates Helmuth Kiesel's book devoted to this dimension of Döblin's writing.) For Kleinschmidt, Döblin did not advance during his exile years, especially in narrative strategies, but employed previous techniques in a more self-reflexive manner, a new "Privatheit" with which he tried to reach clarity about his own position. Döblin did not change his previous attitudes toward the Weimar Republic. But when he wrote *November 1918*, he made the point that he, too, had been part of the Weimar establishment, and he included himself in the satirical picture he painted of the past, for instance in the character of Stauffer and the other writers portrayed. The text reveals Döblin's ongoing preoccupation with the failure of the Weimar democracy. In Kleinschmidt's view *November 1918* is, like Döblin's other novels, an open text, one that does not try to hide the gestation process in which the author confronts his material, but instead makes a point of revealing it (123). It is however Döblin's text that determines the historical perspective, not vice versa: the facts of reality do not determine the narrative process, but instead the narrative process determines what to include from reality based on its needs (124). Thus, Kleinschmidt says, one might understand *November 1918* as a kind of "epic ballad" (126). It could be understood as an oral narration, as an attempt to reach out for an audience that Döblin knew was not there, but that he needed to imagine when he wrote his work.

Ernst Ribbat's article "Döblin, Brecht und das Problem des historischen Romans"[15] compares *November 1918* as a historical novel with Brecht's *Dreigroschenroman* and his Caesar and "Tui" projects. If Brecht's projects eventually ended in failure, it was in good part because they were more ambitious than those of the other authors of the German exile, except perhaps Döblin. Ribbat analyzes the first volume *Bürger und Soldaten 1918*, the text that was praised by Brecht. If one looks at *November 1918* from the perspective of the original first volume, one arrives at very different results than by looking backward from the last volume, *Karl und Rosa*, which explains in part the divergence of views on *November 1918*. The first part is more homogeneous than the subsequent volumes; it is much more assured in its language, more colorful and precise in its depiction of characters and events (38). What the first volume shows, according to Ribbat, is the effect of the crisis on various people and groups of people, an awareness of what the term "revolution" really meant in the reality of experience (39). In the subsequent two volumes, this perspective on the reality of the revolution is expanded and decisively altered by bringing in the decision-makers, the politicians, together with the ordinary people. As Ribbat formulates it: "Die Realität der Geschichte als eines umfassenden Prozesses, in dem jeder einzelne Opfer und Mitwirkender ist, Einfluß ausüben kann und doch ohnmächtig ist — diese Erkenntnis ist im ganzen Werk dargestellt" (40). "Erkenntnis" is the crucial word here: Reading *Bürger und Soldaten* gives one an understanding of what the revolution in Germany was, and what it could have been (41). For Ribbat, the later parts of the work provide this awareness only from time to time, with private and public stories going in different directions. Ribbat sees a successor to Döblin in Uwe Johnson, who in his novel *Jahrestage* is more successful than Döblin at bringing history to reality as both a private and a public matter (42).

Wulf Koepke, in his article "Spontane Ansätze zur Überwindung der Individuation,"[16] also concentrates on the first volume, and compares Döblin with Brecht. Koepke's basic point is that the work develops its own dynamic out of the fundamental rhythm of its language. This dynamic builds up to the individual scenes and gradually comes to carry the structure of the entire work. *Bürger und Soldaten* is still determined by Döblin's philosophy of nature as he expounds it *Unser Dasein:* the personified earth takes on human features, and human beings emerge from the earth and return to it, literally, in the trench warfare of the First World War. The decisive processes within the human being are subconscious, below the threshold of consciousness, on a level with vegetative processes. The first part, or book, of *Bürger und Soldaten* describes collective processes, while in book 2, individuals begin to emerge from this collective stream of events ("Abläufe"). Individuals act more often than not as stumbling blocks for these streams of events. Döblin calls them "Querschläger" (obliquely striking projectiles), which deviate or stop the action rather than initiate it. The ultimate such force in the following volumes will be Friedrich Ebert, whom the narrator calls the "Verhinderer," or preventer, because he prevents the revolution from happening, and reverses the flow of events into a retrograde direction.

In the later volumes the basic rhythm of the text that is established in *Bürger und Soldaten* is modified and then replaced by another, which is determined by the transcendental perspective. Still, it is the "Mit- und

Gegeneinander der Kräfte," rather than architectonic structures, that determine form and orientation of this gigantic text (32).

For Helmut F. Pfanner, the concepts that he names in the title of his article "Sachlichkeit und Mystik" determine from the beginning Döblin's search for the truth about the failed revolution.[17] Pfanner too starts with *Bürger und Soldaten* and postulates a sudden shift from objective description and reporting to deep mystical vision ("mystische Tiefenschau") (79–80). For the characters Friedrich Becker and Rosa Luxemburg, the experiences of suffering and failure are the beginning of an inner rebirth (82). It follows from the analysis of the text, according to Pfanner, that the double-layered narration reflects fundamentally different attitudes toward life: objectivity and mysticism, which in the end emerges as the correct attitude (83).

Scholars such as Pfanner, Koepke,[18] and Ribbat see two different Döblins at work in *November 1918*: Döblin as the narrator of the failed revolution, most evident in *Bürger und Soldaten,* and Döblin the professing Christian, whose concerns dominate the last volume, *Karl und Rosa.* The theme of revolution was taken up again by two later dissertations, Christina Althen's *Machtkonstellationen einer deutschen Revolution,*[19] and Anna Kuhlmann's *Revolution als "Geschichte."*[20] For Althen, *November 1918* is still informed by the ethos of *Unser Dasein* (35). Her thesis is that the concept of power is key to interpreting *November 1918* (81), and in her view the novel's architecture shows the power structures and power elites (85). She differentiates between *Macht* and *Gewalt* (power and force or violence): *Macht* being associated with governmental and military authorities, and *Gewalt* with the masses, but in the case of the military the two overlap. She points out the inertia of the masses, who do not act, leaving all involvement to the leading figures. The text is didactic and is designed to move us in the manner of the legend, the satire, or the didactic play (206). The increasingly critical attitude is not only directed at the revolutionaries, their opponents, and the masses, but also at Friedrich Becker and his downfall, and this shows, according to Althen, a much more critical reception of Kierkegaard than has generally been connected with Döblin (240). Becker is a Faustian figure, and he will be measured not only according to Kierkegaardian categories, but also as a successor to Nietzsche, and to the philosopher's solipsism and "Ichsucht" as well (242). Becker is not a model. In this world of baffling contrasts, ambiguities, and contradictions, only one positive character stands out: the American president Wilson.

Anna Kuhlmann treats *November 1918* as the exemplary historical novel or *Geschichtsroman.* She investigates the fundamental questions that surround the genre: history versus fiction, the genre as bound to realism, and — a crucial aspect — the historical novel as a self-reflexive genre. As a historical novel, *November 1918* has to be read in a double manner: both as historiography and as fiction, even though the two modes of reading clash. The historiographical paradigm is the failed revolution, with all its mythological and eschatological associations: the revolution as a totally new beginning, destruction and rebirth, and as a process leading to an ultimate age of peace beyond history. Döblin wants to demonstrate that the "revolution" of 1918/19 failed to achieve this new beginning, and consequently never brought real peace to Germany. The narrator stresses again and again that nothing has changed in spite of the violent upheavals, and that leads him and his author Döblin to conclude that such political uprisings are in vain; the only possible transformation is transcendent, a leap into God's grace. All human action and striving is futile without the grace of God. The three protagonists striving for a true revolutionary transformation, Woodrow Wilson, Rosa Luxemburg, and Friedrich Becker, meet their deaths as political and religious martyrs seeking the redemption of both themselves and humanity. The failed revolution opens the perspective both on the repetition of history — the Second World War following on the First — and the metaphysical outlook for the human soul beyond history.

Richard Humphrey, in *The Historical Novel as Philosophy of History,*[21] offers two major contributions to the understanding of *November 1918*. He places the novel in the succession of Willibald Alexis's *Ruhe ist die erste Bürgerpflicht* and Theodor Fontane's *Vor dem Sturm,* emphasizing that the setting, the big city of Berlin, is the necessary environment for the events that occur. He also points out the Prussian military tradition as a precondition of events, and the features that *November 1918* shares with the traditional historical novel going back to Walter Scott. There is, however, one major innovation in this narrative work: the function of the masses. Whereas riotous and revolutionary masses have been part of historiography and historical fiction since the French Revolution, Döblin questions not only how "revolutionary" crowds can really be, but also — and even more pointedly — the function and efficacy of the political leadership, or rather the lack thereof. For Döblin the revolution was characterized by the absence of leadership, or at least by the leaders' inability to initiate and direct revolutionary actions. On the contrary, "Verhinderer" like Ebert and the generals, who are out to prevent action, are the most successful leaders. In this general framework, Humphrey brings in Friedrich Becker as a leader without followers, a leader whose message does not stir the masses to revolution.

Roland Dollinger's chapter on *November 1918* in his 1994 book *Totalitarität und Totalitarismus im Exilwerk Döblins* is titled "Geschichte als Heilsgeschichte."[22] Dollinger sees a clear break between the novel's first three volumes and *Karl und Rosa* (156), and analyzes the biographical reasons, as described by Döblin in his 1949 account of his 1940 flight to exile, *Schicksalsreise*. History, personal history in particular, seems at first, as portrayed in the first three volumes, senseless and chaotic, but gradually, and most evidently in *Karl und Rosa*, the events take on the character of omens, portents, and signs (Dollinger's word is *Zeichen*) that point in definite directions. For as Döblin himself relates in *Schicksalsreise*, out of the vividly described chaos of his flight into exile a new understanding ("Erkenntnis") emerged. Döblin's isolation during his flight continued in Los Angeles, where he had few friends and literary contacts, and this isolation, for him the essential trait of exile, led to his encounter with Jesus Christ and the Christian God. This meant the final break with all collective solutions to the historical crisis, such as the socialist revolution and the search for a Jewish homeland. As early as in his 1931 *Wissen und Verändern!*, Döblin had made it clear that he opposed violent class struggle as a way to reach the goal of peace; similarly, although he supported Neo-Territorialism as a peaceful way to a Jewish homeland in peace, he did not support the movement if it involved constant struggle and warfare in Palestine, as was becoming the evident case.

In *November 1918*, says Dollinger, Döblin's narrative strategy can at first be defined as "polyphonic narration," an epic panorama of the conflicting forces of German society at this critical juncture of history (165). In the course of his writing, however, and most evidently in the last volume, tension arises between this presentation of the historical moment as the nucleus of the later evolution toward National Socialism, and the didactic narrative of the Christian salvation of Friedrich Becker. The text is characterized by a pronounced self-reflexivity on the part of the narrator/author, who remembers the events and has a very personal stake in their outcome. He keeps commenting and asking himself (and others) what went wrong, what caused the revolution to bog down and ultimately fail. Here he assigns the heaviest guilt to the Social Democrats, and he later considers Hitler's army to be the direct successor to Noske's troops. *November 1918*, says Dollinger, is built upon a dialectical process of the mutual illumination of the past and the present.

Dollinger analyzes the interplay of the different discourses in the text, public and private, that define the personalities of the characters as well as their political positions, as evident for instance in the language of Ebert, Liebknecht, and the military. The most complex combination of discourses appears in the portrayal of Rosa Luxemburg, whose political thoughts and pronouncements stand side by side with her most intimate thoughts. Friedrich Becker's change of language from the humanist to the mystical Christian is clearly marked.

In this multiperspectival, polyphonic linguistic structure, according to Dollinger, the voice of the narrator becomes increasingly didactic and one-dimensional, and this interferes with the complexities of the characters' voices. Dollinger considers this a consequence of exile, as if the painful loss of Döblin's former readership had left its formal traces in the work (178). Instead of the dialogues of the characters, and the dialogues between narrator and reader, a direct address from the narrator to the reader is substituted. The narrator evolves, and his evolution is parallel to that of Friedrich Becker, ending in *Karl und Rosa* in a *Heilsgewißheit:* this is where we have to go. On a formal level, one can observe in *November 1918* a gradual reduction of montage elements, that is, the insertion of historical documents, and a stronger self-affirmation of the narrator and his message, a message that leads beyond history. Again, this can be attributed at least in part to Döblin's isolation in exile.

For Dollinger, the vast array of figures in this panoramic epic can be ordered around one fundamental question: are they ready to accept guilt and responsibility for this catastrophe and work for a radical change, or will they try to maintain the status quo? Döblin himself kept asking this question, and at times caused scandal by doing so, as when he implicated the exiles themselves in a speech during the celebration of his sixty-fifth birthday in Los Angeles. This is strongly reminiscent of Friedrich Becker. Dollinger sees here the impact of Kierkegaard and the transition from an aesthetic to an ethical mode of existence. Becker, however, is anything but an ideal figure. His pronounced *Innerlichkeit* and his refusal to take a stand for the revolution are typically "German" and contribute to the revolution's failure and the rise of National Socialism (190). Becker's newfound religiosity with its masochistic aspects and his readiness to give in to a mystical self-effacement is alarmingly close to the masochistic yielding of the masses to a dictator. According to Dollinger, Becker's transformation into a Christian preacher is, in the final analysis, "Geschichtsmüdigkeit," an attempt at an escape from history that would leave humanity to the "others," those who live by violence, expressing the resignation of a fatalistic observer of history.

Dollinger finds that Rosa Luxemburg, the other protagonist of *Karl und Rosa,* appears in a very unusual light. Besides Döblin's emphasis on her masochistic traits, and on her anti-Leninist thought, Dollinger stresses the point that Döblin wanted to make a fictive Christian out of the historical Jewess (198). Döblin seemed to want to free Luxemburg from the accusations of her enemies that she was the cause of the destruction of the fatherland, and to cleanse her of the image of the devilish Jewish seductress. Her Christian conversion transforms her socialism into a peaceful Christian socialism, and herself into a saint; by turning away from Judaism and assuming the role of a Christian martyr, she becomes a figure of identification. But for Dollinger, both Döblin's conversion and that of his Rosa Luxemburg character stand at the end of a long process that involved a good deal of Jewish self-hate (202). For Döblin, says Dollinger, "Juden kommen nur als Volk vor" (208): when he realized that the dream of a Jewish homeland, as he had envisaged it, was impossible, he began to cut his ties with Judaism, which had always been difficult and uneasy in any case. Dollinger detects an anti-Semitic strain in *November 1918*, visible among other places in Becker's belief that one has to be purified from one's own Jewishness, a process exemplified by the Rosa Luxemburg character.

For Dollinger, neither Becker nor Luxemburg is an ideal figure: although both of them point in the right direction, both reveal serious flaws as well. Nonetheless, the radical transformation of society and individuals that was needed in 1918 was even more urgently needed at the time of Döblin's writing of *November 1918*. Indeed, one could argue that 1945 turned out to be another failed opportunity.

In his study "Allegorie und Psychomachie,"[23] Matthias Luserke draws an unexpected literary parallel between Friedrich Maximilian Klinger's fragment of 1803 *Das zu frühe Erwachen des Genius der Menschheit* and Döblin's *November 1918*. In each of the texts, set in 1789 and 1918 respectively, Luserke sees the exemplification of Adorno and Horkheimer's thesis: "Rationalität schlägt in Mythologie zurück" (263). After the self-destruction of 1789, Klinger states, the writer has the responsibility to advance to the place of horrors, into darkness (instead of toward the light of reason) to determine the origins of insanity and the mania for domination (263). The writer is armed with the instrument of allegory to depict the psychomachia, the battle of the souls, of satanic forces unleashed by the self-destructive Enlightenment and the revolution. The "Genius der Menschheit," Klinger's guide through the chamber of horrors, arrives before the "Thron des Verhüllten," but receives no answers to a long list of questions. For Klinger, Luserke says, the experience of the revolution is connected with the unreconcilable loss of divine presence ("Entgöttlichung") in the world (265). From this vantage point, Luserke sees *No-*

vember 1918 in a new light: Döblin's God reveals himself and speaks at the beginning of the novel, but he proves to be an anthropomorphic, completely powerless God — in other words no God at all — and is never again seen to speak in the novel (265). With the second volume, *Verratenes Volk*, the representations of psychomachia begin. Döblin moves toward a privatization and eschatologization of revolution, defaming and demonizing it and the geniuses who drive it, as is evident in the depiction of Rosa Luxemburg's struggle with Satan. Possibly, Luserke says, instead of being oriented toward the telos, the goal and result of the revolution, Döblin's real question concerns its origins, and going back one step, the origins of the war and its senseless, devastating slaughter, which made the revolution as inevitable as it was impossible.

Helmuth Kiesel devotes the third part of his book *Literarische Trauerarbeit*, more than two hundred pages, to *November 1918*.[24] The first part of his examination deals with narrative strategies, structures, themes, and styles in a more general way; he then proceeds to a specific analysis of the fictive or fictionalized revolution, and of Rosa Luxemburg and Friedrich Becker. Kiesel retraces in precise details Döblin's complex writing process, his manner of using his historical sources, the novel's publication history, and the changing figure of the author/narrator, whose transformation from the chronicler of the 1918/19 events to the author of a "Welttheater" is reflected in Döblin's gradual turning away from the modern techniques so much in evidence in his previous works, such as montage, interior monologue, and *erlebte Rede*. History appears within the horizon of myth, and as the text progresses, it reveals itself increasingly as a "christliches Welttheater" in which the text has the primary function of completing the "sichtbare Welt," which is imperfect and incomplete, with the invisible one (311–17). In the course of the events, the author/narrator arrives at the point (in volume 3) where he tells a story between heaven and hell, and "Geschichte" becomes "Heilsgeschichte" (316). Kiesel offers a long examination of Döblin's use of the images and figures of Christian mythology, finally arriving at the critical point, that of Döblin's style. Many reviewers have criticized the obvious use of clichés and trivial situations, images, and language (336–40). Kiesel finds reasons for this in Döblin's conscious avoidance of intellectualizing and in his aim to achieve a popular style, one that touches real people instead of talking over their heads. However, compared to Brecht, Döblin was much less assured in using the idiom of the common people, especially after he had left the sphere of the Berlin vernacular, and it is unmistakable that at times he reached too deeply into the truly trivial, for instance in several episodes of the Stauffer story.

In Kiesel's view, one of the major thrusts of Döblin's novel of the revolution is the incessant attempt to quell it, to end it as soon as possible, or to prevent its eruption in the first place, in the name of law and order. Even the revolutionaries themselves submit to "law and order." This begins to be evident in *Bürger und Soldaten* on a small scale before it takes the form of actions by the government and the military. As far as the revolutionaries are concerned, Kiesel says, Döblin stresses the common discrepancy between revolutionary talk and (un)revolutionary deed (361). Döblin brings this discrepancy into sharp focus through the figure of Karl Radek, the Bolshevist emissary who observes with cynical reason the failure of the German revolution (365). Radek tries to win Karl Liebknecht over to the strategies of Lenin, with tragic results, as Liebknecht wavers between his original pacifism and Lenin's method of violent action. Lenin's long shadow hovers over the German revolution, and the inevitable comparison with events in Russia make the outcome look even more dismal, yet the implied criticism of Lenin's violence never ceases. Döblin can never get comfortable with the regress of humanity into bestiality, evident both in the Russian wars and in the *Freikorps* actions sanctioned by Noske. The latter lead eventually to the murder of Liebknecht and Luxemburg, which would take on such tremendous significance for German history — the first of many political murders and acts of terror in the Weimar period and after. The narrative tone begins to shift from satire and wit to the pathos of tragedy, ending, however, with the rather grotesque chapter "Totentanz," the danse macabre of the margraves, electors, and kings of the history of Brandenburg-Prussia whose monuments stood on both sides of the *Siegesallee* (392–97).

Kiesel's last two sections are devoted to Rosa Luxemburg and, most prominently, to Friedrich Becker. Döblin's characterization of Luxemburg has been criticized from a variety of angles (398–404). The key, according to Kiesel, is that Döblin presents Luxemburg as a modern Antigone (402). What Döblin had in mind when he described her sorrow was not to describe a mental illness, but to demonstrate the psychic and ethical depth, or seen in another light, the radicalism and "Unheilbarkeit" of her mourning (403). It is irritating for many readers, however, to see the narrator oscillate between factual descriptions, often taken almost verbatim from letters and other documents, and hallucinatory states of mind that include angels and devils, so that medical explanations are presented alongside theological ones, without discernable transitions. Luxemburg's mourning appears as the "Rechtsanspruch eines Toten an die Lebenden," as Becker explains the situation of Antigone (411). Rosa's suffering is not private; her mourning of her dead lover must be seen in connection with her radical opposition to Lenin's ideology of violence, her realization of the traditional militaristic character of his dictatorship, her refusal to accept the principle of violence, and her modification of the idea of class struggle, a point of special interest for Döblin (416). Rosa struggles with Satan and Satanism. Satan is as handsome and attractive as he is horrible. The final battle between Rosa's angel, the cherub, and Satan for Rosa's soul leaves her transformed, as remorse and repentance replaces the pride that was in her soul (424). While for Karl Liebknecht, in his and Rosa's final scene in the novel, Milton's Satan remains the true revolutionary and enlightener, Rosa understands his fatal blindness against Satan's machinations and sees the source of true enlightenment.

Kiesel sees Döblin's protagonist Friedrich Becker as having to carry a double burden (427–86): first, the more general one of a historically-based figure faced with an existential crisis due to the war and revolution (as many people found themselves to be at the time), and second, a particular one due to his being a projection-figure for the author, one onto whom Döblin loaded his own religious difficulties (427). Kiesel notes that Becker's story, if separated from the rest of the text, would be long and substantial enough for a novel in itself. As Antigone and Rosa Luxemburg were "Töchter der Trauer," so is Friedrich Becker the exemplary "Sohn der Trauer," the seriously wounded soldier who is experiencing a physical, psychological, and ethical crisis when the revolution makes itself heard in the small Alsatian town. Kiesel traces Becker's long path to the end. Johannes Tauler, the Alsatian mystic who becomes Becker's "Virgil," his guide through the underworld of the revolution, attracted Döblin's attention because of his insistence on suffering as the gate to a new life, on the three paths to God, which are purification and retreat from the world; the internalization of the sufferings of Christ; unification with God through the force of the love of Christ; and on the "Lebenswende" and inner transformation these make possible. Kiesel says that Tauler, for Döblin, reinforces the message of Kierkegaard and becomes his "pseudonym" (432–40). Becker's journey begins in the train from the Alsace to Berlin, with his turn away from his previous aestheticism, symbolized by Richard Wagner's *Tristan und Isolde* (443–46), and his rejection of the hubris of Sophocles' verse (cited in a faulty translation) "Nichts ist gewaltiger als der Mensch" (441–42). His guilt feelings and new humility open his soul up for a slow and painful rebirth. The first stage, the ethical stage in Kierkegaard's sense, will not be able to provide a new foundation. The first stage away from the previous aesthetic humanism — the ethical stage in Kierkegaard's sense — will not be able to provide a new foundation. A "leap" into the religious stage becomes inevitable for Friedrich Becker, and this is what the text of *November 1918* describes.

One of the irritants of Döblin's text is his insistence on the omnipresence of Satan in the world and his broad descriptions of Satanism. It becomes clear in Becker's three encounters with Satan in different forms that he is not dealing with the "Demonic," which is a power of nature, of the cosmos, but with Evil, with Satan as the antagonist. Becker's previous aesthetic/ethical authorities, the great writers like Sophocles, Goethe, and Kleist, and the great classical artists, are found insufficient; he is exposed to the onslaught of evil without any support. Döblin draws upon the long tradition of literary devil figures, as he had done before in *Wallenstein*, and shows Satan in animal disguises, but he shies away from the realm of the grotesque, and the comic in general, when he approaches this area (457–64). According to Kiesel there is an element of anti-modernism in Döblin's manifestation of evil, particularly as compared with its portrayal in Thomas Mann's *Doktor Faustus*. However, other prominent writers of the time who shared Döblin's views come to mind, for instance Georges Bernanos and Elisabeth Langgässer. This new insistence on the presence of radical evil and guilt can be explained as part of the crisis and impasse of enlightenment. Enlightened modernity attempts to illuminate the causes of rebarbarization in the spirit of religion (464).

Becker, with a new Christian faith and awareness after his journey through remorse and mourning in his "cave," wants to re-enter the world and to prove himself anew; to find out what is possible for a man who has been through war and is determined not to forget the dead (475). This brings about his visit to the Gymnasium and the fateful Greek lesson on *Antigone*. In Becker's explanation of the tragedy, the crucial conflict is that between the authority of the state and of the divine (476). Here Döblin has Becker reject Hegel's dialectics and the claims for the right of the state in both Hegel's philosophy and in Marxism. Instead, Antigone is elevated as the valid model for mourning and action. Becker's path after the end of the fighting in 1919 is not an example to follow, although he is a lone Christian in a "verwahrlosten Zeit" (483). Kiesel sums up Döblin's program for an ethical — and needed — revolution: it is firmly and without concessions pacifistic, without being at all fatalistic or defeatist (484). The similarities with *Wang-lun* are striking.

It remains in question, however, whether ethical revolution is possible or whether it remains an oxymoron, and, as far as *November 1918* is concerned, whether it suffices to bind the two threads of the events together, the political revolution and the path to a Christian faith. So far, critics have always taken sides, choosing either the beginning in *Bürger und Soldaten 1918* or the outcome in *Karl und Rosa*, as their favored point of view.

A recent attempt to bring these points of view together was made by Wulf Koepke in his "Die Überwindung der Revolution: *November 1918*."[25] Without denying the obvious fact that Döblin's views and attitudes changed while he was writing *November 1918*, he considers the idea of "revolution" as fundamental for the book; however, it soon becomes evident that revolution means a transformation of people, and not just of political conditions, and that this transformation has to take place within each individual human being. Three paths to such a change are outlined in the text, connected with three protagonists: the American President Wilson is "der große Vernünftige," who wants to bring about a world of peace through reason, establishing a world governed and formed by human reason. Döblin's third part *Heimkehr der Fronttruppen* narrates the failure of his mission. Rosa Luxemburg arrives at the end, in the view of Döblin, at an anarchist conception of society, a society without the coercion of state power, based on voluntary association and solidarity, a society that, furthermore, lives in harmony with the forces of nature. However, Döblin had gone on to a worldview of Good and Evil, of God and Satan, Heaven and Hell. Western civilization is Satanic hubris. The only way to salvation is through the recognition of guilt and Christian humility, in order to come closer to God through Christ. This attempt is personified in Friedrich Becker, whose search and erring never ends, until the vision of the heavenly Jerusalem at the moment of his death.

It remains unresolved whether these three paths are mutually exclusive. *November 1918* remains a multi-faceted, complex, and in part enigmatic work, and true to Döblin's way of writing, it urges its readers to think for themselves.

Notes

[1] The continuing debate about "trilogy" vs. "tetralogy" found a Salomonic solution in Werner Stauffacher's edition in the *Ausgewählte Werke*, where Stauffacher offers the text in four volumes, but numbers them I, II,1, II,2, and III.

[2] Published in *Internationales Alfred-Döblin-Kolloquium 1980–1983*, ed. Werner Stauffacher (Bern: Peter Lang, 1986). Three of the four Basel papers, and five of the eight New York papers were devoted to *November 1918*.

[3] Heinz D. Osterle, "Alfred Döblins Revolutionstrilogie *November 1918*," *Monats-hefte* 62 (1970), 1–23; also in *Zu Alfred Döblin*, ed. Ingrid Schuster, LWG-Interpretationen 48 (Stuttgart: Ernst Klett Verlag, 1980), 160–176.

[4] Hans Mayer, "'Eine deutsche Revolution. Also keine.' Über Alfred Döblins wieder-entdecktes Erzählwerk *November 1918*," *Der Spiegel* 33 (1978): 124ff., and "Alfred Döblins Erzählwerk *November 1918*" in H. M. *Die umerzogene Literatur: Deutsche Schriftsteller und Bücher 1945–1967* (Berlin: Siedler-Verlag, 1988), 66–70.

[5] Wolfgang Düsing, "Das Epos der Weimarer Republik. Döblins Romanzyklus *November 1918*," in *Schriftsteller und Politik in Deutschland*, ed. Werner Link (Düsseldorf: Droste-Verlag, 1979), 49–61.

[6] *Erfahrung Exil: Antifaschistische Romane 1933–1945*, eds. Sigrid Bock and Manfred Hahn (Berlin/Weimar: Aufbau Verlag, 1979); Roland Links, "Mit Geschichte will man etwas. Alfred Döblin: *November 1918*," 328–51. There was a later similar vol-ume by the same editors, *Erfahrung Nazideutschland: Romane in Deutschland 1933–1945* (Berlin/Weimar: Aufbau-Verlag, 1987), that analyzed novels of the "Inner Emi-gration" and the resistance. Both volumes were projects of the Akademie der Wissen-schaften.

[7] Manfred Auer, *Das Exil vor der Vertreibung: Motivkontinuität und Quellenproble-matik im späten Werk Alfred Döblins* (Bonn: Bouvier Verlag Herbert Grundmann, 1977), 56–102.

[8] Auer, *Das Exil vor der Vertreibung*, 179–197, offers as an example an appendix showing how Döblin excerpted and used facts and passages from *Die deutsche Revo-lution* by Eduard Bernstein. Other observations on the manuscripts and sources are found in the footnotes.

[9] Otto Keller, "Tristan und Antigone. Gestus, Verfremdung und Montage als Medien der Figurengestaltung in Döblins 'November 1918,'" *Internationale Alfred-Döblin-Kolloquien 1980–1983*, ed. Werner Stauffacher, 10–19; Heinz D. Osterle, "Auf den Spuren der Antigone: Sophokles, Döblin, Brecht," ibid, 86–115.

[10] Wolfgang Frühwald, "Rosa und der Satan. Thesen zum Verhältnis von Christen-tum und Sozialismus im Schlußband von Alfred Döblins Erzählwerk *November 1918*," *Internationale Alfred-Döblin-Kolloquien 1980–1983*, ed. Werner Stauffacher, 239–56.

[11] Heidi Thomann Tewarson, "Alfred Döblins Geschichtskonzeption in *November 1918. Eine deutsche Revolution*. Dargestellt an der Figur Rosa Luxemburgs in *Karl und Rosa*," *Internationale Alfred-Döblin-Kolloquien 1980–1983*, ed. Werner Stauf-facher, 64–75.

[12] David Dollenmayer, "Der Wandel in Döblins Aufassung von der deutschen Revo-lution 1918–1919," *Internationale Alfred-Döblin-Kolloquien 1980–1983*, ed. Werner Stauffacher, 56–63.

[13] David Dollenmayer, *The Berlin Novels of Alfred Döblin* (Berkeley/Los Angeles/London: U of California P, 1988), 124–78).

[14] Erich Kleinschmidt, "Parteiliche Fiktionalität. Zur Anlage historischen Erzählens in Alfred Döblins *November 1918*," *Internationale Alfred-Döblin-Kolloquien 1980–1983*, ed. Werner Stauffacher, 116–32.

[15] Ernst Ribbat, "Döblin, Brecht und das Problem des historischen Romans. Überlegungen im Hinblick auf *November 1918*," *Internationale Alfred-Döblin-Kolloquien 1980–1983*, ed. Werner Stauffacher, 34–44.

[16] Wulf Koepke, "Spontane Ansätze zur Überwindung der Individuation. Zur Struktur von Döblins *Bürger und Soldaten 1918*," *Internationale Alfred-Döblin-Kolloquien 1980–1983*, ed. Werner Stauffacher, 20–33.

[17] Helmut F. Pfanner, "Sachlichkeit und Mystik: Zur Erzählhaltung in Alfred Döblins Revolutionsroman," *Internationale Alfred-Döblin-Kolloquien 1980–1983*, ed. Werner Stauffacher, 76–85.

[18] Wulf Koepke, "Schwierigkeiten bei der Beurteilung von Döblin's *November 1918*," in *Exil: Wirkung und Wertung*, edited by Donald G. Daviau and Ludwig M. Fischer (Columbia, SC: Camden House, 1985), 195–202.

[19] Christina Althen, *Machtkonstellationen einer deutschen Revolution: Alfred Döblins Geschichteroman "November 1918,"* Münchener Studien zur literarischen Kultur in Deutschland, vol. 18 (Frankfurt: Peter Lang, 1993).

[20] Anna Kuhlmann, *Revolution als "Geschichte": Alfred Döblins "November 1918": Eine programmatische Lektüre des historischen Romans.* Communicatio vol. 14 (Tübingen: Niemeyer, 1997).

[21] Richard Humphrey, *The Historical Novel as Philosophy of History: Three German Contributions: Alexis, Fontane, Döblin* (London: Institute of German Studies, University of London, 1986).

[22] Roland Dollinger, *Totalität und Totalitarismus im Exilwerk Alfred Döblins*, Epistema: Würzburger Wissenschaftliche Schriften, Reihe Literaturwissenschaft, 126 (Würzburg: Königshausen & Neumann, 1994), 156–218.

[23] Matthias Luserke, "Allegorie und Psychomachie. Revolutionsdeutung in Klingers 'Genius'-Fragment und Döblins Roman 'November 1918,'" *Internationale Alfred-Döblin-Kolloquien Münster 1989–Marbach a. N. 1991*, ed. Werner Stauffacher (Bern: Peter Lang, 1993), 262–70.

[24] Helmuth Kiesel, *Literarische Trauerarbeit: Das Exil- und Spätwerk Alfred Döblins* (Tübingen: Max Niemeyer, 1986) 273–486.

[25] Wulf Koepke, "Die Überwindung der Revolution: *November 1918.*" *Internationales Alfred-Döblin-Kolloquium Bergamo 1999*, ed. Torsten Hahn (Jahrbuch für Internationale Germanistik A vol. 51, Bern: Peter Lang, 2002), 243–59.

14: *Hamlet oder Die lange Nacht nimmt ein Ende*

D ÖBLIN'S LAST NOVEL *Hamlet oder Die lange Nacht nimmt ein Ende* was written during the transition from American exile to his return to Germany. The action is centered around Edward, a seriously wounded and mutilated British soldier, returning to his family in England and his attempts to begin a new life. It is, on the surface of it, a *Heimkehrerroman*, as they were written in large numbers after both world wars. In reality, Döblin aims at something very different, but the theme of the return home should not be forgotten.

Döblin brought the unfinished manuscript with him when he arrived in Baden-Baden in November 1945, and completed it in 1946. Because he was busy trying to publish his many other works from the exile years, he decided to wait before offering *Hamlet* to the public, but by the time he was ready to do so, the other books had been rejected or ignored by the reading audience, so that publishers did not dare attempt another experiment with a book that promised no profit. Thus the manuscript remained unpublished until it was rescued by Peter Huchel and the East German publisher Rütting & Loening. When it was published in 1956, after ten years' delay, it still generated controversy and a wide range of reactions, and a West German edition followed in 1957. After Döblin's death in the same year, the initial debate on the book and the realization that there would be no more new novels by Döblin turned the later reviews into assessments of Döblin's entire oeuvre. Scholarly studies on Döblin began to include mention of *Hamlet* while it was still new enough to be sold in bookstores, but it was not their main focus. This changed only in the seventies. However, while the works of the German exiles in general suffered from the prejudice that they were backward and inferior, *Hamlet* seemed to be intriguingly modern, and it has more recently even been called "postmodern." However, after a time, scholarly interest declined somewhat, and interesting aspects of the work remain unexplored.

Adolf Steinmann published his dissertation, *Alfred Döblins Roman "Hamlet oder Die lange Nacht nimmt ein Ende": Isolation und Öffnung,* in 1971.[1] The study has two parts: the first titled "Einholen der Vergangenheit," capturing and retrieving the past; the second could be described by the book's subtitle, "Isolation und Öffnung." The thesis of the first part is that the "accident," the Japanese suicide bomber that causes the mutilation of Edward and the death of his closest friend, is not without precedent and brings a latent crisis to the surface. *Hamlet* is closely connected to Döblin's own biography, says Steinmann, but he offers the biographical facts last in order not to detract from the consideration of the novel as a novel (136–61). Still, the biographical aspect of the text may account for both its intensity and some of its inconsistencies, and is of major significance not only in this novel, but, as Steinmann indicates, in previous novels by Döblin as well.

Edward considers his severe injury to be a death, one from which he is reborn to a second life as a "new man." While this recalls *Manas* and *Berlin Alexanderplatz,* Edward's need for a "Daseinserhellung" is of a different kind (3). Steinmann takes up Robert Minder's thesis of Döblin as a writer between Orient and Occident: Edward's goal is to reach the East, and his injury throws him back into the West, from which he had tried to escape. There, among his family, Edward is cast in the situation of a Hamlet, but without the ghost's revelations. He wants and needs to find out the deeper causes of his trauma, which are connected with his parents' marriage. In order to divert his attention, his father proposes that they tell each other stories at the get-togethers in the evenings; however, these stories, intended to hide the ugly truth, instead reveal it, and Edward's searching mind dismantles the fictions and the role-playing of the family members. The marriage of the parents is definitively shattered, and they go to their death, but not before achieving an "Aufhebung der Angst durch den Glauben" (135). Edward is able to leave the world of fiction behind, and a new life begins for him.

On the way to self-revelation and self-acceptance, both Edward and his parents must overcome the lure of preconceived images. "Du sollst dir kein Bildnis machen" is for Steinmann one of the cornerstones of Döblin's "cure" for his characters, albeit in a different sense from what Max Frisch meant when he used this same biblical quote in his *Tagebuch* and in the novel *Stiller,* works that were published in the interval between the writing and the publication of *Hamlet.* Frisch meant that our world, dominated by the mass media, leads us to believe in preconceived images, even on the personal level: we form a fixed image of a person, instead of trying to find out who she or he really is. Döblin, on the other hand, was thinking of role-playing that hides the true character of a person, even from her- or himself. Steinmann integrates into his treatment of *Hamlet* analysis of some of the stories told in the novel, especially "Theodora," but he does not pay much attention to the correspondences between the novel's action and the stories, beyond the direct bearing of the story-telling on Edward's search for the truth.

Manfred Auer, in his chapter on *Hamlet* in his *Das Exil vor der Vertreibung*,[2] draws a close connection between *November 1918* and *Hamlet*, as the two books tell two sides of one story, of Döblin's own story. The two works taken together represent a spectrum of Döblin's experimental style (103). Auer finds *Hamlet* in particular to be one of the most interesting of Döblin's works in terms of narrative technique (103). Auer recognizes that the generic classification of *Hamlet* as a "Rahmenzyklus" raises some problems and points to significant differences between Döblin and the Boccaccio model.

Auer discusses in detail the structural elements of the novel. In a first section, he describes the action; in a second one he analyzes the stories told by the characters. Although Döblin's *Hamlet* is not a drama, the action proceeds in scenes and can be described in terms of the characters' dialogues and monologues (many of them by the Hamlet figure Edward), together with short inner monologues connected with the stories. Therefore, says Auer, *Hamlet* reveals a dramatic structure after all, through the tension about the outcome, Edward's finding of the truth, and its unforeseen consequences.

Auer defines the connection of the two levels, the action and stories told, as a "Simultanstruktur" that should make these connections evident at first sight. *Hamlet* reverts to the model of the novella cycle, where storytelling is used as the means of conflict resolution. While Auer believes this is the express purpose of Döblin's text, he says it has the opposite results. He proceeds to a precise examination of the specific functions and integration of the different stories, which shows substantial differences between them, and even an evolution in the course of the text, which leads, however, to contradictions and structural disintegration in the later part of the novel. One point is clear: *Hamlet* is an analytical novel that makes unusual demands on the reader (135). Only a very close reading and a detailed analysis reveal its complex interrelationships.

According to Auer, *Hamlet* resumes themes and motifs from all the previous works since 1933. It takes up numerous points of *Pardon wird nicht gegeben*, but even more striking is its closeness to *November 1918*. This is exemplified by the similarities between the fates and personalities of Friedrich Becker and Edward Allison, especially their "Selbstfindung" or "Ich-Suche." Differences should not be overlooked, of course; Edward does not feel guilt and the need to get involved, as Becker does; Edward remains an observer and a harsh judge of others. Whereas love in many forms is an essential ingredient of the action in the *November* trilogy, it is reduced in *Hamlet* to the mother-son relationship of Edward and Alice and her love-hate marriage to Gordon, Edward's father. Taken as a whole, says Auer, *Hamlet* unifies, compresses, and psychologizes entire units of plot and motif complexes going back to *Pardon wird nicht gegeben,* and can be regarded as a summation of Döblin's essential themes from his earliest works (142).

Finally, Auer turns to two central complexes, the religious dimension and the psychoanalytic one. For Auer, Döblin's change of the ending — so that Edward returns to life instead of entering a monastery — has much more significance than previous scholars, including Riley, have admitted. Auer does not see Edward as a religious figure; except in the version where Edward ends up in a monastery, Edward's concept of a fate determining our lives cannot be called "Christian." The religious figure of the novel is Edward's mother, Alice; however, there seems to be an implicit criticism of her faith as being too sure of itself, never questioning itself. On the other hand, Edward/Hamlet is the "Gottsucher" in the manner of Kierkegaard. Edward follows Kierkegaard's "Redlichkeit und Wahrheit" in his search for himself and the truth, and he likens himself to Kierkegaard's Hamlet and to the "German" interpretation of Hamlet that emphasizes the searching and philosophical aspects of his personality. Although there is no evidence that Döblin followed Freud's methods in his analysis of the "Hamlet" situation, the parallels are undeniable, as is Döblin's familiarity with Freud's writings. On the whole, it is striking how Auer downplays the religious dimensions in favor of the psychological and sociopolitical ones.

Roland Links's evaluation of *Hamlet* is remarkable.[3] The family Allison needs a "Lebenslüge" to be able to exist, and this lie can be seen as a symbol for an entire society (202). When Edward shatters the family's lie, he shatters his parents' social and ideological system. The novel, says Links, raises fundamental problems of our society. He sees the book's problematics as decisive for the century and for the survival of mankind, and believes that this, and its profoundly humanistic answer, raise it far above the average in spite of its artistic weaknesses Döblin's personal pessimism (202). The book became greater than its author; Döblin outdid himself, and this is the reason for its peculiar form (203). With a remarkable *Redlichkeit,* honesty, the narrator depicts a world doomed to destroy itself, and succeeds in rescuing the humaneness of humanity.

Jules Grand, who in his book *Projektionen in Alfred Döblins Roman "Hamlet oder Die lange Nacht nimmt ein Ende"*[4] mentions Steinmann as his major reference point, emphasizes these "projections," the stories told and their meanings. He offers first a detailed description of Edward's injury and illness, of his double shock, the one caused by his injury in the bombing, and the deeper shock from his childhood. In following Edward/Hamlet's pursuit of the truth, Grand also describes the past history and unsolved problems of Edward's parents Gordon and Alice and of their relationship, and the eventual "explosion" of the family. This enables him to understand the functions and meanings of the various stories told as projections, as reflections of current and past problems and conditions. The story "Prinzessin von Tripoli," told by Gordon, reflects his assessment of the situation in the Allison house, his view of his son, and Gordon's relationships to women, whom he sees mostly in a negative light. The story ends with a wish-fulfilling marriage of Jaufré and Petite Lay. In the medieval legend that Gordon retells and refashions, the minstrel Jaufré Rudel never reaches the unknown yet beloved Princess until the moment of his death. In Gordon's version, in contrast, Jaufré possesses Petite Lay, and this symbolizes Gordon's ultimate victory over his rival Edward, who has attracted the love of his mother Alice. Beyond the many projections contained in the story, Grand considers also its philosophical meaning: all characters are in search of themselves, their own identity. For Gordon, their destiny is "fate": they are powerless to change it. But the author/narrator makes it explicit for the reader that, on the contrary, we are responsible for our destiny, and we are able to change it. Thus the biggest mistake Gordon and the others make is hiding behind illusions and easy pretexts, and the confrontation with the truth, which is what they might call their real fate, will come over them nolens volens.

For Grand, the mother figure in the story "Die Mutter auf dem Montmartre" does not understand the reasons for her suffering and the meaning behind the seemingly senseless events of the war and the postwar period. Only the Christian faith, which Döblin himself found during his deep crisis of 1940 in Mende, would lift her out of her despair, as it will later lift Edward's mother Alice from her crisis. The story indicates the path but not the goal.

In the same way, Grand analyzes the various stories in their connection with the person who tells them and the situation at the moment when they are told. His last commentary is devoted to the Theodora legend. This legend, which Alice partially tells Edward and then completes in a letter, reveals the "two souls" in Alice's breast — purity and animalistic passion — and her arrogance, her *Hochmut*, in believing she can save the savage man who has degraded her. She needs to find the way to saintly humility, which includes sexual abstinence and even the eventual transformation from Theodora to Theodorus. Grand follows the various implications of this complex story, which seems to point out the way not how to live this life but how to transcend it. The projections, all told, are for Grand revelations of the self, of the characters, but ultimately of the creator of these characters, Döblin. Together they are a summary of Döblin's life and work, and a confession of his guilt and sins. The human being has to accept the coexistence of good and evil within us. For Grand, this is the truth behind the lies that we have to accept: "Im Grunde wissen alle Personen des Romans, welches die Wahrheit ist, aber es fehlt ihnen der Mut, sich für sie zu entscheiden. Mit Wahrheit ist aber auch der Glaube an den Menschen, an Gut und Böse, an Wertverwirklichung und Verantwortung und der Glaube an die Existenz der Liebe gemeint" (165). The lack of faith brings about aggressiveness, egotism, irresponsible behavior, the will for revenge and brutality, and thus war. In this egotistical hubris is the root of man's guilt, which can only be overcome by love — the idea and nature of true love being the quest of the protagonists in all of Döblin's works after 1933, if not before. Grand's discussion of this profound problem provides a fitting end to his search for the central point of the novel (180–96).

The peculiar structure of *Hamlet* provides the point of departure for Wolfgang Düsing's study "Döblins 'Hamlet oder Die lange Nacht nimmt ein Ende' und der Novellenroman der Moderne."[5] Düsing defines it as a *Novellenroman*, which is different from a *Novellenzyklus* in the tradition of Boccaccio, as the *Novellenroman* goes beyond the telling of stories in a small group of people, or in a situation like the Arabian Nights, where Sheherazade tells stories to save her life. The *Novellenroman* offers a plot that is centered around a protagonist and advances mainly through the telling of the stories. Düsing exemplifies this with Hermann Broch's *Die Schuldlosen*, but he mentions other more contemporary examples as well. For Broch, he says, the *Novellenroman* is "eine epische Antwort auf Grundprobleme der modernen Gesellschaft" (271). *Die Schuldlosen* presents the decomposition of reality leading to a decomposition of the characters' identity, in a montage of novellistic vignettes (272). Broch's protagonist Andreas shows inner development, and the inserted stories make possible a leitmotiv technique that works by glimpses into the past and omens of the future: a total system binding the individual stories and the frame together (273). It generates a multiperspectival portrayal that enables the author to present the "Identitätszerfall" of the characters.

For Düsing, Döblin's variant of the *Novellenroman* is characterized by its medical background: the protagonist needs to be healed — or to heal himself — from the shock and trauma of his war injury, and by doing so discovers the deeper lying conflicts of his family, which prevented him from becoming his own person. The text is characterized by the close interconnection between the fate of the characters and the stories they tell (276), stories whose interpretations determine the events and can lead to altered versions with different outcomes — both of the stories and of the fates of the characters. There are stories told to the whole group and others told or written from one single person to another. All the stories are ambiguous and open to several interpretations. The characters change during the time of the action, and new stories or new versions of previous stories indicate these changes. Edward's initial inquiries in search of the truth do not receive clear answers, but lead to ever more unexpected and complex outcomes. If both conclusions of the novel could be considered valid, it would be an indication of the deep ambiguity and impenetrability that remain (280). But Düsing prefers the first version, in which Edward enters the monastery. This structural inconclusiveness, notes Düsing, may be a reason for the attraction of the *Novellenroman* for contemporary writers.

In his chapter "Identitätszerstörung und Rekonstruktion" in his book *Erinnerung und Identität*, Düsing delves into the intricacies of the interconnections between the stories and Edward's healing process, focusing on the double trauma: the wound from the war and the early childhood memories.[6] Of particular interest is the relation of role-playing to the search for identity, and the *Hamlet* play-in-the-play in which Edward wants to unmask his father. His Kierkegaardian "Redlichkeit" destroys the family, but offers Edward a chance for a new life — however, the question remains: which life? For Düsing, both alternative endings of the novel — Edward's retreat into a monastery and his return to life in the city — are symptoms of unresolved conflicts, as both, the active and the contemplative forms of life, must come together to make the individual whole and fully liberated from the traumatic past. The solution Döblin is after, the reaching of both possibilities, is a utopian goal. And for Düsing this is also why Döblin's novels cannot have closure (172).

In her short study "Es war die Liebe, es war die Welt, es war der Mensch," Ute Karlavaris-Bremer sheds some light on one aspect of Alice's love in *Hamlet*: the use Döblin made of the newspaper articles on the suicide of the dancer and film star Lupe Velez — which occurred while Döblin was living in Hollywood — for a montage in *Hamlet*.[7] This short insertion in the second half of the novel not only continues the montage techniques prevalent in *Berlin Alexanderplatz*, but is effectively used as a foil for the depiction of Alice's love and fate, and possibly as a hidden allusion to the fate of Frieda Kuhnke, who bore Döblin's "forgotten" child and died soon afterwards. The montage brings to light the entire complex of sex, love, and guilt, and the contradictions of human relationships in general.

Karlavaris-Bremer's hint at the evidence of montage ties in with several studies on the narrative techniques of *Hamlet*. Bettina Kümmerling, in her article "Analytische und synthetische Erzählweise: Zur Struktur von Döblins Roman 'Hamlet oder Die lange Nacht nimmt ein Ende,'" looks for the reasons for the obvious differences between the two parts of the novel.[8] In the first part, analytic narrative techniques prevail: the stories told, Edward's reflections on these stories, and his relentless and aggressive efforts to find the truth combine to build a complex structure in terms of time, of meaning, and of worldview. This is in keeping with Edward's "psychoanalytic" perspective where the truth keeps eluding him, in large part because the other characters don't want to reveal it. But according to Kümmerling, analytic forms need to be complemented by synthetic forms, and vice versa. The second part, which shows Gordon's and Alice's fates after their breakup, was considered a literary embarrassment by most critics, but according to Kümmerling is necessary for the completion of Edward's quest to find himself and to find his way back into society. Kümmerling goes on to analyze the element of the *Märchen* as an indication of Döblin's *Überrealität,* hyperreality, but also as a realm that Edward has to leave behind. In sum, the novel and its various layers and narrative strategies, as heterogeneous as they may seem at first, form a meaningful whole and convey a message that goes far beyond a simple call for the acknowledgment of guilt and a conversion to Christianity. On the contrary, Kümmerling sees the multiple narrative perspectives as a call to the readers to form their own judgment on the events and the message of the text.

Otto Keller, in his "Diskurskritik in Alfred Döblins Roman 'Hamlet oder Die lange Nacht hat ein Ende' oder das Problem der Montage," takes the presence of the montage principle for granted and uses it to critique the notion of the hero.[9] Döblin's subversion of the idea of a hero of the novel is a radical critique of Western novel writing principles, and justifies the claim that he offers something new in this text that could have been, as he said in his *Epilog,* the beginning of a new direction for his writing. Horst Steinmetz, in his "Hamlet oder die lange Nacht der Intertextualität," pursues the problem of intertextuality.[10] After discussing the problems of working with Kristeva's concept of intertextuality, he points out that it can be productive in analyzing twentieth-century texts, and that *Hamlet* is a prime example of an intertextual composition

(239). There is a consensus that the action is realized through references to other texts and that it follows the paradigm of Shakespeare's *Hamlet.* Steinmetz notes that the texts exert such a dominating force on *Hamlet* that they profile the novel's structure, which justifies the designation *Novellenroman,* a term Düsing had already applied to the work (240). This gives the novel a certain "indirectness"; it appears as if the characters cannot act for themselves, but only as the characters of the stories that they tell, and that they are driven, if not determined, by their stories and the figures that they create. The stories, quotes, and allusions make up the novel's reality: the figures have no other reality than that given in the texts (241). They are characterized by a "Sucht nach Texten" (242). For Gordon and Alice, life comes to an end when it is revealed that they tried to construe their identities with the wrong texts (243). Since one's identity can never be captured by a single pre-existing story, there are constant attempts to change the stories as they are being told, and to expand from one story to several stories. This is especially true for the endings of the stories, and no story has more versions and endings than Alice's Theodora legend. Edward's quest implies a quest for liberation from the texts, and when he finally understands that *Hamlet* was made up of the wrong texts and that he should go beyond all texts, his life is really at an end, and his decision to enter a monastery is the only logical outcome: it means death. But Döblin changed the ending, and if a new life is to begin for Edward, it must be a life with new texts.

Steinmetz compares *Hamlet* with Max Frisch's novels of the same period, *Stiller, Homo Faber,* and *Mein Name sei Gantenbein,* where intertextuality enters largely not through pre-existing texts, but through stories that the protagonists project of themselves. They try to reach their identities through stories that they invent themselves. All of these texts, however, express a crisis of the self and its identity, a crisis that arises because textuality undermines reality's unambiguous meaning (246).

Notes

[1] Adolf Steinmann, *Alfred Döblins Roman "Hamlet oder Die lange Nacht nimmt ein Ende": Isolation und Öffnung* (Zurich: AKU-Fotodruck, 1971).

[2] Manfred Auer, *Das Exil vor der Vertreibung: Motivkontinuität und Quellenproblematik im späten Werk Alfred Döblins* (Bonn: Bouvier Verlag, 1977), 102–53.

[3] Roland Links, *Alfred Döblin: Leben und Werk* (Berlin: Volk und Wissen, 1976), 196–205.

[4] Jules Grand, *Projektionen in Alfred Döblins "Hamlet oder Die lange Nacht nimmt ein Ende"* (Frankfurt: Herbert Lang/Peter Lang, 1974).

[5] Wolfgang Düsing, "Döblins 'Hamlet oder Die lange Nacht nimmt ein Ende und der Novellenroman der Moderne," *Internationale Alfred-Döblin-Kolloquien Münster 1989 – Marbach a. N. 1991,* ed. Werner Stauffacher (Bern: Peter Lang, 1993), 271–82.

[6] Wolfgang Düsing, *Erinnerung und Identität: Untersuchungen zu einem Erzählproblem bei Musil, Döblin, und Doderer* (Munich: Wilhelm Fink, 1982), 149–72.

[7] Ute Karlavaris-Bremer, "Es war die Liebe, es war die Welt, es war der Mensch." Entdeckungen und Überlegungen zu einer Episode in Döblins 'Hamlet'-Roman," *Internationales Alfred-Döblin-Kolloquium Lausanne 1987,* ed. Werner Stauffacher (Bern: Peter Lang, 1991), 181–88.

[8] Bettina Kümmerling, "Analytische und synthetische Erzählweise: Zur Struktur von Döblins Roman 'Hamlet oder Die lange Nacht nimmt ein Ende,'" *Internationales Alfred Döblin-Kolloquium Lausanne 1987,* ed. Werner Stauffacher, 165–80.

[9] Otto Keller, "Diskurskritik in Alfred Döblins Roman 'Hamlet oder Die lange Nacht hat ein Ende' oder das Problem der Montage," *Internationale Alfred-Döblin-Kolloquien 1984–1985,* ed. Werner Stauffacher, 93–101.

[10] Horst Steinmetz, "Hamlet oder die lange Nacht der Intertextualität," *Internationales Alfred-Döblin-Kolloquium Leiden 1995,* ed. Gabriele Sander (Bern: Peter Lang, 1997), 237–46.

15: Döblin's Impact on Other Writers

DÖBLIN THE WRITER is known to be avant-garde, unconventional, ever changing, and multi-faceted. How could he possibly serve as a model, as a "master" for younger generations of writers? He did serve this purpose, but relatively little attention has been paid to his impact. Günter Grass did much to change the idea of Döblin as unsuccessful with his 1967 speech, "Über meinen Lehrer Döblin." Yet little has been done since then to follow it up. What Matthias Prangel stated in 1987 — "[Es] ist noch beinahe ungeklärt, welche Bedeutung Döblin seinerseits für Zeitgenossen und Nachgeborene hatte und hat"[1] — has not lost its validity.

Gabriele Sander tracks down some traces of Döblin's influence on other writers in her study "Spurensuche in 'döblinener Waldung.' Über den Einfluß Döblins auf die Literatur der zwanziger Jahre und der Nachkriegszeit."[2] Her survey reaches from Lion Feuchtwanger and Bertolt Brecht[3] to Uwe Johnson and Alexander Kluge. She emphasizes the mutual effects between Döblin and Hans Henny Jahnn, whose novel *Perrudja,* written during the same period as *Berlin Alexanderplatz,* shows not only the impact of Joyce's *Ulysses,* but also that of previous novels by Döblin, especially *Wang-lun* and *Berge Meere und Giganten.* Among postwar authors influenced by Döblin, Sander singles out Wolfgang Koeppen, for instance *Tauben im Gras* (136–38), and Arno Schmidt, who expressed his admiration for Döblin's work in many different ways and whose earlier works are clearly marked by his readings of Döblin (138–41). Other authors who exhibit the effects of "Döblinismus" are Hans Erich Nossack, Wolfdietrich Schnurre, Ernst Kreuder, Uwe Johnson, and, of course, Günter Grass.

Jan Misinsky examines one aspect of this last connection in his study, "Apokalyptische Utopie. Alfred Döblin und Günter Grass."[4] Misinsky concentrates on what he calls the "anti-utopia" of *Berge Meere und Giganten,* which is for him a clearly negative indictment of human technology and "progress." "So distanziert sich Döblin in seiner apokalyptischen Utopie sowohl von der Technik — im Namen der Natur — als auch von der Politik — im Namen der Moral. Sein Werk *Berge Meere und Giganten* ist ein Science-Fiction-Roman, in dem die 'Science' der Menschheit nichts als Böses bringt" (156). Misinsky views Günter Grass's 1986 novel

Die Rättin as going a decisive step further: after the coming nuclear war humankind is replaced by the rule of the rats. Grass inserts into his history of the rats the history of the Matzerath-Bronski family, the Baltic expedition of the feminists in *Der Butt,* Grimm's fairy tales and the dying forests in the Federal Republic, and finally the criminal case of the Lübeck painter-forger Malskat. The narrator, who observes these events from a space station, in unable to intervene. While Döblin's anti-utopia was pessimistic, but left room for a renewal of humankind, Grass's Cassandra warnings are marked by an "Abwertung des Menschen" (162), which, however, still contains all the eternal hope of the classical utopias: that what he foresees will not come true.

Earlier, Ingrid Schuster had examined the impact of *Wang-lun* on writers during the Weimar period.[5] She placed the Wu-wei of *Wang-lun* in the context of the pacifism of Ernst Toller, Lion Feuchtwanger, Ludwig Rubiner, and Oskar Maria Graf. Parallels are apparent in Ernst Toller's *Masse-Mensch* and in Graf's *Die Heimsuchung* (1925), with the sect of "die Sanften," and later, in *Die Erben des Untergangs,* with "die Stillen" (47–48). The opposition between violence and the power of "Nicht-Widerstreben" is crucial for Lion Feuchtwanger's play *Warren Hastings* (1916) and for Ludwig Rubiner's play *Die Gewaltlosen.* Brecht, on the other hand, while admiring *Wang-lun,* never subscribed to its non-violence, and he may have influenced Feuchtwanger in changing this aspect when they reworked *Warren Hastings* into *Kalkutta, 4. Mai* (1927). Among later authors, Arthur Koestler has acknowledged his debt to Döblin, especially for *The Gladiators* (50–51).

There are some direct adaptations of Döblin's texts. Apart from film versions, Holger Teschke's 1987 theater play *Berliner November: Ein deutscher Bilderbogen nach Motiven aus Alfred Döblins November 1918* is of considerable interest, as Anne Kuhlmann shows in her article "Zweimal deutscher November. Revolutionshistoriographie und Intertextualität bei Alfred Döblin und Holger Teschke."[6] Both authors articulate the aporia of text and reality (177). In Teschke's theatrical scenes, continuity, still a goal and a framework in Döblin's narration, is completely abandoned.

Sabine Kyora analyzes some aspects of the reception and non-reception of Döblin's works by GDR writers.[7] In the 1960s, *Berlin Alexanderplatz* and its narrative voice seems to have exerted the most influence, as can be seen in texts by Uwe Johnson and Günter Kunert. The locale of Berlin was an additional attraction. In general, Döblin seems to have been less attractive as a model than, for instance, Kafka, because Döblin was politically less controversial, as only those of his works were published that did not disturb the authorities, at least until 1981 and the publication of *November 1918*. It would certainly be worthwhile to investigate traces of linguistic and stylistic similarities with Döblin in works of the younger generation of the eighties.

Finally the empirical study by Gebhard Rusch on the presence of Döblin's works on the German book market and of his name among writers confirms a persistent perception: Döblin is still known as a writer, but as one of the past.[8] The title *Berlin Alexanderplatz* is better known than the author's name, largely because of Rainer Werner Fassbinder's 1979 television series, which was subsequently released as a film. *Berlin Alexanderplatz* is the only title that is mentioned by any group of readers in Rusch's study. Döblin's books sell very little compared with books by Hermann Hesse, Kafka, Thomas Mann, even Heinrich Mann. When writers today are asked about earlier writers who have influenced them, Döblin's name is rarely mentioned. In libraries, the only Döblin title in any demand is *Berlin Alexanderplatz*. However, this is by no means a definitive measure of Döblin's real influence on other writers, whether direct or indirect: that history has not yet been written. It is a difficult undertaking, as very few writers — with the exceptions of Bertolt Brecht and Günter Grass — have openly acknowledged that they learned from Döblin's writings. But it is hoped that this book contributes some facts and ideas toward that goal.

Notes

[1] Matthias Prangel, *Alfred Döblin*, Sammlung Metzler, vol. 105 (2nd ed., Stuttgart: J. B. Metzler, 1987), 121.

[2] Gabriele Sander, "Spurensuche in 'döblinener Waldung.' Über den Einfluß Döblins auf die Literatur der zwanziger Jahre und der Nachkriegszeit," *Internationale Alfred-Döblin-Kolloquien Münster 1989–Marbach a. N. 1991,* ed. Werner Stauffacher (Bern: Lang, 1993), 128–53.

[3] There is much more to the Brecht-Döblin connection than has been considered so far. Cf. Otto F. Best, "'Epischer Roman' und 'Dramatischer Roman.' Einige Überlegungen zum Frühwerk von Alfred Döblin und Bert Brecht," *Germanisch-Romanische Monatsschrift* 53 (1972): 281–309; "'Zertrümmerung der Person.' Galy Gay (Brecht) und Franz Biberkopf (Döblin) im Vergleich," *Internationales Alfred-Döblin-Kolloquium Leipzig 1997,* ed. Ira Lorf and Gabriele Sander (Bern: Peter Lang, 1999), 97–104.

[4] Jan Misinsky, "Apokalyptische Utopie. Alfred Döblin und Günter Grass," *Internationale Alfred-Döblin-Kolloquien Münster 1989–Marbach a. N. 1991,* ed. Werner Stauffacher (Bern: Peter Lang, 1993), 154–64.

[5] Ingrid Schuster, "Die Wirkungen des Wang-lun in der Weimarer Republik," *Internationale Alfred-Döblin-Kolloquien 1980–1983,* ed. Werner Stauffacher (Bern: Peter Lang, 1986), 45–53.

[6] "Zweimal Deutscher November. Revolutionshistoriographie und Intertextualität bei Alfred Döblin und Holger Teschke," *Internationales Alfred-Döblin-Kolloquium Leipzig 1997,* ed. Ira Lorf and Gabriele Sander (Bern: Peter Lang, 1999), 167–77.

[7] Sabine Kyora, "'Das Döblinsche Syndrom.' Die Döblin-Rezeption als Beispiel für die Rezeption der klassischen Moderne in der DDR," *Internationales Alfred-Döblin-Kolloquium Leipzig 1997,* ed. Ira Lorf and Gabriele Sander (Bern: Peter Lang, 1999), 179–89.

[8] Gerhard Rusch, "Die literarische Wirklichkeit Alfred Döblins 1997. Eine Explorationsstudie zur Bedeutung des literarischen Wissens im Buchmarkt," *Internationales Alfred-Döblin-Kolloquium Leipzig 1997,* ed. Ira Lorf and Gabriele Sander (Bern: Peter Lang, 1999), 191–210.

Conclusion

THERE ARE TWO "SCHOOLS" among Döblin scholars; one of them calls him a "Proteus" and emphasizes the changes in his views and in the nature of his texts. The second maintains that, in spite of these undeniable changes, he always remained the same. This is only the first indication how varied the views on Döblin and his oeuvre have been. From the first reviewers to the most recent scholars, hardly anyone writing on Döblin remains neutral. As he himself liked debates and controversy, his texts still elicit a partisan response, pro or con. He still causes emotional reactions with his manner of writing, he baffles with the inconclusive outcome of his narratives, and his philosophy of nature, his political views, and his religious beliefs remain controversial. It is to be expected, therefore, that the reception of his novels cannot be summed up in a few neat statements.

The difficulties begin with the very use of the term "novel." Döblin was not happy with it, and would have preferred "epic," but that would be a misnomer as well. When he called *November 1918* an "Erzählwerk," a narrative work, he may have found the best term — but then, this is a vague generic term that includes everything that is narrated.

Critics have not missed the point that Döblin's narrative works had a message, some of them a rather didactic message at that. The messages seemed to be political, but not only political: the texts expressed a total worldview and urged the reader to change. One of the basic patterns in these texts is decadence and destruction versus renewal. However, Döblin's messages were rarely expressed without ambiguity. His novels were a challenge to his readers to change their views on life and in so doing to change themselves. But Döblin did not give them ready-made precepts: they had to find their own way. The most striking instance of this was Döblin's "open letters" to the then-student Gustav René Hocke, published in 1931 as *Wissen und Verändern!* Hocke had asked Döblin for advice what to do and how to act in the desperate and confusing situation of the last Weimar years. What he got was an analysis of the political landscape, especially socialism, and its history; the reasons for the "Untertanengeist," the submissiveness of the Germans to authority; and hints at Döblin's political philosophy. Döblin concluded with the statement: if you think this through, you will know what to do and how to act.

A major point of interest for the critics of Döblin's first published novel, *Die drei Sprünge des Wang-lun,* was the idea of Wu-wei: non-resistance, or non-violent resistance. But they could not fail to notice the ambiguity of the narrator toward this idea. Although he seemed to affirm it, the plot and the changes in the attitudes of Wang-lun himself emphasized the problematic and potentially negative aspects of this fundamentally noble idea.

These are examples of the fundamental problems readers have with Döblin's texts. One of the reasons for conflicting messages and open endings is that the novels resemble a process of reflection by the author/narrator. He attacks a problem or conflict, and in the course of the action, begins to gain clarity about himself and the problem. This is most clearly demonstrated in the last novel, *Hamlet,* where the characters gain insight into themselves and others by means of telling stories. There are similarities between this process and psychoanalysis, as many scholars have noted. Döblin's novels are not the *results* of a previous process of "becoming," of reflection and gestation; instead, they themselves represent this process, and their endings are often like the beginning of another story, as Döblin himself confirmed.

The theme of "becoming," of transformation, of revolution, is central to Döblin's stories. The grand theme of Expressionism was "der neue Mensch," the transformed human being, sometimes seen as Nietzsche's "Übermensch," sometimes conceived in a more peaceful incarnation. Döblin's continual urge and need to change and to transform himself can be regarded as a variant of this epochal idea. It finally led him to his own transformation into a confessing Christian.

Döblin's philosophy of nature and his ambivalent attitude toward modern technological progress and the ideas of Western civilization in general are discernable in most of his novels and have intrigued the early reviewers and the later critics alike. However, it is noteworthy that both Döblin's non-fiction books on this subject, *Das Ich über der Natur* and *Unser Dasein,* and the three novels that most directly confront these complex issues, *Wadzek, Berge Meere und Giganten,* and *Amazonas,* as well as the important essay *Prometheus und das Primitive,* have found what may be called a very reluctant reception, and it is only recently that scholars have tackled these issues in a more comprehensive manner.

One of the controversial issues emanating from Döblin's worldview, his views on the system of conflicting natural forces and on the human being as part of these natural conflicts, is the question of "Gewalt," of violence. Scenes of violence abound in his works, especially in *Wallenstein*, which was written under the impression of the slaughter of the First World War. There are also many impressively or even repellingly violent scenes in *Wang-lun, Berge Meere und Giganten,* and *Amazonas,* to name the most obvious examples. Did Döblin the author enjoy writing these scenes? This is still a controversial issue. It is undeniable, and has been noted by many critics, that the author and narrator clearly sympathize with the victims, the poor and the downtrodden. There is also the idyllic utopia that appears at the end of violent narratives like *Berge Meere und Giganten,* a return of the human race to a peaceful existence in harmony with nature. Here again, critics have asked whether these idylls are an expression of escapism and regression, or whether they are a vision of a truly humane and peaceful world.

It has been noted that, although Döblin himself was considered the typical intellectual, the writer of the big city who confronted life with common sense and a sober rational mind, there was always another side of him: an attraction to mysticism, which was connected with his conception of nature, just as the big city demanded rationality. Both of these sides are apparent in his writings, and invite his readers to stress the aspects that appeal to them more than the others.

There is a curious paradox in Döblin's life and work: he was a Berliner and had his roots in that city. Indeed he himself stated that he never wanted to leave it, except for short trips. Therefore, his exile beginning in 1933 was all the more catastrophic for him, and scholars have noted with a degree of justification that the texts he wrote after 1933 are not of the same caliber as those before, or at least that their language is uneven, and "damaged" by exile, as it were. However, when one considers Döblin's novels, it is fascinating to see that he mostly chose material from previous historical periods or from far-away lands and foreign cultures. It has been noted how much Döblin was able to immerse himself in eighteenth-century Chinese culture and mentality in *Wang-lun,* how close he came to the thoughts and feelings of the German during the Thirty Years' War in *Wallenstein,* and that he presented such a convincing picture of the sceneries of South America, of the Barbaric European colonizers, and the Indians, in *Amazonas.* He liked to travel in his mind, with the help of books, maps, and artifacts in museums, much more than in reality. The question arises whether these imaginary voyages were escapes from reality or not; and although this remains controversial, the scholarly consensus is that all of Döblin's depictions of past eras, foreign lands, mythical stories (in *Manas,* for instance), are reflections of his present and have close connections with its conditions and conflicts.

There are a few major recurring themes in Döblin's narratives: man versus the powers of nature; decay or destruction versus renewal; war and other violent conflict and its horrible destruction and the suffering of its victims, including the lasting trauma of war veterans (most prominent in *Berlin Alexanderplatz* and *Hamlet*); flight and exile (present even long before 1933); the vision of a peaceful community of mutual respect and solidarity; the need and search for redemption, for salvation, either in nature, away from the human race, or as a search for God's grace.

There is a consensus by now on Döblin's significance as one of the great epic writers of the twentieth century. However, Döblin's work has never become "mainstream," his place in literary history is uncertain, and in spite of his undeniable importance, Döblin's work is little known outside the German-speaking areas. He has remained an outsider, in contrast to his contemporary and "rival" Thomas Mann. This book, which has attempted to offer a view of the many ways in which his novels have been read and understood, is meant to be an invitation to a further acquaintance with this writer who still has the ability to surprise his readers with unexpected new ideas.

Bibliography

Editions of Döblin's Works

Ausgewählte Werke in Einzelbänden. Olten/Freiburg, now Zürich/Düsseldorf: Walter-Verlag.

Includes:

Amazonas. Roman. Ed. Werner Stauffacher, Freiburg/Olten: Walter-Verlag, 1988.

Babylonische Wandrung oder Hochmut kommt vor dem Fall. Ed. Walter Muschg. Olten/Freiburg, 1962.

Berge Meere und Giganten. Ed. Gabriele Sander. Düsseldorf/Zürich, 2003.

Berlin Alexanderplatz. Die Geschichte vom Franz Biberkopf. Ed. Werner Stauffacher. Düsseldorf/Zürich: Walter Verlag, 1996.

Briefe. Edited by Heinz Graber. 1970.

Briefe II. Ed. Helmut Pfanner. Düsseldorf/Zürich: Walter Verlag, 2001.

Der deutsche Maskenball. Von Linke Poot. Ed. Heinz Graber. Olten/Freiburg: Walter Verlag, 1972.

Drama — Hörspiel — Film. Ed. Erich Kleinschmidt. Olten/Freiburg: Walter Verlag, 1983.

Die drei Sprünge des Wang-lun. Ed. Walter Muschg. Olten/Freiburg: Walter Verlag, 1960.

Hamlet oder Die lange Nacht nimmt ein Ende. Ed. Walter Muschg and Heinz Graber. Olten/Freiburg: Walter Verlag, 1966.

Jagende Rosse. Der schwarze Vorhang und andere Erzählwerke. Ed. Anthony W. Riley. Olten/Freiburg: Walter Verlag, 1981.

Kleine Schriften I (1902–1921). Ed. Anthony W. Riley. 1985.

Kleine Schriften II (1922–1924). Ed. Anthony W. Riley. 1990.

Kleine Schriften III. Ed. Anthony W. Riley. Düsseldorf/Zürich: Walter Verlag, 1999.

Kritik der Zeit. Rundfunkbeiträge 1946–1952. Ed. Alexandra Birkert. Olten/Freiburg: Walter Verlag, 1992.

Manas. Epische Dichtung. Ed. Walter Muschg. Olten/Freiburg: Walter Verlag, 1961.

November 1918. Eine deutsche Revolution. 4 vols. Ed. Werner Stauffacher. Olten/Freiburg: Walter Verlag, 1991.

Pardon wird nicht gegeben. Ed. Walter Muschg. Olten/Freiburg: Walter Verlag, 1960.

Reise in Polen. Ed. Heinz Graber. Olten/Freiburg: Walter Verlag, 1968.

Schicksalsreise. Bericht und Bekenntnis. Ed. Anthony W. Riley. Solothurn/Düsseldorf: Walter Verlag, 1993.

Schriften zu jüdischen Fragen. Ed. Hans-Otto Horch. Solothurn/Düsseldorf: Walter Verlag, 1995.

Schriften zu Leben und Werk. Ed. Erich Kleinschmidt. Olten/Freiburg: Walter Verlag, 1986.

Schriften zur Ästhetik, Poetik und Literatur. Ed. Erich Kleinschmidt. 1989.

Schriften zur Politik und Gesellschaft. Edited by Heinz Graber. 1972.

Unser Dasein. Ed. Walter Muschg. Olten/Freiburg: Walter Verlag, 1964.

Wadzeks Kampf mit der Dampfturbine. Ed. Anthony W. Riley. Olten/Freiburg: Walter, 1982.

Wallenstein. Ed. Erwin Kobel. Düsseldorf/Zürich: Walter Verlag, 2001.

Wissen und Verändern! Ed. Heinz Graber. Olten/Freiburg: Walter Verlag, 1972.

English Translations

Alexanderplatz, Berlin. The Story of Franz Biberkopf. Trans. Eugene Jolas. New York: Viking Press, 1931.

The Three Leaps of Wang Lun. A Chinese Novel. Trans. C. D. Godwin. Hong Kong: Chinese University Press, 1991.

Journey to Poland. Trans. Joachim Neugroschel. New York: Paragon House, 1991.

Men without Mercy. Trans. Trevor and Phyllis Blewitt. London: Gollancz, 1937.

Destiny's Journey. Trans. Edna McCown. New York: Paragon House, 1992.

A People Betrayed. November 1918. A German Revolution. Trans. John E. Woods. New York: Fromm International Publications, 1983.

Karl and Rosa. Trans. John E. Woods. New York: Fromm International Publications, 1983.

Secondary Literature

Alfred Döblin zum 70. Geburtstag. Wiesbaden: Limes Verlag, 1948.

Alfred Döblin. text & kritik 13/14 (Special issue): 1966.

Althen, Christina. *Machtkonstellationen einer deutschen Revolution: Alfred Döblins Geschichtsroman "November 1918."* Frankfurt: Peter Lang, 1993.

Anders, Günther. "Der letzte Roman. Gebrauchsanweisung für Döblins Buch *Babylonische Wandrung oder Hochmut kommt vor dem Fall.* In G. A. *Mensch ohne Welt: Schriften zur Kunst und Literatur,* 31–41. Munich: C. H. Beck, 1984.

———. "Der verwüstete Mensch. Über Welt- und Sprachlosigkeit in Döblins *Berlin Alexanderplatz.*" In G. A. *Mensch ohne Welt: Schriften zur Kunst und Literatur,* 3–30. Munich: C. H. Beck, 1984.

Arnold, Armin. *Alfred Döblin.* Köpfe des 20. Jahrhunderts 129. Berlin: Morgenbuch Verlag, 1996.

Auer, Manfred. *Das Exil vor der Vertreibung: Motivkontinuität und Quellenproblematik im späten Werk Alfred Döblins.* Bonn: Bouvier Verlag, 1977.

Baacke, Dieter. "Erzähltes Engagement. Antike Mythologie in Döblins Romanen." *text & kritik* 13/14 (1966): 22–31.

Banchelli, Eva. "'Berlin Alexanderplatz' und der Großstadtroman der amerikanischen Moderne: Reflexe, Anregungen, Polemiken." *Internationale Alfred-Döblin-Kolloquien Münster 1989–Marbach a. N. 1991,* ed. Werner Stauffacher, 206–16. Bern: Peter Lang, 1993.

Bartscherer, Christoph. *Das Ich und die Natur: Alfred Döblins literarischer Weg im Licht seiner Religionsphilosophie.* Literatur- und Medienwissenschaft 55. Paderborn: Igel Verlag Wissenschaft, 1997.

Baumann-Eisenack, Barbara. "Zu Gebrauch und Funktion des Mythos in Alfred Döblins 'Babylonische Wandrung oder Hochmut kommt vor dem Fall' (1934)." *Internationale Alfred-Döblin-Kolloquien Münster 1989–Marbach a. N. 1991,* ed. Werner Stauffacher, 233–42. Bern: Peter Lang, 1993.

Bayerdörfer, Hans-Peter. "Alfred Döblin: *Berlin Alexanderplatz.*" In *Interpretationen: Romane des 20. Jahrhunderts,* vol. 1, 158–94. Stuttgart: Reclam, 1933.

———. "Der Wissende und die Gewalt. Alfred Döblins Theorie des epischen Werkes und der Schluß von *Berlin Alexanderplatz.*" *Deutsche Vierteljahrsschrift* 44 (1970): 318–53.

Bekes, Peter. *Berlin Alexanderplatz: Interpretationen.* Oldenbourg Interpretationen mit Unterrichtshilfen, vol. 74. Munich: Oldenbourg, 1995.

Best, Otto F. "'Epischer Roman' und 'Dramatischer Roman.' Einige Überlegungen zum Frühwerk von Alfred Döblin und Bert Brecht." *Germanisch-Romanische Monatsschrift* 53 (1972): 281–309.

———. "'Zertrümmerung der Person.' Galy Gay (Brecht) und Franz Biberkopf (Döblin) im Vergleich." *Internationales Alfred-Döblin-Kolloquium Leipzig 1997,* ed. Ira Lorf and Gabriele Sander, 97–104. Bern: Peter Lang, 1999.

———. "Zwischen Orient und Okzident. Döblin und Spinoza. Einige Anmerkungen zur Problematik des offenen Schlusses von *Berlin Alexanderplatz.*" *Colloquia Germanica* 12 (1979): 94–105.

Blessing, Karl Herbert. *Die Problematik des "modernen Epos" im Frühwerk Alfred Döblins.* Deutsche Studien 19. Meisenheim am Glan: Anton Hain, 1972.

Bock, Sigrid, and Manfred Hahn, eds. *Erfahrung Exil: Antifaschistische Romane 1933–1945.* Berlin/Weimar: Aufbau Verlag, 1979.

Brecht, Bertolt. *Tagebücher 1920–1922* (Frankfurt: Suhrkamp, 1975).

Brüggemann, Heinz. "*Berlin Alexanderplatz* oder 'Franz, Mieze, Reinhold, Tod & Teufel.' Rainer Werner Fassbinders filmische Lektüre des Romans von Döblin. Polemik gegen einen melodramatischen Widerruf der ästhetischen Moderne." In *Rainer Werner Fassbinder,* edited by Heinz Ludwig Arnold, 51–65. *text & kritik* 103. Munich: text & kritik, 1989.

Delgado, Teresa. "Poetische Anthropologie. Interkulturelles Schreiben in Döblins *Amazonas*-Trilogie und Hubert *Fichtes Explosion. Roman der Ethnologie.*" *Internationales Alfred-Döblin-Kolloquium Leipzig 1997,* ed. Lorf and Sander, 151–66. Bern: Peter Lang, 1999.

Denlinger, Ardon. *Alfred Döblins "Berge Meere und Giganten": Epos und Ideologie.* Amsterdam: B. R. Grüner, 1977.

Detken, Anke. *Alfred Döblins "Berlin Alexanderplatz" übersetzt: Ein kontrastiver multilingualer Vergleich.* Palaestra 299. Göttingen: Vandenhoeck & Ruprecht, 1997.

Dollenmayer, David B. *The Berlin Novels of Alfred Döblin.* Berkeley/Los Angeles/London: U of California P, 1988.

———. "Heroismuskritik in einem Frühwerk von Döblin: 'Wadzeks Kampf mit der Dampfturbine.'" *Internationale Alfred-Döblin-Kolloquien 1980–1983,* ed. Werner Stauffacher, 270–79.

———. "Der Wandel in Döblins Auffassung von der deutschen Revolution 1918–1919." *Internationale Alfred-Döblin-Kolloquien 1980–1983,* ed. Werner Stauffacher, 56–63. Bern: Peter Lang, 1986.

———. "'Wessen Amerikanisch?' — Zu Eugene Jolas' Übersetzung von *Berlin Alexanderplatz.*" *Internationale Alfred-Döblin-Kolloquien Münster 1989–Marbach a. N. 1991,* ed. Werner Stauffacher, 192–205. Bern: Peter Lang, 1993.

Dollinger, Roland. *Totalität und Totalitarismus im Exilwerk Döblins.* Epistema: Würzburger Wissenschaftliche Schriften, Reihe Literaturwissenschaft, 126. Würzburg: Königshausen & Neumann, 1994.

Dronske, Ulrich. *Tödliche Präsens/zen: Über die Philosophie des Literarischen bei Alfred Döblin.* Würzburg: Königshausen & Neumann, 1998.

Düsing, Wolfgang. "Döblins 'Hamlet oder Die lange Nacht nimmt ein Ende und der Novellenroman der Moderne." *Internationale Alfred-Döblin-Kolloquien Münster 1989–Marbach a. N. 1991,* ed. Werner Stauffacher, 271–82. Bern: Peter Lang, 1993.

———. "Das Epos der Weimarer Republik. Döblins Romanzyklus *November 1918." Schriftsteller und Politik in Deutschland,* ed. Werner Link, 49–61. Düsseldorf: Droste-Verlag, 1979.

———. *Erinnerung und Identität: Untersuchungen zu einem Erzählproblem bei Musil, Döblin und Doderer.* Munich: Wilhelm Fink, 1982. (On Döblin, 103–72.)

Duytschaever, Joris. "Joyce — Dos Passos —Döblin: Einfluß oder Analogie?" *Materialien zu Alfred Döblins "Berlin Alexanderplatz,"* edited by Matthias Prangel, Suhrkamp Taschenbuch 268. Frankfurt: Suhrkamp, 1975, 136–49.

Elshorst, Hansjörg. *Mensch und Umwelt im Werk Alfred Döblins.* Munich, 1966. (Diss. Munich 1964.)

Erhardt, Jacob. *Alfred Döblins "Amazonas"-Trilogie.* Worms: Georg Heintz, 1974.

Falk, Werner. "Der erste moderne deutsche Roman. *Die drei Sprünge des Wang-lun* von Alfred Döblin." *Zeitschrift für deutsche Philologie* 89 (1970): 510–31.

Fang-hsiung Dscheng. *Alfred Döblins Roman "Die drei Sprünge des Wang-lun" als Spiegel des Interesses deutscher Autoren an China.* Frankfurt: Peter Lang, 1979.

Fromm, Georg. "Hiobs Wachhund. Die erste Hiob-Paraphrase in Alfred Döblins *Berlin Alexanderplatz." Internationales Alfred-Döblin-Kolloquium Paris 1993,* ed. Michael Grunewald, 213–26. Bern: Peter Lang, 1995.

———. "Die Isaak-Paraphrase in Alfred Döblins *Berlin Alexanderplatz." Internationales Alfred-Döblin-Kolloquium Leiden 1995,* ed. Gabriele Sander, 159–68. Bern: Peter Lang, 1997.

Frühwald, Wolfgang. "Rosa und der Satan. Thesen zum Verhältnis von Christentum und Sozialismus im Schlußband von Alfred Döblins Erzählwerk *November 1918." Internationale Alfred-Döblin-Kolloquien 1980–1983,* ed. Werner Stauffacher, 239–56. Bern: Peter Lang, 1986.

Gathge, Roderich. "Die Naturphilosophie Alfred Döblins: Begegnung mit östlicher Weisheit und Mystik." *Internationale Alfred-Döblin-Kolloquien 1984–1985,* ed. Werner Stauffacher, 16–29.

Graber, Heinz. *Alfred Döblins Epos "Manas."* Basler Studien zur deutschen Sprache und Literatur 34. Bern: Francke, 1967.

Grand, Jules. *Projektionen in Alfred Döblins Roman "Hamlet oder Die lange Nacht nimmt ein Ende."* Frankfurt: Herbert Lang/Peter Lang, 1974.

Grass, Günter. "Über meinen Lehrer Döblin." *Über meinen Lehrer Döblin und andere Vorträge,* LCB Editionen vol. 1. Berlin: Literarisches Colloquium, 1968. 7–26. Originally published in *Akzente* 14, 4 (August 1967): 290–309.

Grunewald, Michel, ed. *Internationales Alfred-Döblin-Kolloquium Paris 1993.* Jahrbuch für Internationale Germanistik, series A, vol. 41. Bern: Peter Lang, 1995.

Hahn, Torsten. "'Vernichtender Fortschritt.' Zur experimentellen Konfiguration von Arbeit und Trägheit in *Berge Meere und Giganten. Internationales Alfred-Döblin-Kolloquium Bergamo 1999,* ed. Torsten Hahn. Bern: Peter Lang, 2001, 107–29.

Hahn, Torsten, ed. *Internationales Alfred-Döblin-Kolloquium Bergamo 1999.* Jahrbuch für Internationale Germanistik, series A, vol. 51. Bern: Peter Lang, 2002.

Haag, Achim. "Fassbinder ver-filmt *Berlin Alexanderplatz.* Bilder und Töne jenseits ihrer Vorlage: Wider eine Dogmatik der Literaturverfilmung." *Internationale Alfred-Döblin-Kolloquien Münster 1989–Marbach a. N. 1991,* ed. Werner Stauffacher, 298–316. Bern: Peter Lang, 1993.

Hecker, Axel. *Geschichte als Fiktion: Alfred Döblins "Wallenstein" — eine exemplarische Kritik des Realismus.* Epistema: Würzburger Wissenschaftliche Schriften, Reihe Literaturwissenschaft, 21. Würzburg: Königshausen & Neumann, 1986.

———. "Döblins *Wallenstein* und Flauberts *Salammbô.* Ein strukturaler Vergleich." *Internationale Alfred-Döblin-Kolloquien 1984–1985,* ed. Werner Stauffacher, 196–214.

———. "Die Realität der Geschichte und die 'überreale Sphäre' des Romans. Überlegungen und Thesen zum Problem der Fiktionalität in Döblins Romanprogramm und seinem 'Wallenstein.'" *Internationale Alfred-Döblin-Kolloquien 1980–1983,* ed. Werner Stauffacher, 280–92.

Herchenröder, Max. "Berge, Meere und Giganten." *Alfred Döblin zum 70. Geburtstag,* ed. Paul E. H. Lüth, 48–57. Wiesbaden: Limes Verlag, 1948.

Hilman, Roger. "Döblin's 'Symphony of the Big City': *Berlin Alexanderplatz* and the Historical Novel." In *The Modern German Historical Novel: Paradigms, Problems, Perspectives,* edited by David Roberts and Philip Thomson, 97–108. New York/Oxford: Berg, 1991.

Horkheimer, Max, ed. *Studien über Autorität und Familie.* Paris, 1936.

Humphrey, Richard. *The Historical Novel as Philosophy of History: Three German Contributions: Alexis, Fontane, Döblin.* Bithell Series of Dissertations 10. London: The Institute of Germanic Studies, University of London, 1986. (On *November 1918*: 127–49.)

Hüppauf, Bernd. "The Historical Novel and a History of Mentalities: Alfred Döblin's *Wallenstein* as a Historical Novel." In *The Modern German Historical Novel: Paradigms, Problems, Perspectives,* edited by David Roberts and Philip Thomson. New York/Oxford: Berg, 1991.

Kaemmerling, Ekkehart. "Die filmische Schreibweise." *Materialien zu Alfred Döblin "Berlin Alexanderplatz,"* ed. Matthias Prangel, 185–98.

Karlavaris-Bremer, Ute. "Döblin und die Berlinerin. Frauengestalten in Alfred Döblins Berliner Romanen," *Internationale Alfred-Döblin-Kolloquien 1984–1985,* ed. Werner Stauffacher, 176–84. Bern: Peter Lang, 1988.

———. "Es war die Liebe, es war die Welt, es war der Mensch." Entdeckungen und Überlegungen zu einer Episode in Döblins 'Hamlet'-Roman." *Internationales Alfred-Döblin-Kolloquium Lausanne 1987,* ed. Werner Stauffacher, 181–88. Bern: Peter Lang, 1991.

Kaya, Nevzat. "'Tellurische Rationalitätskritik': Zur Weiblichkeitskonzeption in Alfred Döblins *Berge Meere und Giganten,*" *Internationales Alfred-Döblin-Kolloquium Bergamo 1999,* ed. Torsten Hahn, Bern: Peter Lang, 2002, 131–49.

Keller, Otto. "Diskurskritik in Alfred Döblins Roman 'Hamlet oder Die lange Nacht hat ein Ende' oder das Problem der Montage." *Internationale Alfred-Döblin-Kolloquien 1984–1985,* ed. Werner Stauffacher, 93–101. Bern: Peter Lang, 1988.

———. *Döblins Montageroman als Epos der Moderne: Die Struktur der Romane Der schwarze Vorhang, Die drei Sprünge des Wang-lun und Berlin Alexanderplatz.* Munich: Wilhelm Fink, 1980.

———. "Tristan und Antigone. Gestus, Verfremdung und Montage als Medien der Figurengestaltung in Döblins 'November 1918.'" *Internationale Alfred-Döblin-Kolloquien 1980–1983,* ed. Werner Stauffacher, 10–19. Bern: Peter Lang, 1986.

Kiesel, Helmuth. "Döblin und das Kino. Überlegungen zur Alexanderplatz-Verfilmung." *Internationale Alfred-Döblin-Kolloquien Münster 1989–Marbach a. N. 1991,* ed. Werner Stauffacher, 284–97. Bern: Peter Lang, 1993.

———. *Literarische Trauerarbeit: Das Exil- und Spätwerk Alfred Döblins.* Tübingen: Max Niemeyer, 1986.

Klein, Otto. *Das Thema Gewalt im Werk Alfred Döblins: Ästhetische, ethische und religiöse Sichtweise.* Hamburg: Verlag Dr. Kovac, 1995.

Kleinschmidt, Erich. "Parteiliche Fiktionalität. Zur Anlage historischen Erzählens in Alfred Döblins *November 1918.*" *Internationale Alfred-Döblin-Kolloquien 1980–1983*, ed. Werner Stauffacher, 116–32. Bern: Peter Lang, 1986.

Klotz, Volker. *Die erzählte Stadt: Ein Sujet als Herausforderung des Romans von Lesage bis Döblin.* Munich: Carl Hanser, 1969.

Kobel, Erwin. *Alfred Döblin: Erzählkunst im Umbruch.* Berlin/New York: Walter de Gruyter, 1985.

Kodjio, Pierre Nenguie. "Döblins Reflexionen zur technischen Zivilisation. Das Beispiel des *Wadzek*-Romans," *Internationales Alfred-Döblin-Kolloquium Bergamo 1999*, edited by Torsten Hahn (Bern: Peter Lang, 2002), 75–85.

Koepke, Wulf. "Der Beginn von Döblins Babylonischer Wanderung." *Internationales Alfred-Döblin-Kolloquium Paris 1993*, ed. Michel Grünewald, 67–84. Bern: Peter Lang, 1995.

———. "Spontane Ansätze zur Überwindung der Individuation. Zur Struktur von Döblins *Bürger und Soldaten 1918.*" *Internationale Alfred-Döblin-Kolloquien 1980–1983*, ed. Werner Stauffacher, 20–33. Bern: Peter Lang, 1986.

———. "Die Überwindung der Revolution: *November 1918*," *Internationales Alfred-Döblin-Kolloquium Bergamo 1999*, edited by Torsten Hahn (Bern: Peter Lang, 2002), 243–59.

Kojima, Hajime. "Bemerkungen zu Alfred Döblins Roman 'Die drei Sprünge des Wang-lun.'" *Internationale Alfred-Döblin-Kolloquien 1984–1985*, ed. Werner Stauffacher, 10–15.

Komar, Kathleen. "Technique and Structure in Döblin's *Berlin Alexanderplatz.*" *German Quarterly* 54 (1981): 318–34.

Koopmann, Helmut. "Der Schluß des Romans *Berlin Alexanderplatz* — eine Antwort auf Thomas Manns *Zauberberg*?" *Internationale Alfred-Döblin-Kolloquien Münster 1989–Marbach a. N. 1991*, ed. Werner Stauffacher. 179–91. Bern: Peter Lang, 1993.

Kort, Wolfgang. *Alfred Döblin.* Twayne World Authors Series 290. New York: Twayne Publishers, 1974.

———. *Alfred Döblin: Das Bild des Menschen in seinen Romanen* (Bonn: H. Bouvier, 1970).

Kreutzer, Leo. *Alfred Döblin: Sein Werk bis 1933.* Stuttgart: W. Kohlhammer, 1970.

Kuhlmann, Anna. *Revolution als "Geschichte": Alfred Döblins "November 1918." Eine programmatische Lektüre des historischen Romans.* Communicatio vol. 14. Tübingen: Max Niemeyer, 1997.

————. "Zweimal Deutscher November. Revolutionshistoriographie und Intertextualität bei Alfred Döblin und Holger Teschke." *Internationales Alfred-Döblin-Kolloquium Leipzig 1997,* ed. Ira Lorf and Gabriele Sander, 167–77. Bern: Peter Lang, 1999.

Kümmerling, Bettina. "Analytische und synthetische Erzählweise: Zur Struktur von Döblins Roman 'Hamlet oder Die lange Nacht nimmt ein Ende.'" *Internationales Alfred-Döblin-Kolloquium Lausanne 1987,* ed. Werner Stauffacher, 165–80. Bern: Peter Lang, 1986.

Kyora, Sabine. "'Das Döblinsche Syndrom.' Die Döblin-Rezeption als Beispiel für die Rezeption der klassischen Moderne in der DDR." *Internationales Alfred-Döblin-Kolloquium Leipzig 1997,* ed. Ira Lorf and Gabriele Sander, 179–89. Bern: Peter Lang, 1999.

Links, Roland. *Alfred Döblin: Leben und Werk.* Berlin: Volk und Wissen, 1976.

————. "Mit Geschichte will man etwas. Alfred Döblin: *November 1918.*" *Erfahrung Exil: Antifaschistische Romane 1933–1945,* ed. Sigrid Bock and Manfred Hahn, 328–51. Berlin/Weimar: Aufbau Verlag, 1979.

Lorf, Ira. "'Hier war man im echten Urwald.' Zur Verarbeitung ethnographischen Wissens in einem 'nicht-exotistischen' Text Döblins." *Internationales Alfred-Döblin-Kolloquium Paris 1993,* ed. Michel Grunewald, 113–25. Bern: Peter Lang, 1995.

————. *Maskenspiele: Wissen und kulturelle Muster in Alfred Döblins "Wadzeks Kampf mit der Dampfturbine" und "Die drei Sprünge des Wang-lun.* Bielefeld: Aisthesis Verlag, 1999.

————. "Wissen — Text — kulturelle Muster. Zur literarischen Verarbeitung gesellschaftlicher Wissenbestände in Alfred Döblins Roman *Wadzeks Kampf mit der Dampfturbine.*" *Internationales Alfred-Döblin-Kolloquium Leiden 1995,* ed. Gabriele Sander, 83–94. Bern: Peter Lang, 1997.

Lorf, Ira, and Gabriele Sander, eds. *Internationales Alfred-Döblin-Kolloquium Leipzig 1997.* Jahrbuch für Internationale Germanistik, series A, vol. 46. Bern: Peter Lang, 1999.

Luserke, Matthias. "Allegorie und Psychomachie. Revolutionsdeutung in Klingers 'Genius'-Fragment und Döblins Roman 'November 1918.'" *Internationale Alfred-Döblin-Kolloquien Münster 1989–Marbach a. N. 1991,* ed. Werner Stauffacher, 262–70. Bern: Peter Lang, 1993.

Maierhofer, Waltraud. "Zur Repräsentation der Frau und des Weiblichen in Döblins *Wallenstein.*" *Internationales Alfred-Döblin-Kolloquium Leiden 1995,* ed. Gabriele Sander, 95–114. Bern: Peter Lang, 1997.

Martini, Fritz. "Alfred Döblin." In *Deutsche Dichter der Moderne,* ed. Benno von Wiese, 321–69. Berlin: Erich Schmidt, 1965.

————. "Berlin Alexanderplatz." In *Das Wagnis der Sprache: Interpretationen deutscher Prosa von Nietzsche bis Benn.* Stuttgart: Ernst Klett, 1954.

Mayer, Dieter. *Alfred Döblins "Wallenstein": Zur Geschichtsauffassung und zur Struktur.* Munich: Wilhelm Fink, 1972.

Mayer, Hans. "Alfred Döblins Erzählwerk *November 1918.*" In H. M., *Die umerzogene Literatur,* 66–70. *Deutsche Schriftsteller und Bücher 1945–1967.* Berlin: Siedler-Verlag, 1988.

———. "'Eine deutsche Revolution. Also keine.' Über Alfred Döblins wiederentdecktes Erzählwerk *November 1918.*" *Der Spiegel* 33 (1978): 124ff.

Melcher, Andrea. *Vom Schriftsteller zum Sprachsteller? Alfred Döblins Auseinandersetzung mit Film und Rundfunk (1909–1932).* Frankfurt: Peter Lang, 1996.

Meyer, Jochen. *Alfred Döblin 1878–1978: Eine Ausstellung des Deutschen Literaturarchivs im Schiller-Nationalmuseum Marbach am Neckar.* Munich: Kösel Verlag, 1978.

Minder, Robert. "Döblin zwischen Osten und Westen." In R. M., *Dichter in der Gesellschaft: Erfahrungen mit deutscher und französischer Literatur,* 155–90. Frankfurt: Insel, 1966.

———. "Marxisme et psychoanalyse chez Alfred Döblin. A propos de son dernier Roman *Pardon wird nicht gegeben.*" *Revue de l'enseignement des langues vivantes* 54 (1937): 209–21. Also in R. M. *Die Entdeckung deutscher Mentalität,* ed. Manfred Bayer, 267–82. Leipzig: Reclam, 1992.

Misinsky, Jan. "Apokalyptische Utopie. Alfred Döblin und Günter Grass." *Internationale Alfred-Döblin-Kolloquien Münster 1989–Marbach a. N. 1991,* ed. Werner Stauffacher, 154–64. Bern: Peter Lang, 1993.

Mitchell, Breon. *James Joyce and the German Novel 1922–1933.* Athens, OH: Ohio UP, 1976.

Müller-Salget, Klaus. *Alfred Döblin: Werk und Entwicklung.* Bonn: Bouvier, 1973; 2nd rev. ed. 1988.

———. "Zur Entstehung von Döblins *Berlin Alexanderplatz.*" *Materialien zu Alfred Döblins "Berlin Alexanderplatz,"* ed. Matthias Prangel, 117–35. Suhrkamp Taschenbuch 268. Frankfurt: Suhrkamp, 1975.

Muschg, Walter. *Die Zerstörung der deutschen Literatur.* Bern: Francke, 1956.

———. *Tragische Literaturgeschichte.* Bern: Francke, 1948.

O'Neill, Patrick. *Alfred Döblin's "Babylonische Wandrung": A Study.* Bern: Peter Lang, 1974.

———. "The Anatomy of Crisis. Alfred Döblin's Novel *Pardon wird nicht gegeben.*" *Seminar* 14 (1978): 195–214.

———. "*Babylonische Wandrung.*" In *Zu Alfred Döblin,* ed. Ingrid Schuster, 149–59. Stuttgart: Klett, 1980.

Ogosawara, Yoshihito. *"Literatur zeugt Literatur"*: *Intertextuelle, motiv- und kulturgeschichtliche Studien zu Alfred Döblins Poetik und dem Roman "Berlin Alexanderplatz."* Frankfurt: Peter Lang, 1996.

Osterle, Heinz D. "Alfred Döblins Revolutions-Trilogie *November 1918*." *Monatshefte* 62 (1970): 1–23.

―――. "Auf den Spuren der Antigone: Sophokles, Döblin, Brecht." *Internationale Alfred-Döblin-Kolloquien 1980–1983*, ed. Werner Stauffacher, 86–115. Bern: Peter Lang, 1986.

Pfanner, Helmut F. "Der entfesselte Prometheus oder die Eroberung Südamerikas aus der Sicht Alfred Döblins." *Literatur und Geschichte: Festschrift für Wulf Koepke zum 70. Geburtstag*, ed. Karl Menges, 155–70. Amsterdam/Atlanta: Rodopi, 1998.

―――. "Sachlichkeit und Mystik: Zur Erzählhaltung in Alfred Döblins Revolutionsroman." *Internationale Alfred-Döblin-Kolloquien 1980–1983*, ed. Werner Stauffacher, 76–85. Bern: Peter Lang, 1986.

―――. "Die Widerspiegelung der Exilerfahrung in Alfred Döblins *Babylonischer Wandrung*." *Internationales Alfred-Döblin-Kolloquium Lausanne 1987*, ed. Werner Stauffacher, 68–82. Bern: Peter Lang, 1991.

Prangel, Matthias. *Alfred Döblin*. Sammlung Metzler 105. 2nd rev. ed., Stuttgart: J. B. Metzler, 1987.

―――. "Franz Biberkopf und das Wissen des Wissens. Zum Schluß von *Berlin Alexanderplatz* unter der Perspektive einer Theorie der Beobachtung der Beobachtung." *Internationales Alfred-Döblin-Kolloquium Leiden 1995*, ed. Gabriele Sander, 169–80. Bern: Peter Lang, 1997.

―――, ed. *Materialien zu Alfred Döblins "Berlin Alexanderplatz."* Suhrkamp Taschenbuch 268. Frankfurt: Suhrkamp, 1975.

Rasch, Wolfdietrich. "Döblins *Wallenstein* und die Geschichte." In W. R., *Zur deutschen Literatur seit der Jahrhundertwende: Gesammelte Aufsätze*, 228–42. Stuttgart: J. B. Metzler, 1976.

Reid, James, H. *"Berlin Alexanderplatz — A Political Novel." German Life & Letters* 21 (1967/68): 214–23.

Reif, Wolfgang. *Zivilisationsflucht und literarische Wunschräume: Der exotistische Romane im ersten Viertel des 20. Jahrhunderts.* Stuttgart: J. B. Metzler, 1975.

Renzi, Luca. "Alfred Döblins Dampfturbine: Symbol, Gleichnis, Mythos, Realität. Gesellschafts- und Zukunftskritik im Roman *Wadzeks Kampf mit der Dampfturbine* (1918)." *Internationales Alfred-Döblin-Kolloquium Bergamo 1999*, edited by Torsten Hahn (Bern: Peter Lang, 2002), 55–74.

Ribbat, Ernst. "Döblin, Brecht und das Problem des historischen Romans. Überlegungen im Hinblick auf *November 1918.*" *Internationale Alfred-Döblin-Kolloquien 1980–1983,* ed. Werner Stauffacher, 34–44. Bern: Peter Lang, 1986.

———. "Ein globales Erzählwerk. Alfred Döblins Exotismus." *Begegnung mit dem Fremden: Grenzen — Traditionen — Vergleiche. Akten des VIII. Internationalen Germanisten-Kongresses Tokyo 1990,* vol. 7. 426–33. Munich: Iudicium Verlag, 1991.

———. "Ein globales Erzählwerk. Alfred Döblins Exotismus," in *Begegnung mit dem 'Fremden': Grenzen — Traditionen — Vergleiche,* Akten des VIII. Internationalen Germanisten-Kongresses Tokyo 1990, vol. 7 (Munich: Iudicium Verlag, 1991), 426–33.

———. *Die Wahrheit des Lebens im frühen Werk Alfred Döblins.* Münster: Aschendorff, 1970.

Riley, Anthony W. "Nachwort" in Alfred Döblin, *Wadzeks Kampf mit der Dampfturbine, Ausgewählte Werke in Einzelbänden,* ed. Riley, 365–93. Olten/Freiburg: Walter-Verlag, 1982.

Rost, Andreas. "Fassbinder ver-filmt *Berlin Alexanderplatz.* Bilder und Töne jenseits ihrer Vorlage: Von 'Sachzwängen' und 'Zwangsjacken' einer filmischen Ästhetik." *Internationale Alfred-Döblin-Kolloquien Münster 1989–Marbach a. N. 1991,* ed. Werner Stauffacher, 317–30. Bern: Peter Lang, 1993.

Rusch, Gebhard. "Die literarische Wirklichkeit Alfred Döblins 1997. Eine Explorationsstudie zur Bedeutung des literarischen Wissens im Buchmarkt." *Internationales Alfred-Döblin-Kolloquium Leipzig 1997,* ed. Ira Lorf and Gabriele Sander, 191–210. Bern: Peter Lang, 1999.

Ryan, Judith. "From Futurism to 'Döblinism.'" *German Quarterly* 54 (1981): 415–26.

Sander, Gabriele. *"An der Grenze des Wirklichen und Möglichen . . .": Studien zu Alfred Döblins Roman "Berge Meere und Giganten."* Frankfurt: Peter Lang, 1988.

———. "Spurensuche in 'döblinener Waldung.' Über den Einfluß Döblins auf die Literatur der zwanziger Jahre und der Nachkriegszeit." *Internationale Alfred-Döblin-Kolloquien Münster 1989–Marbach a. N. 1991,* ed. Werner Stauffacher, 128–53. Bern: Lang, 1993.

———, ed. *Alfred Döblin: Berlin Alexanderplatz.* Erläuterungen und Dokumente. Stuttgart: Reclam, 1998.

———, ed. *Internationales Alfred-Döblin-Kolloquium Leiden 1995.* Jahrbuch für Internationale Germanistik, series A, vol. 43. Bern: Peter Lang, 1997.

Scholvin, Ulrike. *Döblins Metropolen: Über reale und imaginäre Städte und die Travestie der Wünsche.* Weinheim/Basel: Beltz, 1985.

Schöne, Albrecht. "Döblin: *Berlin Alexanderplatz*." In *Der deutsche Roman: Vom Barock bis zur Gegenwart,* ed. Benno von Wiese, vol. 2, 291–325. Düsseldorf: August Bagel, 1963.

Schoonover, Henrietta S. *The Humorous and Grotesque Elements in Alfred Döblin's "Berlin Alexanderplatz."* Frankfurt: Peter Lang, 1977.

Schröter, Klaus. *Alfred Döblin in Selbstzeugnissen und Bilddokumenten.* Rowohlts Monografien 266. Reinbek: Rowohlt, 1978.

Schuster, Ingrid. "Die Wirkungen des Wang-lun in der Weimarer Republik," *Internationale Alfred-Döblin-Kolloquien 1980–1983,* ed. Werner Stauffacher, 45–53. Bern: Peter Lang, 1986.

———. "Alfred Döblins 'chinesischer Roman.'" *Wirkendes Wort* 20 (1970): 339–46.

———. *China und Japan in der deutschen Literatur 1890–1925.* Munich/Bern: Francke, 1977.

———. "Die drei Sprünge des Wang-lun." In *Zu Alfred Döblin,* ed. Schuster, 82–97. Stuttgart: Ernst Klett, 1980.

———. "Die Wirkungen des *Wang-lun* in der Weimarer Republik." *Internationale Alfred-Döblin-Kolloquien 1980–1983,* ed. Werner Stauffacher, 45–53.

———, ed. *Zu Alfred Döblin.* Stuttgart: Ernst Klett, 1980.

Schuster, Ingrid, and Ingrid Bode, eds. *Alfred Döblin im Spiegel der zeitgenössischen Kritik.* Bern/Munich: Francke Verlag, 1973.

Schwimmer, Helmut. *Alfred Döblin: Berlin Alexanderplatz. Interpretationen für Schule und Studium.* Munich: Oldenbourg, 1973.

———. "Erlebnis und Gestaltung der Wirklichkeit bei Alfred Döblin." Diss. Munich, 1960.

Sebald, Winfried Georg. "Alfred Döblin oder Die politische Unzuverlässigkeit des bürgerlichen Literaten." *Internationale Alfred-Döblin-Kolloquien 1980–1983,* ed. Werner Stauffacher, 133–39.

———. *Der Mythos der Zerstörung im Werk Alfred Döblins.* Stuttgart: Ernst Klett, 1980.

———. "Preussische Perversionen. Anmerkungen zum Thema Literatur und Gewalt, ausgehend vom Frühwerk Alfred Döblins." *Internationale Alfred-Döblin-Kolloquien 1980–1983,* ed. Werner Stauffacher, 231–38.

Sperber, George Bernard. *Wegweiser im "Amazonas."* tuduv studien, Sprach- und Literaturwissenschaften, vol. 2. Munich: tuduv, 1975.

Stauffacher, Werner. "'Komisches Grundgefühl' und 'Scheinbare Tragik.' Zu 'Wadzeks Kampf mit der Dampfturbine.'" *Internationale Alfred-Döblin-Kolloquien 1980–1983,* ed. Stauffacher, 168–83.

————, ed. *Internationale Alfred-Döblin-Kolloquien 1980–1983*. Jahrbuch für Internationale Germanistik, series A, vol. 14. Bern: Peter Lang, 1986.

————, ed. *Internationale Alfred-Döblin-Kolloquien 1984–1985*. Jahrbuch für Internationale Germanistik, series A, vol. 24. Bern: Peter Lang, 1988.

————, ed. *Internationales Alfred-Döblin-Kolloquium Lausanne 1987*. Jahrbuch für Internationale Germanistik, series A, vol. 28. Bern: Peter Lang, 1991.

————, ed. *Internationale Alfred-Döblin-Kolloquien Münster 1989–Marbach a. N. 1991*. Jahrbuch für Internationale Germanistik series A, vol. 33. Bern: Peter Lang, 1993.

Steinmann, Adolf. *Alfred Döblins Roman "Hamlet oder Die lange Nacht nimmt ein Ende": Isolation und Öffnung*. Zürich: AKU-Fotodruck, 1971.

Steinmetz, Horst. "Hamlet oder die lange Nacht der Intertextualität." *Internationales Alfred-Döblin-Kolloquium Leiden 1995*, ed. Gabriele Sander, 237–46. Bern: Peter Lang, 1997.

Strelka, Joseph. "Der Erzähler Alfred Döblin." *German Quarterly* 33 (1960): 197–210.

Tatar, Maria. "'Wie süß ist es sich zu opfern.' Gender Violence and Agency in Döblin's *Berlin Alexanderplatz*." *Deutsche Vierteljahrsschrift für Literaturwissenschaft und Geistesgeschichte* 66 (1992): 491–518.

Tewarson, Heidi Thomann. *Alfred Döblin: Grundlagen seiner Ästhetik und ihre Entwicklung 1900–1933*. Bern: Peter Lang, 1979.

————. "Alfred Döblins Geschichtskonzeption in *November 1918. Eine deutsche Revolution*. Dargestellt an der Figur Rosa Luxemburgs in *Karl und Rosa*." *Internationale Alfred-Döblin-Kolloquien 1980–1983*, ed. Werner Stauffacher, 64–75. Bern: Peter Lang, 1986.

Wichert, Adalbert. *Alfred Döblins historischer Roman: Zur Poetik des modernen Geschichtsromans*. Stuttgart: J. B. Metzler, 1978.

Zheng Fee. *Alfred Döblins "Die drei Sprünge des Wang-lun": Eine Untersuchung zu den Quellen und zum geistigen Gehalt*. Regensburger Beiträge zur deutschen Sprach- und Literaturwissenschaft, series B, vol. 49. Frankfurt: Peter Lang, 1991.

Zhonghua Luo. *Alfred Döblins "Die drei Sprünge des Wang-lun, ein chinesischer Roman?* Frankfurt: Peter Lang, 1991.

Ziolkowski, Theodore. *Dimensions of the Modern Novel: German Texts and European Contexts*. Princeton NJ: Princeton UP, 1969.

Index